The Collected Writings of Walt Whitman

WALT WHITMAN

The Correspondence

VOLUME VI: A SUPPLEMENT

with a COMPOSITE INDEX

Edited by Edwin Haviland Miller

NEW YORK UNIVERSITY PRESS   1977

Library of Congress Catalog Card Number: 76–25786

ISBN: 0-8147-5415-5

Manufactured in the United States of America

Library of Congress Cataloging in Publication Data

Whitman, Walt, 1819-1892.
　Walt Whitman, The correspondence.

　Includes an index as well as corrections and
additions to vols. 1-5 of The correspondence.
　　1. Whitman, Walt, 1819-1892–Correspondence.
2. Poets, American–19th century–Correspondence.
I. Whitman, Walt, 1819-1892. The correspondence.
II. Miller, Edwin Haviland. III. Title.
PS3231.A3 1977　　　811'.3 [B]　　　76-25786
ISBN 0-8147-5415-5

The Collected Writings of Walt Whitman

GENERAL EDITORS

Gay Wilson Allen and Sculley Bradley

ADVISORY EDITORIAL BOARD

Roger Asselineau   *Harold W. Blodgett*

Charles E. Feinberg   *Clarence Gohdes*

Emory Holloway   *Rollo G. Silver*   *Floyd Stovall*

Preface

In the last of the five volumes of *The Correspondence of Walt Whitman,* which was published in 1969, I began the Preface with the brave words that its publication completed a task launched in 1957 with the appearance of *Walt Whitman's Correspondence—A Checklist.* Fate has decreed otherwise, for now there is a *Supplement.*

Since 1969 over ninety letters and postcards have become available, in a few instances the originals of letters transcribed from auction records, in others letters listed in the various volumes as "Whitman's Lost Letters," and in others letters previously unrecorded and unknown.

The *Supplement* includes the earliest extant letter, written in 1841, which was acquired several years ago by the Library of Congress, as well as what may well be all surviving letters written to Ernest Rhys and H. Buxton Forman, which have been added to the superb Whitman holdings of the Berg Collection in the New York Public Library.

I am deeply indebted to Dr. Lola L. Sladitz, that model of curators, for permission to print these letters. Charles E. Feinberg, whose magnificent collection of Whitmania is now housed in the Library of Congress, has continued "in retirement" to acquire letters with an enthusiasm that never grows old.

Although the letters gathered in this *Supplement* will not alter in any dramatic way the outlines of the poet's life, they add details to the story, particularly of his publishing activities in the later 1880s. It is useless to speculate how, in the hands of future biographers and critics, these letters may contribute new insights or deeper understanding. What is demonstrable is that these volumes now include almost 2900 letters of America's greatest poet.

After spending over twenty years in gathering, preparing, and publishing Whitman's letters, and after a "furlough" of several years, it is refreshing to return once more to the personal communications of a man of many moods and many poses. In public Whitman struck various postures—the rough, the good gray poet, the venerable sage of Camden in his littered "shanty"—and, as some of the letters here indicate, he was concerned, perhaps overly concerned, with the image he projected—aspects of his complex personality which are discussed in the Introduction. At the same time there was that stubborn (he would have said Dutch) integrity that led Whitman in personal communications to write not for future generations of unknown readers, but to write simply and unselfconsciously. Whitman respected his correspondents too much to strike poses. Walt was egomaniacal—as who is not?—but he was also a warm human being—and the best evidence is in the letters.

I am indebted to the following institutions for permission to print Whitman letters in their collections: the Henry A. and Albert A. Berg Collection, the New York Public Library; the Charles E. Feinberg Collection, the Library of Congress; the Library of Congress; the University of Pennsylvania; and the University of Southern Illinois.

The following individuals have allowed me to print letters in their possession: Professor Richard F. Giles, Mrs. Roy L. Marston, Sr., and Mrs. Pearl Stone.

It is always a pleasure to acknowledge, however inadequately, those who have assisted me: Gay Wilson Allen, who has continued to be a remarkable friend and associate; John C. Broderick, Chief of the Manuscripts Division of the Library of Congress; Charles E. Feinberg; Professor Jerome L. Loving; Professor Randall Waldron; and Professor William White, the editor of the *Walt Whitman Review.* I am particularly indebted to Gloria A. Francis, Chief of the Gifts and Rare Book Division of the Detroit Public Library, and to Professor Artem Lozynsky, of Temple University, who are preparing a history of Whitman at auction; they graciously provided me with prints of records pertaining to letters.

I am obliged to various librarians at the New York University Library and at the New York Public Library. And, finally, it is a pleasure rather than a duty to state once again how delighted I have been with my long association with the New York University Press.

*   *   *

In the *Supplement* I have followed the editorial procedures outlined in the first volume, and the format, including the appendices, is identical.

For the convenience of readers and scholars, this volume contains a composite index to the six volumes of *The Correspondence of Walt Whitman.*

Users of these volumes should be informed of two important matters. The materials marked Feinberg are now in the Library of Congress. The abbreviation *CB* (which for the sake of consistency remains unchanged in this volume) refers to what I called *The Commonplace-Book;* it is, perhaps more accurately, called a *Daybook* in the forthcoming publication of the New York University Press, *Daybooks and Diaries of Walt Whitman.*

Riverdale, New York   E.H.M.

CONTENTS

PREFACE   *vii*

INTRODUCTION   *xi*

APPENDIX:

    Notes to Tables 1 and 2   *xxiii*

A LIST OF WHITMAN'S CORRESPONDENTS   *xxxvii*

ILLUSTRATIONS   *xli*

The Correspondence   3

APPENDICES:

    A. A List of Manuscript Sources and Printed Appearances   63

    B. A Check List of Whitman's Lost Letters   66

    C. A Calendar of Letters Written to Whitman   68

    D. Chronology of Walt Whitman's Life and Work   70

    E. A List of Corrections and Additions to Volumes I-V   73

COMPOSITE INDEX TO VOLUMES I-VI   79

Introduction

WALT WHITMAN'S INCOME, 1876-1892

On January 26, 1876, an article entitled "Walt Whitman's Actual American Position" appeared in a small New Jersey newspaper, the *West Jersey Press*. The reporter claims that Whitman's poems "have fallen stillborn in this country. They have been met, and are met today, with the determined denial, disgust and scorn of orthodox American authors, publishers and editors, and, in a pecuniary and worldly sense, have certainly wrecked the life of their author."

The article reviews Whitman's career in sketchy fashion, occasionally quoting the poet directly. He was "worth some money and 'doing well,' " until his head buzzed with the "notion that he must make pieces or lyrics, 'fit for the New World.' " With the publication of *Leaves of Grass* in 1855 he ran into troubles. Because critics charged him with writing indecent poems, he had to print his poetry at his own expense.

During the war Whitman was "a hard-working unpaid army nurse and practical missionary," and "in the overstrained excitement and labors of those years were planted the seeds of the disease that now cripples him."

    ... that he got work in 1865 at Washington as a clerk in the Interior Department, but was turned out forthwith by Secretary Harlan declaredly for his being the author of the "Leaves"–that he received an appointment again, but after some years was again discharged–being taken ill–that he left Washington, and has now lived for a while in a sort of half-sick, half-well condition, here in Camden–and that he remains singularly hearty in spirit and good natured, though, as he himself grimly expressed it lately, "pretty well at the end of his rope"–are parts of his history that we will merely mention.

    And now, since that beginning over twenty years have passed away, and Whitman has grown gray in the battle. Little or no impression, (at least ostensibly,) seems to have been made. Still he stands alone. No established publishing house will yet print his books. Most of the stores will not even sell them.

The report in the *West Jersey Press* details Whitman's plight in 1876. Magazines like the *Atlantic Monthly* "will not touch him," his poems "are returned with insulting notes," "established American poets studiously ignore" him, and "friendly" notices in England are not reprinted in the American press. "We have now said enough to suggest the bleakness of the actual situation. . . . But the poet himself is more resolute and persevering than ever," as he prepares a two-volume edition of his works, the sixth edition of *Leaves of Grass* and a miscellany to be called *Two Rivulets.*

The last sentence of the article is scarcely ordinary journalism: "Walt Whitman's artist feelings for deep shadows, streaked with just enough light to relieve them, might find no greater study than his own life." [1]

On January 26, 1876, Whitman sent the article to William Michael Rossetti, perhaps the staunchest of his English admirers. Rossetti printed excerpts from the report in the *West Jersey Press* in *The Athenaeum* on March 11, and included these two sentences from Whitman's letter: "My theory is that *the plain truth* of the situation here is best stated. It is even worse *than* described in the article." [2]

The allegations in the *West Jersey Press,* then, had found by March 1876 an international audience.

Whitman had achieved his purpose. For, as Clifton Joseph Furness proved years ago in *Walt Whitman's Workshop,* the poet wrote the article in the *West Jersey Press.*

As a former journalist and editor, Whitman understood the role of the newspaper in American life, and throughout his career exploited its potential fully. Probably no American poet has received such extensive newspaper coverage. If his countrymen did not read his poetry, they knew a lot about a man named Walt Whitman. That Americans are on a first-name basis with Walt is attributable as much to the anecdotes he sent to newspapers throughout his life as to the personal nature of his poetry.

The lot of the "Old, poor, and paralyzed" poet was not publicized for the first time in the *West Jersey Press.* On November 18, 1875, an old friend from Pfaffian days, Edwin Einstein, wrote to him: "I would not trouble you with this letter, were it not that I saw mentioned in the N.Y. Sun the other day the fact that you were in very needy circumstances, if that is so will you let me know, and myself and a few other of your old friends would be glad to aid you to the best of our ability."

Instead of replying casually to Einstein's friendly query, Whitman carefully wrote out a trial copy before he sent off a letter on November 26:

---

1 *West Jersey Press,* January 26, 1876, reprinted by Furness, 245-246.
2 *Corr.,* III, 20; the italics are WW's.

My paralysis has left me permanently disabled, unable to do any thing of any consequence, and yet with perhaps (though old, not yet 60) some lease of life yet. I had saved up a little money, & when I came here, nearly three years ago, I bought a nice cheap lot, intending to put on a small house to haul in, & live out the rest of my days.

I had, & yet have, a sort of idea that my books, (I am getting ready, or about have ready, my complete writings, in two volumes—*Leaves of Grass,* and *Two Rivulets)* will yet henceforth furnish me reliably with sufficient for grub, pocket money, &c., if I have my own shanty to live in. But my means, meagre at the best, have gone for my expenses since, & now, while not hitherto actually wanting, (& not worrying much about the future either,) I have come to the end of my rope, & am in fact ridiculously poor.[3]

Whether Einstein and his friends made a contribution to Whitman we do not know, although the only substantial deposit in his bank account in 1875 was the sum of $75.00 entered on December 11.

On December 30, 1875, the poet made a similar statement to Jeannette L. Gilder, the editor of *The Critic:* "Pecuniary matters thin & meagre, (but not in want)." On January 2 in the following year the New York *Herald* commented: "He is poor in purse, but not in actual want."

When Whitman sent the article to the *West Jersey Press,* he had two purposes, to call attention to his economic lot and to advertise the so-called Centennial Edition. The publicity served his purposes perhaps better than he had anticipated, since he had no way of knowing that the article would set off what almost amounted to an Anglo-American debate. Was Whitman poor and neglected, unhonored and insulted in his native land? Did Americans neglect him while English admirers supported him? Was he a poet martyr in truth, or was he crying wolf? For months there were charges and countercharges, particularly in the pages of the New York *Tribune,* which carried favorable notices as well as Whitman's own (unsigned) review of his work in February 1876. Later the newspaper carried the hostile notices of Bayard Taylor which were answered by John Burroughs and William D. O'Connor.

A century later there is no reason to be as fervid as the lovers and haters in 1876, unless we are determined to see Whitman as a martyr to the Gilded Age or to take pot shots at the unending self-promotion of a man who quite accurately and disarmingly characterized himself as a furtive hen.

In 1876 Whitman's economic lot was, if not desperate, certainly unpromising. However, his newspaper account was at times more dramatic than accurate. From January 1873, when he suffered a stroke that left him a cripple, until August 31, 1874, he remained on the government payroll. He

3 *Corr.,* II, 343 and n. Only the draft letter is extant.

paid Walter Godey, his substitute, $50.00 a month, while he continued to receive his yearly salary of about $1600.00. When his services were terminated on July 1, 1874, he was granted two-months' terminal pay.[4]

After he moved in 1873 to Camden to live with his brother George, he paid his sister-in-law Louisa $30.00 a month for the first few months and then $15.00 or $16.00. According to his tabulations in the *Daybooks* he paid the latter sum from 1874 to 1878. Whitman's "Board Acc't" in the *Daybooks* makes clear that he paid board only when he was in Camden.

He opened a bank account at the National State Bank in Camden in December 1873 with a deposit of $704.00. In the following year he deposited $1967.80 and made withdrawals amounting to $1555.00. In addition to the payments to Godey and Louisa Whitman, and probably to the printers of his 1876 books, he withdrew $450.00 to purchase a lot [5] on which, as he informed Einstein, he planned to build himself a shanty, apparently believing at the time that he would continue to receive his salary from the Interior Department. At the end of 1874 the balance in his account was $1116.80.

That his economic situation changed with the loss of his Washington post is dramatically revealed in the bank records. In 1875 he deposited $129.14 and withdrew $645.00. At the end of the year the balance was $600.16.

When in November 1875 Whitman returned to Washington for the first time in over two years, sixteen friends sent a petition to the Secretary of the Treasury: "We respectfully ask that Walt Whitman, 'the Good Gray Poet,' may be appointed to a position in the Treasury Department." According to the docket in the National Archives, "The Secretary says give the applicant a place Jany 1, '76 if possible." [6] If his friends did not, Whitman did know that he could not hold down a clerical post, although it is quite possible that he put the friends up to it. He returned to Camden "much refreshed" [7] after his vacation, and about this time decided to take his case to the public through the newspapers.

We tend sometimes to think of Whitman as a disorderly, easygoing man, although readers of his poetry know that he artfully orders the disorderly and calculatingly celebrates the spontaneous and impulsive. Surviving photographs of his Mickle Street quarters and the garrulous accounts of his Boswell, Horace Traubel, reveal that he lived surrounded by books, newspapers, and what-not piled in every corner, every chair and table. Yet Whitman always seemed able to find what he wanted with little effort, disorder perhaps being in the eyes of the beholder.

4 *Corr.,* II, 307; Allen, 461.
5 *Corr.,* II, 308.
6 *Corr.,* II, 342-343n.
7 *Corr.,* II, 344.

In public, Whitman appeared affable, Olympian, perhaps cosmic, but in private he was a meticulous bookkeeper, as the *Daybooks* establish. He knew to the penny how much he paid his sister-in-law for board and how much the tax collectors cheated him of annually. He handled hundreds of orders for his books with only a few trivial mishaps. In these transactions he noted receipt of the money for the purchase and receipt of the book by the purchaser. When he mailed a package of books he also sent off a postcard. As he occasionally reminded admirers, on his mother's side he was of Dutch descent, and, although he never exactly admitted it, he respected his and the other fellow's money.

Whitman's literary executors, Dr. Richard Maurice Bucke, Thomas B. Harned, and Horace Traubel, preserved almost everything they found in the Mickle Street home; recipients kept his letters and cards; and Traubel recorded his almost daily conversations with the poet beginning in March 28, 1888. Such frugality makes it possible to reconstruct with reasonable accuracy Whitman's actual financial position from 1876 until his death, by drawing primarily on the following sources: *The Correspondence of Walt Whitman* and *Supplement; The Commonplace Book* (to be issued as *Daybooks and Diaries of Walt Whitman*); the bankbook of the National State Bank in Camden (Feinberg-LC); "Accounts of Sales and Copyright—*Leaves of Grass* and *Specimen Days,*" the records of David McKay, the Philadelphia publisher, (Pennsylvania); Horace Traubel, *With Walt Whitman in Camden* (1906-1964), five volumes.

With everything expressed in dollars and cents, Table 1 seems perhaps to simplify too much, but it tells a story, in numbers rather than emotions. The income has been placed in five categories: Book Orders, or purchases of books from Whitman himself; Royalties, or returns from publishers; Publication, or earnings from magazines and newspapers; Gifts; Miscellaneous. Notes to Tables 1 and 2, at the conclusion of the essay, supply the data upon which these compilations are based.

Whitman's income from 1876 to 1892 totalled $20,610.10. His average income during these years was $1270.00.[8] This was not a large sum, but in an era when one could buy a two-story house for $1750.00, it was not small.

The average income, however, smooths out fluctuations. For three years (between 1877 and 1879) Whitman received less than $500.00 annually, and for three other years his income was under $1000.00 (1881, 1883, 1884). Only for four years did the amount go above $2000.00. As Table 1 indicates, in 1882 for the first but last time in his career he received substantial royalties, but only after a Boston district attorney, and the extensive newspaper

---

8 I have arrived at this calculation by eliminating the necessarily incomplete records for 1892.

TABLE 1. WHITMAN'S ANNUAL INCOME, 1876-1892

YEAR	BOOK ORDERS	ROYALTIES	PUBLICA- TION	GIFTS	MISCEL- LANEOUS	TOTALS
1876	$1552.83		$78.15	$150.00		$1780.98
1877	266.24					266.24
1878	343.79		30.00	65.00		438.79
1879	189.63		65.30		50.00	304.93
1880	766.14	40.50	53.00	175.00	90.00	1124.64
1881	476.12	25.00	243.00	70.00	135.00	949.12
1882	89.00	1439.30	67.00		525.00	2120.30
1883	65.00	329.66	100.00	50.00	100.00	644.66
1884	97.00	163.04	125.00	200.00	280.00	865.04
1885	118.00	118.77	350.20	746.01		1332.98
1886	190.45	120.21	360.00	728.32	742.00	2140.98 [9]
1887	95.50	128.05	233.00	1513.87	694.00	2664.42
1888	76.46	277.91	277.00	232.77	139.00	1003.14
1889	419.39	452.11	95.00	478.15		1444.65
1890	592.00	102.95	196.00	413.65	874.45	2179.05
1891	455.55	196.63	223.00	192.00		1067.18
1892	283.00					283.00
TOTALS	$6076.10	$3394.13	$2495.65	$5014.77	$3629.45	$20610.10

coverage, aroused the interest of buyers who up to that time had ignored the poetry. From 1885 to 1887 English and American friends contributed large sums of money after campaigns were organized by William Michael Rossetti and Edward Carpenter in England and Sylvester Baxter and W. S. Kennedy in the United States.

As this compilation makes clear, Whitman had no alternative if he were to be self-supporting but to be a publisher-salesman. The largest earnings came from book sales—roughly 30 percent. These figures are to some extent misleading since I have not tabulated the costs he incurred in printing his own books. (Whitman as Publisher needs to be studied, not only in the years 1876 to 1892 but also in the earlier period, if we are to have the whole story.)

The second most important source of income was the gifts—about 20 percent. From these two sources he received more than 50 percent of his income. But it should be noted that 60 percent of the gifts came in the three-year period from 1885 to 1887, and that sources in England were responsible for almost 60 percent of these donations.

Although there is no way of checking, probably Whitman recorded most of the substantial monetary gifts either in the *Daybooks* or in letters to the donors. I have not attempted to place a monetary value on services and

---

9 In *Corr.*, IV, 61n, I estimated that WW's income for the year "amounted to at least $2,289.06." An error in recording and reexamination of the data have produced a somewhat smaller amount.

TABLE 2. SOURCES OF INCOME (AMERICAN, ENGLISH, OTHER: A, E, O)

YEAR		BOOK ORDERS	ROYALTIES	PUBLICA- TION	GIFTS	MISCEL- LANEOUS	TOTALS
1876	A	$457.00		$60.00	$150.00		$667.00
	E	1080.83		18.15			1898.98
	0	15.00					15.00
1877	A	120.25					120.25
	E	130.99					130.99
	O	15.00					15.00
1878	A	178.55		30.00	65.00		273.55
	E	120.24					120.24
	O	45.00					45.00
1879	A	78.00		50.00		50.00	178.00
	E	91.63		15.30			106.93
	O	20.00					20.00
1880	A	457.50	40.50	43.00	175.00	90.00	806.00
	E	215.14		10.00			225.14
	O	93.50					93.50
1881	A	207.50	25.00	243.00	70.00	135.00	680.50
	E	240.87					240.87
	O	27.75					27.75
1882	A	75.00	1439.30	67.00		525.00	2106.30
	E	14.00					14.00
	O						
1883	A	27.00	329.66	100.00	50.00	100.00	606.66
	E	35.00					35.00
	O	3.00					3.00
1884	A	81.00	163.04	125.00		280.00	649.04
	E	16.00					16.00
	O				200.00		
1885	A	113.00	66.77	205.00	60.00		444.77
	E	5.00	52.00	145.20	686.01		888.21
	O						
1886	A	126.00	120.21	360.00	155.00	742.00	1503.21
	E	35.40			573.32		608.72
	O	29.05					29.05
1887	A	78.00	76.91	233.00	800.00	694.00	1881.91
	E	8.50	51.14		713.87		773.51
	O	9.00					9.00

YEAR	BOOK ORDERS	ROYALTIES	PUBLICA-TION	GIFTS	MISCEL-LANEOUS	TOTALS
1888 A	71.66	221.08	257.00	10.00	139.00	698.74
E		56.83	20.00	222.77		299.60
O	4.80					4.80
1889 A	404.39	452.11	95.00	155.00		1108.50
E	15.00			323.15		338.15
0						
1890 A	479.00	102.95	196.00	135.00	874.45	1787.40
E	88.00			278.65		366.65
0	25.00					25.00
1891 A	374.05	196.63	223.00			793.68
E	68.70			192.00		260.70
O	12.80					12.80
1892 A	283.00					283.00
E						
O						
TOTALS						
A	$3610.90	$3234.16	$2287.00	$1825.00	$3629.45	$14586.51
E	2165.30	159.97	208.65	2989.77		5523.69
O	29990			200.00		499.90

nonmonetary gifts. Money was raised by Thomas Donaldson and Philadelphia friends to purchase a horse and buggy in 1885;[10] Whitman apparently provided Mrs. Mary Davis with living accommodations in return for her services; and Dr. Bucke paid for the services of some of the male attendants in the poet's last years.

Income from articles and poems he submitted to newspapers and magazines averaged out at somewhat better than $155.00 annually. It should not be overlooked that after the Boston incident he seemingly was more successful in placing his poems and prose.

The items in the Table under Miscellaneous include returns from Whitman's lectures on Abraham Lincoln, Robert Ingersoll's speech at a benefit that was an impressive money-raiser, the sale of property, etc.

In 1876 and again in 1886 there was much discussion in print on both sides of the Atlantic about Whitman's neglect by his countrymen in contrast with the support he received abroad. Table 2 indicates what income came from American and English sources. In this table "Other" refers primarily to

10 Since his friends raised the money ($125.00) for a specific purpose, I have not considered this gift as income, until WW sold the horse and buggy in 1888 for $130.00. See Notes to Tables 1 and 2, 1888, Miscellaneous.

the purchases and gifts of Canadian and Irish friends, as well as to purchasers from other countries, as indicated in the notes to Tables 1 and 2.

The totals in Table 2 reveal that almost 75 percent of Whitman's income was derived from American sources, roughly 25 percent from English sources.

While it is true that in 1876 and 1877 and again in 1885 Whitman received more money from English than from American sources, and while in 1886 and 1887 he received generous support from English admirers, there was no continuity in this support, most of it stemming from the campaigns in 1876 and 1885 and 1886. There were continuing contributions, in the form of annual birthday gifts beginning in 1885, from Edward Carpenter and his friends and to a lesser extent from Dr. John Johnston and J. W. Wallace, who organized a Whitman Fellowship in Bolton, England. But it was Americans who supplied him with the largest proportion of his income.

Table 2 does not do justice to the contributions of Dr. Bucke, whose principal gifts were probably nonmonetary. Bucke was Whitman's host for several months during the most extended vacation he enjoyed following the paralysis of 1873, and more than any one else Bucke tried to ease Whitman's physical discomforts in the last few years of his life.

The preservation of Whitman's bank book makes it possible to watch the tightening economic situation for three years before it was gradually reversed beginning in 1880.

TABLE 3–BANK DEPOSITS AND WITHDRAWALS [11]

YEAR	DEPOSITS	WITHDRAWALS	BALANCE
1875			$600.94
1876	$1282.30	$1132.00	751.24
1877	188.70	505.00	434.94
1878	486.30	825.50	95.74
1879	175.00	100.00	170.74
1880	991.63	100.00	1062.37
1881	747.37	494.00	1315.74
1882	2072.90	540.25	2848.39
1883	650.00	700.00	2798.39
1884	693.63	2271.54	1220.48
1885	1011.25	66.95	2164.78
1886	1654.71	300.00	3519.49
1887	2565.19	286.25	5798.43
1888	907.61	1035.53	5670.51
1889	1318.08	631.38	6357.21
1890	1868.30	188.66	8036.85
1891	770.11	1844.19	6962.77
1892	$416.25	$1500.00	$5879.02

11 WW's bank book was not consistently balanced on the last day of the year. I have placed the entries, deposits and withdrawals, on an annual basis.

It is not possible to match the receipts listed in Table 1 and the deposits recorded in the bank statements. Sometimes Whitman deposited large sums as they were received, but usually he deposited some checks and postal orders and cashed others for current expenses. In a few instances when the data in the notes to Tables 1 and 2 are arranged chronologically, receipts from book orders and other known sources are considerably smaller than bank deposits. I have not speculated as to the sources of additional income, preferring caution to conjecture.

After 1880 the money in the bank began to accumulate steadily, and surprisingly rapidly, in view of the nominal receipts of money cited in Table 1. Whitman lived modestly, making no unusual or extravagant expenditures, yet he managed to contribute to the support of his feeble-minded brother Edward as well as to make yearly gifts to his sisters, Hannah Heyde and Mary Van Nostrand, and to other friends. The only extravagance was the mausoleum he ordered in the late 1880s. Yet Horace Traubel was, for him, unusually unkind when he commented in 1889: "Whenever he gets a little flutter of hope that he may live longer, . . . he seems to start in at once to husband what money he has so he may not get stranded. His economies last a day or two. Then he lets himself go again. This is the only frailty in him which rubs me." [12]

Expenditures were substantial in 1884 when he purchased his home on Mickle Street and did extensive remodeling; in 1888 when he was printing at his own expense *Complete Works* and *November Boughs;* and in 1891 when he paid $1500.00 for his mausoleum. The withdrawal of the same amount in 1892 was probably the final payment for the tomb, part of the settlement which Harned arranged after Whitman and the contractor had a disagreement as to price.[13]

.   .   .

The compilations of Whitman's income and disbursements supplement the story of his life as it is told in his letters and other documents, and in their own way they constitute a drama themselves.

The publicity in the *West Jersey Press* paid off handsomely, producing a return in 1876 from book sales which he never had again. The earnings in 1876 carried him through the next three years when his income fell below $500.00. During this period withdrawals from the bank were steady and substantial, and by the end of 1878 the bank balance had fallen to $95.74.

12 Traubel, IV, 340.

13 Harned's recollection of the circumstances in 1919 make it appear that he settled the matter out of his own pocket (Barrus, 340-341; Allen, 540). WW admitted that he owed the contractor $4,000.00 (*Corr.,* V, 225), but evidently was unwilling to settle at that amount. At any rate the bank withdrawal indicates that he himself paid the final installment for his last home.

Although circumstances were critical Whitman complained surprisingly little, at least in extant letters. Since he paid his sister-in-law Louisa about $180.00 a year for board, his overhead was low, and he even had a kind of second home in these years with the Staffords.

In 1879 he undertook the most extensive journey of his life, going as far West as Colorado, perhaps with some assistance from Colonel John W. Forney, who accompanied him as far as Lawrence, Kansas, where he was to give a lecture.[14] When in 1880 Whitman sold his books with more success than he had experienced since 1876, he turned himself about economically. His bank book makes the point graphically.

The publication of the seventh edition of *Leaves of Grass* and *Specimen Days* made 1882 a banner year. It was followed by two lean years, as royalty payments declined and were not replaced by other sources of income. As the situation deteriorated, Whitman and his friends did not hesitate to call attention to his lot in the newspapers. The result was the period of generous gifts. Whitman, who was a proud and prudent man, took no chances that the giving would continue indefinitely.

When royalties from *Leaves of Grass* and *Specimen Days* leveled off after 1884, he began to make plans to become his own publisher again, and in a few years saw *Complete Works* and *November Boughs* through the presses. Printing costs were substantial,[15] but no doubt the project paid off, although perhaps not so dramatically as in 1876. This time McKay was a substantial purchaser, at a wholesale figure,[16] but it is possible, depending to some extent upon the size of the inventory at the time of Whitman's death, that he would have fared almost as well if he had made McKay his publisher instead of his chief distributor.

Whitman trusted no one with Whitman. He reviewed his own poetry as early as 1855 on the (incontestable) principle that no one understood his purposes as well as he. He supervised every biographical account in his lifetime, even to overseeing the printing of Bucke's "biography," because posterity was to receive and to accept Whitman's portrait of Whitman. Printers, publishers, and editors knew how meticulous he was about punctuation and format, and how carefully he drew up contracts, protecting his rights to future publication and reserving the privilege of selling books directly to customers. As the new letters included in this volume disclose, Whitman gave Ernest Rhys full control over the three editions printed by

14 See *Corr.*, III, 163n.

15 Bills for printing, paper, etc. amounted to at least $788.54; see Traubel, I, 415; II, 261, 309, 418; III, 41, 289, 399, 421. In negotiations with printers and suppliers, Horace Traubel acted as WW's agent: "I stand between him and binders and printers and have many matters of the financial sort to smoothe down on both sides" (IV, 340).

16 See Notes to Tables 1 and 2 in 1889 and 1890. It was McKay who purchased books in 1892.

Walter Scott in England, but coached him in exact detail every step of the way. Against overwhelming odds Whitman somehow managed to keep death waiting until he had prepared what he decreed was to be the definitive text of his poetry, in the so-called Deathbed Edition.

Whitman may have seemed unduly concerned about posterity and his future reputation, but he never neglected the role he had assumed on his father's death in 1855, when he had become head of the household. He cared for his family faithfully throughout his life. In a Last Will and Testament which he drew up in 1888 he provided for his survivors. To his two sisters who were mired in poverty he left bequests of $1000.00 each. After designating smaller sums to the two women to whom he owed much in the way of attention and affection in the twilight years, Mrs. Davis and Mrs. Stafford, he directed that the residue of his estate be used for the care of the most helpless member of the Whitman family, Edward, who was now institutionalized in New Jersey.

In the late 1880s Whitman carefully planned and then supervised the erection of a lavish mausoleum in Harleigh Cemetery which seemed a tribute to the ornateness and vanity of the Gilded Age rather than to the achievements of a democratic poet of humble origins. The tomb was an extravagance, the cost certainly excessive for a man of Whitman's means. Although the contractor finally settled for less, the original price was $4000.00, which was more than twice the price of his "shanty." If some of the disciples were surprised, perhaps shocked, there was nothing inconsistent in Whitman's desire to have an enduring monument.

The mausoleum was no more grandiloquent and vain than that wonderfully witty and self-inflating line in the first edition of *Leaves of Grass:* "Walt Whitman, an American, one of the roughs, a kosmos." Because it was his father's business, Whitman knew a lot about construction. When *Leaves of Grass* was germinating in the 1850s, Whitman was in Brooklyn, at home, assisting his father and then gradually replacing him as his father's health failed. In planning the tomb he was again about his father's business. It was to be the last and the finest of the Whitman homes.

For Whitman directed that the remains of his parents be buried at his side. He accomplished at death what life for complex reasons had denied, the reunion of mother, father, and child: that eternal trio finally at peace in an eternal home. His instructions provided that they be surrounded by other members of the family, and as the years passed they were joined by Edward, George, and Hannah, as well as by Louisa and her son, Walter Orr Whitman.

A child went forth and at last returned a poet, a son, a brother who became a "father."

Appendix

The reconstruction presented in this essay understates Whitman's income during the years surveyed by probably 10 or 15 percent, perhaps more. As systematic as Whitman appears to have been in the entries in his *Daybooks,* which generally refer to mail orders and gifts sent by check or postal orders, there is no reason to believe that he consistently recorded the sales of books or the gifts of people who came to his house in Camden.

The dollar amounts Whitman received and paid must be viewed in terms of the period, though no doubt prices fluctuated between 1876 and 1892. In judging Whitman's income we have to bear in mind that when he held clerical posts in Washington in the 1860s and early 1870s he earned between $1200.00 and $1600.00 annually; that in 1873 and 1874 he could hire a substitute for as little as $50.00 a month; that he paid for board $15.00 or $16.00 a month; and that in 1884 he had a room wallpapered for $3.25 and purchased a house for $1750.00. He sold many of his books for $5.00 or more—a high price in those days and for many decades later.

It is perhaps impossible (or at any rate beyond my competency) to translate the sums Whitman received and spent into present-day equivalencies. The multiple must be, I suspect, at least between five and ten, probably higher.

The notes that follow are voluminous for essentially simple reasons: (1) without the evidence my compilations and statements are arbitrary and, worse, unverifiable; (2) with the evidence at hand it is possible to reinterpret the results by shifting items from one category to another or to place a different construction upon a transaction; and (3) future scholars can correct my errors and add data either overlooked or unavailable.

Whenever I have had to estimate an amount, an E follows the sum. In estimating the price paid for a book, I have chosen the average price for the book in that year. I have estimated the conversion of pounds into dollars generally at a low figure. Understatement has seemed the wiser, if less dramatic, policy.

In order to reduce the number of footnotes, I have placed in parentheses after each item the source of my information. References to the five volumes of *Correspondence* appear with roman numerals followed by page number. References to the *Daybooks* are given by dates: month/day. Letters in the *Supplement* are cited by the appropriate number, preceded by S. When the source of information is a letter to WW, the notation reads: Ltr. with date; these letters are listed in the various volumes in Appendix C, A Calendar of Letters Written to Whitman. To facilitate checking of data, I have arranged the entries alphabetically rather than chronologically within a given year. When poems or articles were paid for a year or so before publication, I have recorded them according to the date of payment, noting in brackets the date of publication.

1876

BOOK ORDERS [17]

American

Abbey, H. (3/22)	5.00
Avery, W. (10/19)	5.00
Ballard, A. (4/21)	10.00
Bangs, Williams (5/29)	2.00E
Belisle, D. W. (3/12)	5.00
Bullard, L. (5/4, 6)	10.00
Burroughs, J. (S758.6; 3/12, 8/1)	10.00
Davis, A. J. (III, 441; 5/4)	20.00E
Giles, A. E. (5/4)	10.00E
Hale, P. (III, 53; 7/11)	10.00
Harrison, J. B. (3/2, 5/5)	10.00
Hay, J. (8/1)	10.00
Hillard, K. (3/12, 7/27)	10.00E
Inglis, J. S. (8/3, 4)	20.00
Johnson, N. M. (III, 440; 3/17)	20.00
Johnston, J. N. (3/2)	10.00
King, H. (10/31, 11/1)	10.00
Linton, W. J. (S778.1; 9/16, 24, 10/11)	10.00
McEntee, J. (3/28)	5.00E
Miller, J. (III, 40; 4/19)	10.00
Morrison, B. G. (III, 440; 4/21)	10.00
Moulton, E. L. C. (III, 65; 12/11)	5.00

Otis, A. B. (3/2)	15.00
Potter, E. J. (12/1)	5.00
Putnam, A. P. (III, 441; 4/26)	10.00
Ritter, F. R. (12/12)	5.00
Sampson, Low (2/18)	9.00
Sanborn, F. B. (4/13)	10.00
Scribner, Armstrong (V, 303; 9/2)	10.00
Seeger, F. (III, 38n, 440, 441; 4/21)	10.00
Smeaton, R. (5/23)	6.00
Stagg, W. A. (III, 441; 11/21)	10.00
Stedman, E.C. (III, 45; V, 303; 3/13, 14)	30.00
Swinton, J. (III, 45; 5/4)	50.00
Trowbridge, J. T. (III, 441; 5/2)	5.00E
Ward, J. Q. A. (III, 45, 441; S749.5; 6/6, 8)	50.00
White, D. S. (12/29)	5.00
Whitney & Adams (9/2)	10.00

English

Buchanan, R. (III, 47-48, 56, 64; 4/28, 9/5)	137.50
Carpenter, E. (III, 41, 43; 4/21)	21.97
Conway, M. D.[18] (III, 57; 6/12, 9/5)	42.92E
Cook, K. (III, 440; 3/21)	20.00
Dixon, T. (3/11)	20.00
Dowden, E. (III, 58-59; 3/2)	69.25

17 Because Swinton, Stedman, Ward, and particularly Rossetti submitted lists of people to whom WW was to mail copies of the Centennial Edition, the list presented here may contain errors. I have tried to record only the names of those who personally ordered copies.

As a general rule I have not recorded in these Notes orders for books which are not confirmed either in the *Correspondence* or in the *Daybooks*.

18 At this time Conway (1832-1907) was living in England.

Gosse, E. (III, 48; 5/19)	10.00E
Hannah, R. (8/23)	5.00E
Leycester, R. (6/5, 12)	11.00E
Lushington, G. (8/31)	27.50E
Lushington, V. (8/31)	27.50E
Oates, C. G. (6/20)	5.47
Rossetti, W. M. (III, 43, 52, 59-60; 4/12?, 5/5, 6/20, 10/10)	571.78
Scott-Moncrieff, E. (III, 42, 440)	5.00
Simpson, T. (III, 42, 440; 4/23, 6/12)	10.00E
Taylor, M. (9/5)	10.00E
Trübner & Co. (6/13)	48.44
Watson, R. S. (S760.5; 8/30)	27.50E
Wallis, G. (6/7)	10.00E

Other

Rolleston, T.W.H. (5/24)	5.00E
Webb, A. (III, 440; 3/11)	10.00

PUBLICATION

American

"A Death-Sonnet for Custer" ["From Far Dakota's Cañons"] (III, 53, 54)	10.00
Excerpts from *Memoranda During the War* (III, 24; 3/16)	50.00

English

"To the Man-of-War-Bird" (III, 23, 56; 6/20?)	18.15E

GIFTS

Burroughs, J. (III, 50; 5/10)	50.00
Anonymous gift (New York *Tribune,* February 10; *SB,* 8 [1956], 245n)	100.00

1877

BOOK ORDERS

American

Aiken, J. R. (12/1)	10.00E
Barton, W. G. (8/5)	5.00E
Bellows, E. D. (III, 102-103; 11/18)	12.00E

Broadbent [& Taylor?] (10/11)	10.00E
Carse, General (7/12)	5.00E
Clarke, W. B. (12/5, 8)	8.00
Claxton, Remsen, & Haffelfinger (12/11)	8.00
Forney, J. W. (10/15)	10.00E
Hutton, L. (3/30)	10.00
Loomis, E. J. (7/27)	5.00
Scott, T. A. (10/15)	10.00E
Scribner & Co. (3/30)	1.00
Strickland, E. F. (11/3)	1.00
Taylor, W. C. (10/11)	10.00E
Waters, G. W. (4/1)	10.00E
Williams & Co. (III, 103-104; 11/30)	5.25

English

Carpenter, E. (10/2, 5, 25)	50.12
Cordery, A. (5/2)	5.00E
Cozens, F. W.[19] (5/3)	11.65
Ellis, E. J. (5/2)	10.00E
Rose, J. A. (III, 96n; 9/16)	11.65
Symonds, J. A. (4/1, 5/3)	20.00E
Trübner & Co. (Ltr. 77/5/31 [LC])	7.57
Vines, S. H. (III, 103; 11/27)	10.00
White, W. H. (5/25)	5.00E

Other

Bucke, R. M. (8/15, 10/17)	15.00E

1878

BOOK ORDERS

American

Brainerd, E. (4/24)	10.00E
Brentano, A. (6/6)	18.00
Central News Co. (1/29)	2.80
Chapman, W. (6/12, 7/11)	10.00
Claxton, Remsen, & Haffelfinger (1/10)	12.75
England, J. W. (7/12)	10.00E
French, A. S. (4/1)	10.00E
Gurney, B. (8/7)	10.00E
Lanier, S. (5/27)	5.00E
Linton, W. J. (7/19)	5.00E
Lippincott, J. B. (4/22)	7.00
Pratt, C. S. (1/24)	5.00E
Putnam's Sons (10/31)	7.00
Ridge, Dr. (1/25)	10.00E

19 In a letter dated August 18 (Feinberg) Rossetti sent WW £4.12s. with instructions to send the two-volume edition to Cozens and Rose. According to WW's notation (9/10) the sum amounted to $23.30.

Rowell, G. P. (8/1)	10.00E
Sarony, (8/2)	30.00E
Scribner, Armstrong (3/5)	7.00
Westermann, B. (11/10)	7.00
Whitney & Adams (3/19)	2.00

English

Dixon, T. (4/3)	5.00E
Jones, H. T. (III, 128; 7/11, 12)	9.70
Rossetti, W. M. (III, 129; 7/12)	24.00
Tottie, O. (III, 129; 7/26)	10.00E
Trübner & Co. (III, 137-138; 9/30, 12/6)	61.55
Wilkinson, E. T. (1/2)	9.99

Other

Bucke, R. M. (1/16, 5/11, 12/11)	25.00E
Fraser, A. S. (1/16)	10.00
Holmes, T. K. (7/13)	10.00E

PUBLICATION

"Gathering the Corn" (III, 137; 10/3, 28)	10.00
"A Poet's Recreation" (III, 129; 7/19)	20.00

GIFTS

Burroughs, J. (1/9)	15.00
Childs, G. W. (III, 142; 12/12)	50.00

1879

BOOK ORDERS
American

Brinton, J. W. (Diary 1879) [20]	10.00
Claxton, Remsen & Haffelfinger (8/20)	6.00
Dillingham, C. T. (9/5)	3.50
Hine, Mrs. (2/25)	10.00E
Johnston & Co., T. (Diary 1879)	10.00E

Kelly, W. H. (8/28)	5.00E
Putnam's Sons (7/14)	7.00E
Sanborn, N. (11/24?)	10.00
Steiger, E. (Diary 1879)	7.00
Vick, J. (2/25)	6.00E
Wilkinson, R. F. (Diary 1879)	3.50E

English

Alexander, A. R. (9/10; Diary 1879)	10.20
Arunachalain, P. (8/5)	19.44
Brooke, W. G. (6/20)	10.00E
Hardie, J. (2/6)	5.00E
Mansfield, E. D. (6/16)	9.72
Thompson, H. E. (11/24; Diary 1879)	5.10
Thompson, J. W. (3/28, 6/16; Diary 1879)	7.67
Trübner & Co. (III, 137n, 157)	24.50E

Other

Alexander, J. (8/9)	5.00E
Bucke, R. M. (Diary 1879)	5.00
Hunt, Dr. (Diary 1879)	10.00

PUBLICATION
American

"Broadway Revisited" (III, 153)	
"Real Summer Openings" (III, 153)	} 45.00
"These May Afternoons" (III, 154, 155)	
"What Best I See in Thee" (III, 170n; Diary 1879)	5.00E

English

"Three Young Men's Deaths" (III, 141n, 159; V, 305)	15.30

MISCELLANEOUS

Lecture: "The Death of Abraham Lincoln" (III, 149-152; Allen, 483-484)	50.00E [21]

20 When WW made his first and last trip to the West, he did not take along his *Daybooks,* but kept a separate Diary.

21 So far as I have been able to determine, WW made no record of the amount he received for this lecture at Steck Hall in New York. Concerned about the number of people who would appear, he asked Burroughs, who took care of arrangements, to choose "some respectable second or third class hall" *(Corr.,* III, 149). I have arbitrarily decided that the collection may have amounted to $50.00, which may be wildly reckless or conservative.

1880

BOOK ORDERS

American

Almy, F. (III, 190-191; 10/27)	10.00
Brough, W. (11/1)	10.00E
Browne, S. T. (10/25)	10.00
Bunner, H. C. (10/27)	10.00E
Cheever, E. C. (III, 445; 10/25)	10.00
Coan, T. M. (3/13, 11/24)	20.00E
Croly, J. C. (2/11)	7.00
Dillingham, C. T. (12/1)	10.50
Dodge, G. E. (11/4)	10.00E
Ehrenfield, C. L. (10/25)	10.00
Ewart, R. H. (V, 307; 3/4)	10.00
Eyvel, G. (6/7)	10.00E
Fields, J. T. (10/25)	10.00E
Foote, C. B. (11/17)	10.00E
Forbes, W. J. (10/25)	10.00E
Furness, H. H. (III, 175-176; 3/30)	10.00E
Gemsanlen, F. W. (11/17)	10.00E
Gillette, F. K. (1/22)	5.00E
Gridley, M. W. (5/6)	20.00E
Hamilton, W. (6/15)	3.50E
Heard, G. (III, 445; 10/25)	10.00
Hitchcock, A. P. (10/22)	10.00E
Hutcheson, D. (III, 445; 11/22)	10.00
Mackenzie, Colin (11/22)	10.00E
Martin, H. A. (10/23)	10.00
Martine, C. A. (12/1)	10.00E
Mills, J. E. (1/15)	10.00E
Mills, W. (1/22)	1.00E
Pierce, C. H. (10/31)	10.00E
Platt, I. H. (10/27)	10.00E
Pope, C. (1/15)	10.00E
Putnam's Sons (1/6, 10/25, 28, 11/18)	24.50
Riggs, C. (10/2)	10.00
Roberts, H. (III, 175; 4/15)	5.00
Savage, M. J. (11/4)	10.00E
Sholes, C. H. (3/12)	10.00E
Stoddard, C. W. (6/26)	10.00
Stott, J. S. (11/17)	7.00E
Tyson, G. (11/17)	20.00E
Watson, B. A. (11/4)	5.00E
Williams & Co. (11/1, 29)	14.00
Williams, T. (3/1)	10.00E
Wolfe, T. F. (5/28)	5.00E
Woodbury, J. P. (12/28)	10.00E
Ziegler, E. S. (3/20)	10.00E

English

Doggett, E. G. (III, 195; 11/23)	10.00E
Locker-Lampson, F. (III, 174; 3/21)	5.00E
Macdonald, K. (III, 445; 6/26)	5.00E
Ruskin, J. (III, 174, 307; 2/16, 19)	50.97
Thompson, E. (2/4)	5.00E
Thompson, J. W. (III, 444; 2/5, 3/13)	1.45
Tonge, C. F. (4/15)	10.00E
Trübner & Co. (3/4, 7/22)	117.72
Walsh, M. A. (5/30)	10.00E

Other

Bucke, R. M. (1/7, 2/19, 3/17, 3/26)	76.50
Mackenzie, J. A. (3/13)	10.00
Pardee, T. B. (6/19)	7.00E

ROYALTIES

Worthington, R. (III, 196-198; 12/5, 6)	40.50

PUBLICATION

American

"My Picture-Gallery" (III, 223n; 10/8)	5.00
"Patroling Barnegat" [published 1881] (III, 204; 10/9)	10.00
"A Riddle Song" (III, 178; 3/21)	10.00
"Summer Days in Canada" (III, 181n; 8/13)	10.00E
Two letters in Philadelphia *Press* (11/19)	8.00[22]

English

"The Dalliance of the Eagles" (III, 158n; 10/9)	10.00

---

22 One of the two letters was probably "Cedar-Plums Like–Names"; see *Corr.,* III, 203n. The editor of *Specimen Days* (see 245n) missed this earlier appearance in the newspaper. I have not identified the other "letter" that appeared in the *Press.* It does not seem likely that it was "Summer Day in Canada."

GIFTS

Burroughs, J. (III, 173; 2/20)	25.00
Childs, G. W. (12/27)	50.00E [23]
Fields, J. T. (III, 172n; Barrus, 189)	100.00

MISCELLANEOUS

Lecture: "The Death of Abraham Lincoln" (III, 178)	90.00

1881

BOOK ORDERS
American

Banning, W. C. (1/13)	10.00E
Booth, B. A. (11/15)	2.00E
Burr, C. B. (1/18)	5.00E
Dillingham, C. T. (4/2)	3.50
Eddy, W. A. (2/27)	12.50
Furness, H. H. (S1003.5; 1/26)	10.00
Furness, W. H. (2/3)	5.00E
Harris, G. W. (3/30)	10.00
Hayes, Jr., J. (1/20)	10.00
Hovey, F. H. (2/27)	10.00E
Kennedy, W. S. (III, 260n; 12/20)	5.00
Lawrence, R. H. (S1015.5; 3/8)	10.00
Lebknecker, A. E. (12/27)	2.00
Moulton, E. L. C. (III, 209; 2/2)	10.00E
Niemeyer, T. W. (S1019.1; 3/17)	10.00E
Paulding, W. J. (6/22)	10.00E
Peck, D. C. (12/10)	10.00E
Ransom, F. H. (2/2)	12.50
Rhoads, J. R. (3/1)	10.00E
Robinson, H. W. (1/17, 6/7)	20.00E
Spencer, J. (3/15)	10.00E
Vedder, E. (2/9)	10.00E
Wiggins, Jr., J. W. (4/8)	10.00E

English

Carpenter, E. (III, 227; 5/30)	15.00E
Fraser, J. (6/11)	10.00E
Scott, J. A. (S998.1; 1/16)	10.00
Shaw, A. D. (4/9)	10.00
Smithton, E. (2/11)	10.00E
Trübner & Co. (3/3, 12/8)	185.87

Other

Bucke, R. M. (1/13)	12.75
Rolleston, T. W. H. (2/12)	5.00
Starr, J. C. (2/17)	10.00

ROYALTIES

Worthington, R. (III, 196-198; 8/11)	25.00

PUBLICATION

"Bumble-Bees and Bird-Music" (III, 223n; 5/5)	20.00
"City Notes in August" (III, 241n; 8/26)	10.00
"The Dead Carlyle" (III, 212; 2/7)	5.00
"Death of Carlyle" (III, 210)	10.00
"How I Get Around at 60 and Take Notes," five parts (III, 202, 205, 216, 222, 254; 1/5, 4/9, 28, 11/16)	71.00
"The Poetry of the Future" (III, 204; 1/15)	100.00
"Spirit That Form'd This Scene" (III, 236n; 5/28)	5.00
"A Summer Invocation" (III, 223n; 5/27, 6/2)	12.00
"A Week at West Hills" (III, 235; 8/4, 26)	10.00

GIFTS

Burroughs, J. (III, 217-218; 3/16)	10.00
Childs, G. W. (12/16)	50.00
Furness, H. H. (4/13)	10.00

MISCELLANEOUS

Lecture: "The Death of Abraham Lincoln" (III, 220-221; 4/13-19)	135.00

1882

BOOK ORDERS
American

Bass, B. C. (5/31)	5.00E
Beckwith, P. D. (7/15)	3.00
Bliss, L. O. (12/18)	5.00E
Callicot, T. C. (III, 284; 5/26)	3.00

---

23 The entry in *Daybooks* reads: "rec'd [*blank*] from G W Childs, for benevolent purposes." In 1878 and 1881 Childs gave WW $50.00 at Christmas time.

Coburn, V. O. (S1095.6; 3/7)	10.00
Dillon, J. R. (7/24)	3.00E
Loomis, Prof. (6/20)	3.00
McGrillis, M. A. (11/18)	3.00E
Martin, H. H. (1/10)	10.00
Noble, L. F. DeH. (III, 282, 288; 5/31)	10.00
Rogers, F. (6/11)	10.00
Stoddart, J. M. (5/8)	10.00

English

Ford, I. O. (10/11)	5.00E
Gilchrist, A. (III, 309; 10/5)	6.00E
White, W. H. (S1171.1; 11/6)	3.00

ROYALTIES

McKay, D.[24]	1294.80
Osgood, J. R.[25] (III, 281)	100.00
Worthington, R. (III, 197n; Ltr. 82/7/25)	44.50

PUBLICATION

"By Emerson's Grave" (III, 274n; 4/29)	3.00
"Death of Longfellow" (III, 273; 4/2)	7.00
"Edgar Poe's Significance" (III, 289; 4/17)	10.00
"How I Get Around at 60 and Take Notes," sixth part (4/2)	7.00
"A Memorandum at a Venture" (III, 274, 276; 4/8, 27)	25.00
"Robert Burns [As Poet and Person]" (III, 318, 12/16)	15.00

MISCELLANEOUS

Sale of lot on Royden Street (11/9)	525.00

1883

BOOK ORDERS
American

Brough, W. (9/12)	4.00
Marsh, E. S. (III, 322)	6.00
Porter & Coates (11/7)	7.00
Proudfit, D. L. (3/16)	10.00E

English

Ford, E. (6/27)	5.00E
Ford, I. O. (12/8)	5.00E
Pease, E. R. (III, 347-348; 8/2)	5.00E
Riley, E. (12/8, 10)	5.00E
Thompson, J. W. (5/10)	15.00E

Other

Whitman, H. N. (11/15)	3.00

ROYALTIES

McKay, D.	329.66[26]

PUBLICATION

"A Backward Glance on My Own Road" [published 1884] (III, 362; 12/27)	12.00
"The Bible As Poetry" (III, 322, 324)	13.00
"An Indian Bureau Reminiscence" (III, 358-359; 12/15)	10.00
"Our Eminent Visitors (Past, Present, and Future," (III, 355-356)	15.00E
"With Husky-Haughty Lips, O Sea!" (III, 357; 11/27-28)	50.00

GIFTS

Childs, G. W. (12/22)	50.00

---

24 In 1882 McKay sold 3,118 copies of *Leaves of Grass* and 925 copies of *Specimen Days;* royalties totaled $1294.80. As recorded in the *Daybooks* (9/26, 10/4, 11/13, 12/1) royalty payments amounted to $1204.78. The discrepancy is attributable to the number of books WW ordered to sell himself ($90.00). He erred in recording 78 cents rather than 80 cents. WW's later claim that he "netted" $1300.00 from the Philadelphia edition is then substantially correct (Traubel, I, 291).

25 The sum from Osgood, the Boston publisher, was a settlement agreed upon after the censorship: WW waived royalties and received the plates, unbound sheets, and $100.00; see Allen, 498-499.

26 Royalties in 1883 were $331.46, but the December payment was reduced by $1.80 presumably because WW purchased one of the books for resale. In 1883 McKay sold 867 copies of *Leaves of Grass* and 558 copies of *Specimen Days.*

MISCELLANEOUS

Dividends from Sierra Grande
Mining Co. (III, 346n; 3/6,
10/3)   100.00

1884

BOOK ORDERS
American

Aldrich, A. (6/12)	3.00
Barnard, J. (2/6)	3.00
Bartlett, J. W. (III, 372; 6/11)	3.00
Bessey, A. (3/4, 8/28)	5.00
Christman, W. M. (11/29)	3.00
Cupples, Upham & Co. (9/19)	5.00
Evans, D. M. (12/22)	3.00
Falkenan, H. (4/24)	3.00
Ginty, A. G. (2/24)	10.00
Hawley, W. A. (6/17)	2.00E
McKee, T. J. (4/18)	10.00
Neal, T. W. (6/6)	3.00
Otis, F. (7/6)	3.00E
Pillsbury, P. (7/19)	3.00E
Randall, J. K. (9/21, 10/3)	15.00
Smith, P. B. (8/19)	5.00
Townsend, P. (2/7)	2.00

English

Lee, J. F. (11/3)	6.00E
Rossetti, W. M. (10/23)	5.00E
Wilkinson, A. M. (7/10, 9/18)	5.00E

ROYALTIES

McKay, D. (7/12, 12/10)   163.04

PUBLICATION

"The Dead Tenor" (III, 382n)	10.00E
"Father Taylor and Oratory" [published 1887] (III, 369, 374; 8/4)	50.00
"If I Should Need to Name, O Western World" ["Election Day, November, 1884"] (III, 379; 10/26)	10.00

"Of That Blithe Throat of
Thine" [published 1885]

(III, 387; 10/17)	30.00
"Red Jacket (from Aloft.)" (III, 378-379)	5.00
"Resurgemus" ["Europe"], (III, 388n)	5.00E
"What Lurks behind Shakspere's Historical Plays?" (III, 377, 378; 8/8)	15.00

GIFTS [27]

Bucke, R. M. (7/6)   200.00

MISCELLANEOUS

Dividends from Sierra Grande Mining Co.[28] (8/21, 9/5)	80.00
Sale of oil portrait by Charles Hine to J. H. Johnston (III, 368-369n, 374, 382, 384; 12/23)	200.00

1885

BOOK ORDERS
American

Bryant, W. C. (5/28)	5.00
Chainey, G. (7/14, 9/8)	23.00
Chaphe (?), Mr.[29]	20.00
Drake, A. B. (1/5)	10.00
Fletcher, A. (6/11)	10.00
Johnston, J. H. (9/6)	2.00
Melotte, G. W. (3/31)	3.00E
O'Reilly, J. B. (3/4)	6.00E
Perry, F. W. (6/11)	3.00E
Randall, J. K. (9/6)	10.00
Robinson, T. B. (3/26)	10.00
Skinner, W. C. (2/7)	3.00
Smith, George (1/20)	5.00
Wyman, A. (12/2)	3.00

English

Abdy-Williams, E. M. (III, 385; 1/7, 3/31)	5.00E

---

27 During the year Thomas Donaldson and friends gave WW $125.00 for the purchase of a horse and buggy and "for horse-keep" (III, 407; 9/15, 18).

28 WW received the eighth and ninth dividends from the stock in 1884 and the first and second in 1883. Five dividends are presumably unaccounted for. I have not ventured an estimate of these receipts.

29 On July 31 (Feinberg) and again on September 11 (Yale) WW's brother, Thomas Jefferson, sent checks for $10.00 to purchase books for a Mr. Chaphe(?).

30 WW complained to Burroughs on December 21, 1885, "I get a miserable return of royalties from McKay, . . .—*not $50 for both books L of G. and S D for the past year*" (*Corr.,* III, 414).

ROYALTIES

American

McKay, D.[30] (III, 401; 7/31,
12/15)   42.77
Worthington, R. (11/5-6)   24.00

English

Scott, W. (III, 407; 11/9)   52.00E

PUBLICATION

American

"Abraham Lincoln" (III, 412;
11/15)   33.00
"Ah, Not This Granite, Dead
and Cold" ["Washington's
Monument, February,
1883"] (III, 387n, 2/20,
5/6)   10.00
"As One by One Withdrew
the Lofty Actors" ["Death
of General Grant"] (III,
387n; 4/2)   30.00
"Booth and 'The Bowery'"
["The Old Bowery"] (III,
403; 8/15)   60.00
"Slang in America" (III, 403n;
9/22; Traubel, II, 232)   50.00
"Some Diary Notes at
Random" (III, 360; 11/11)   10.00
"The Voice of the Rain" (III,
391-392, 394; 6/9)   12.00

English

"Fancies at Navesink" (III,
403; 5/23, 8/29)   145.20

GIFTS

American

Childs, G. W. (1/13)   50.00
Kennedy, W. S. (III, 400n)   5.00
Thayer, W. R. (III, 408)   5.00

English

Carpenter, E., and Ford sisters
(III, 399-400; 8/4)   239.83
Rossetti, W. M. (III, 404, 409,
411; 9/8?, 10/20, 11/28)   446.18

1886

BOOK ORDERS

American

Bushell, W. (5/28, 6/5)   80.00

Evans, A. H. (2/26)   3.00
Fairchild, C. (5/10)   5.00
Garrit (?), J. (5/31)   18.00
Johnston, A. (7/2)   2.00E
Manning, F. L. (3/16)   3.00
Morrison, H. H. (12/22)   3.00
Smith, R. P. (10/9)   11.00
VanDusen, G. (7/6)   1.00E

English

Cook, K. (IV, 19-20; 2/11)   5.20E
Crossfield, J. (2/10)   5.20E
Maxwell, Mrs. (12/19)   10.00E
Taylor, B. (5/10)   10.00E
Wylie, J. (4/28)   5.00E

Other

de Bosis, A. (IV, 38; 7/23)   0.85
Bucke, R. M. (11/24, 12/22)   13.00E
Colles, R. W. (IV, 44-45, 54;
9/18, 11/18)   15.20E

ROYALTIES

McKay, D.   120.21

PUBLICATION

"Army Hospitals and Cases"
[published 1888] (IV, 38,
40-41; 7/26, 8/7)   150.00
"How I Made a Book or Tried
To Last June" (IV, 36, 37,
39; 6/29, 7/10)   80.00
"My Book and I" (IV, 55;
7/22)   50.00
"Robert Burns as Poet and
Person" (IV, 39; 8/6)   70.00
"A Thought on Shakspere"
(IV, 43, 45; 7/27)   10.00

GIFTS

American

Childs, G. W. (IV, 15; 1/1)   50.00
Gross, S. E. (11/30)   100.00
Gunther, Mr. (IV, 25) [31]   5.00

English

Brown, L. M. (IV, 57n) [32]   27.36E
Carpenter, E. and Cambridge
friends (IV, 29-30; 5/29)   216.75
Dowden, E. (IV, 46; 8/24)   9.60E
Rossetti, W. M. (IV, 30;
5/29)   319.61

31 Gunther received a "MS page" *(Corr.,* IV, 25).

32 The pound was worth about $4.80 in 1886. Herbert Gilchrist sent WW a gift of £5 from L.
M. Brown and 14s.6d. from an unnamed Cambridge friend which I have lumped together.

MISCELLANEOUS

Lectures: "The Death of
 Abraham Lincoln"
 Elkton, Maryland (IV, 19;
 2/2)   30.00
 Camden (3/1)   25.00
 Philadelphia (IV, 27-28;
 4/15)   687.00

1887

BOOK ORDERS
American

Biddle, N. T. (IV, 62; 1/2)   5.00
Chandler, Mr. (4/19)   3.00
Colyer, R. (5/11)   3.00E
Hay, J. (3/10; Traubel, III, 91-
 92)   30.00
Loftus, P. J. (12/19)   5.00
Maher, E. (1/8)   12.00E
Robinson, S. B. (1/5)   3.00E
Shiells, R. (9/16)   5.00E
Sizer, N. (6/13)   2.00
Spofford, C. A. (4/12)   2.00E
Wilesell, G. P. (1/31)   3.00E
Williamson, G. M. (IV, 123-
 124)   5.00

English

Lock, T. (1/24, 3/4)   5.00E
Pratt, A. J. (9/8)   3.50E

Other

Bucke, R. M. (1/14)   6.00E
Tratts, E. R. (IV, 88n; 4/26)   3.00E

ROYALTIES
American

McKay, D.   76.91

English

Scott, W. (3/14)   51.14E [33]

PUBLICATION

"As the Greek's Signal Flame"
 New York *Herald* (IV, 136;
 S1639.5; 12/14)   25.00
 Munyon's [published 1888]
 (IV, 136n; 12/7)   10.00

"The Dying Veteran" (IV,
 102, 104; 6/23)   25.00
"New Orleans in 1848" (IV,
 64; 1/16)   25.00
"Shakspere-Bacon Cipher" (IV,
 119; 9/13)   20.00
"Some War Memoranda Jotted
 Down at the Time" (IV,
 61; 1/11)   60.00
"Twilight" (IV, 108; 7/3)   10.00
"November Boughs" (IV, 100;
 5/31)   50.00
"Yonnondio" (IV, 131; 11/15)   8.00

GIFTS
American

Baxter, S., and Boston friends
 (IV, 103, 110, 114, 125;
 6/22)   800.00

English

Brown, L. M. (IV, 132-133;
 11/19)   25.00
Ford sisters (IV, 107; 7/11)   97.40E
Carpenter, E. (5/23)   121.75E
Hales, S. (IV, 425; 3/8)   12.80
Johnston, J., and J. W.
 Wallace (IV, 95-96; 5/28)   48.70
Norman, H. (IV, 63; 1/3)   393.61
Powell, R. E. (IV, 65n)   14.61E

MISCELLANEOUS

Lecture: "The Death of
 Abraham Lincoln" (IV, 84-
 85; 4/13)   600.00
Reading of poetry at
 Contemporary Club (IV, 67;
 2/22)   20.00
Sale of photographs through
 W. Carey (IV, 122-124, 130;
 10/3, 11/2, 12/3)   74.00

1888

BOOK ORDERS
American

Aldrich, T. B. (10/7)   2.00E
Brotherton, Mrs. (10/7)   2.00E
Coaner, Dr. (10/7)   2.00E
Coates, E. (IV, 204; Traubel,
 II, 237, 336)   20.00

---

33 On the basis of WW's translation of pounds into dollars in this year, I have assumed that the pound was valued at $4.87.

Dick & Fitzgerald (IV, 152;
  2/21)   6.66
Gribbins(?) (10/7)   2.00E
Ingram, W. (IV, 228)   2.00E
Klein, J. (IV, 211; 9/10)   13.00
Lindell, E. (10/7)   2.00E
May, F. L. (Traubel, V, 160)   2.00E
Ryman, F. (1/5)   2.00E
Stafford, Edwin (10/7)   2.00E
Wetherbee, Mrs. (10/7)   2.00E
Woodword, T. R. (11/5;
  Traubel, III, 66)   2.00
Züllig, A. A. I. (10/24)   5.00
Unnamed New York purchaser
  (Traubel, I, 447)   5.00

Other
Colles, R. W. (1/27)   4.80E

ROYALTIES
American
McKay, D. (2/29, 10/9)   221.08

English
Scott, W. (IV, 176)   42.40E
Trübner & Co. (IV, 235; 11/8)   14.43

PUBLICATION
American
"Elias Hicks" (IV, 206; 9/6)   15.00
"Old Age's Lambent Peaks"
  (IV, 204; 4/9)   16.00
"To the Year 1889" ["To the
  Pending Year"]
  [published 1889] (IV, 254n;
  12/24)   6.00
Poems and prose published
  from January to May in
  New York *Herald* (IV, 144-
  145n; 5/5; Traubel, I, 439,
  447)   220.00

English
"Twenty Years" (IV, 147-148;
  2/10)   20.00

GIFTS
American
Williamson, G. M. (IV, 436;
  Traubel, II, 403, and III,
  356)   10.00

English
Carpenter, E. (IV, 266n,
  269-270)   174.37
Johnston, Dr. J., and J. W.
  Wallace (Ltr. from Wallace,
  88/5/?)   24.00E [34]
Potter, E. T. (IV, 185)   10.00E
Powell, R. E. (IV, 156)   14.40E

MISCELLANEOUS
Sale of books (Shelley and
  Pepys) to J. H. Johnston
  (IV, 165; 1/20)   9.00
Sale of mare and phaeton (IV,
  206; 9/7)   130.00

1889

BOOK ORDERS
American
Aldrich, T. B. (IV, 309; 3/23)   25.00
Brown, A. N. (IV, 310; 3/23)   6.00E
Bustin, Jr., W. H. (10/7)   5.00E
Carlton, W. (4/29)   10.00
Delabarre, E. B. (10/23)   5.00E
Donaldson, T. (IV, 268;
  88/10/7)   10.00
Donaldson (?), T. (6/18)   1.50
Garrison, Judge (6/7)   19.50
Garrison, Mrs. (IV, 278;
  Traubel, IV, 74)   8.00E
Greeley, N. (1/4)   5.00
Hawley, W. A. (10/31)   12.00E
Johnston, Alma (12/26)   5.00
Johnston, Grace (12/9)   5.00E
Kennedy, W. S. (IV, 344;
  6/5)   4.99
Lychenheim boys (IV, 359n;
  Traubel, V, 368, 371)   12.00
McGee, S. (8/17)   5.00
McKay, D. (IV, 405; 3/[13],
  28, 7/5, 12/11)   187.00
May, F. L. (IV, 336; Traubel,
  V, 160)   6.00E
Palms (?), C. L. (10/7)   5.00E
Putnam, Mrs. H. (Traubel, V,
  461-462)   4.00E
Raymenton, W. H. (10/19)   5.00
Searing, E. W. (6/7)   2.00
Stockton, F. R. (11/8)   2.00
True, Dr. (8/20?; Traubel, V,
  459)   4.00
Wassall, J. W. (IV, 359; 7/23)   6.00

---

[34] The value of the pound is estimated at $4.80. The contribution from Mrs. Powell was £3 and from Johnston and Wallace £5.

Waters, E. C. (12/19) — 6.40
Wormwood, R. F. (IV, 400; 11/19) — 6.00
Unidentified (IV, 343) — 5.00
Unidentified (IV, 347) — 6.00E
Three unidentified purchasers (IV, 390) — 15.00E
Two unidentified purchasers (9/23) — 6.00E

English
Langley, Miss (IV, 304n; 2/26, 3/19, 4/17) — 9.00E
Scull, W. D. (10/26) — 6.00

ROYALTIES

McKay, D.[35] (IV, 266; 1/8, 3/28) — 452.11

PUBLICATION

"Bravo, Paris Exposition!" (IV, 376; 9/18) — 10.00
"A Christmas Greeting" (IV, 404; 12/4) — 11.00
"Death's Valley" [published 1892] (IV, 368; 9/1) — 25.00
"My 71st Year" (IV, 347n; 6/9) — 12.00
"Old Age's Ship & Crafty Death's" [published 1890] (IV, 261, 393; 1/4) — 12.00
"A Voice from Death" (IV, 347; 6/7) — 25.00

GIFTS

American
Kennedy, W. S. (IV, 439, [May 24]) — 5.00
Smith, R. P. (IV, 392; 10/31) — 25.00
Surplus from birthday dinner (6/26) — 125.00

English
Carpenter, E., Ford sisters, and others (IV, 341-342; Traubel, V, 256) — 194.95
Irving, Henry (IV, 348n; 10/1) — 50.00
Johnston, Dr. J., and J. W. Wallace (IV, 345) — 48.70E [36]
Stoker, Abraham (IV, 348n; 10/1) — 25.00
Friend of Carpenter (IV, 270n) — 4.50E

1890

BOOK ORDERS

American
Adams, R. (V, 106; 10/28, 11/5) — 16.00
Blake, J. V. (1/27) — 6.40
Cook, J. W. (2/6) — 6.40
Eckler, P. (6/30) — 5.00E
Kennedy, W. S. (V, 26) — 5.00
Lezinsky, D. L. (V, 106-107; 6/4) — 10.00E
McKay, D. (V, 76, 110-111; 8/27, 10/21) [37] — 300.00
Marsh, E. S. (V, 335; 6/21) — 5.00E
Munyon and M. Philips (1/29, 4/14) — 20.00E
Schilling, A. (12/9) — 5.00
Sears, J. M. (6/3) — 10.00E
Sheppard, Mr. (12/17) — 10.00E
Smith, J. W. (10/13) — 5.00
Smith, R. P. (8/12) — 58.80
Smith, W. H. (V, 136; 12/23) — 6.40
Southwick, F. T. (11/5) — 5.00E
Unidentified (V, 94) — 5.00E

English
Baillee, E. J. (V, 337; 10/20) — 5.00E
Browne, E. (10/6) — 5.00E
Drewry, L. (7/1) — 12.00E

---

35 On January 8, 1889, McKay purchased from WW 950 copies of *November Boughs* at $313.50 ($.33 per copy), less $5.59; see *Corr.,* IV, 266, and 1/8. In this year the royalties from *Leaves of Grass* and *Specimen Days* amounted to $144.20. McKay's order from WW of about fifty copies of the *Complete Works* (1889), I have placed under book orders. McKay paid the discounted price of $4.00 for a book which the poet sold for as much as $10.00 and as little as $6.00.

36 The pound in 1889 was valued at approximately $4.87. Wallace and Johnston contributed £10 and the unnamed friend of Carpenter 22s.6d.

37 McKay ordered from WW 100 copies of the *Complete Works* for sale to a London distributor; see *Corr.,* V, 42.

Forman, H. B. (S2231.1; 5/22)   24.00E
Greenhalgh, R. K. (10/6)   5.00E
Johnston, Dr. J (9/19)   5.00E
Johnstone, T. B. (V, 124;
    11/29)   5.00E
Payne, W. (V, 335; 7/28)   7.00E
Wallace, J. W. (V, 336; 8/28,
    9/11, 30)   15.00E
Wild, F. (12/24)   5.00E

Other
O'Dowd, B. (V, 138; 12/27)   25.00E

ROYALTIES
McKay, D. (4/14)   102.95

PUBLICATION
"A Death-Bouquet" (V, 19n;
    1/8)   10.00
"Old Age Echoes" [published
    1891] (V, 41; 4/24)   60.00
"Old Brooklyn Days" (V, 66)   6.00
"Old Poets" (V, 99, 100)   75.00
"Osceola" (V, 23n; 1/26)   10.00
"A Twilight Song" (V, 24n;
    2/26)   25.00
"Walt Whitman's
    Thanksgiving" (V, 118)   10.00

GIFTS
American
Furness, H. H., and S. W.
    Mitchell (V, 44; 4/29)   100.00
Johnston, J. H. (V, 132)   10.00
Stedman, E. C. (V, 49)   25.00

English
Brown, L. M. (V, 25; 2/10)   25.00
Carpenter, E., Ford sisters, and
    friends (V, 50; 5/26)   203.65
Johnston, Dr. J., and J. W.
    Wallace (V, 63n; 5/26)   50.00E [38]

MISCELLANEOUS
Ingersoll lecture (V, 108;
    10/22)   869.45
Sale of MS. to C. Aldrich (V,
    57; 6/12)   5.00

1891

BOOK ORDERS
American
Barrett, C. E. (V, 157-158;
    1/27)   6.40E
Burke, J. F. (3/5)   2.50
Cabot, M. R. (4/14)   5.00E
Carter, C. F. (3/17)   2.00
Cushing & Co. (4/1)   3.00E
Doherty, D. J. (7/9)   5.00
Fletcher, Dr. (6/2)   6.40E
Foster, S. B. (5/2)   17.80
Funk & Wagnalls (10/27)   4.00
Garland, H. (V, 204; 11/3)   19.20E
Herrick, F. H. (5/6)   6.40
Lloyd, J. W. (12/1)   6.40
McKay, D. (3/31, 9/26, 10/1,
    11/16; Royalty Statement)   252.95
Nicolay, W. J. (2/3)   4.40
Pratt, J. M. (3/27)   2.00
Smith, W. H. (V, 171; 3/2)   12.80
Unidentified (V, 146)   6.40E
Unidentified (V, 163)   5.00E
Unidentified (V, 238)   6.40E

English
Carpenter, E. (Ltr. 91/12/19)   19.20E
Dixon, T. (4/27; Ltr. from
    J. W. Wallace, 91/4/17)   5.00E
Forman, H. B. (V, 247)   15.00
Johnston, Dr. J. (Ltr. 91/6/11)   7.20E
Reynolds, C. (3/29)   12.80
Tuke, H. S. (V, 180-181; 3/24)   6.40E
Wallace, J. W. (Ltr. 91/6/5)   3.10E

Other
Dempsey, J. G. (5/2)   6.40E
Shephard, J. F. (6/15)   6.40E

ROYALTIES
McKay, D.   196.63

PUBLICATION
"American National
    Literature" (3/4)   75.00

---

38 Since WW translated Brown's gift of £5 as $25.00, I have assumed that the pound was worth $5.00 in this year.

"Old Actors, Singers, Show,
&c." (V, 179; 3/22)   16.00
"Old Chants" (V, 183n; 3/15)   12.00
"On, on the Same, Ye Jocund
Twain!" and "Unseen Bud"
(V, 201)   10.00
"The Pallid Wreath" (V, 145;
1/4)   5.00
"Ship Ahoy!" (V, 153; 1/19)   15.00
"Some Personal and Old-Age
Memoranda" (V, 171; 1/6) 90.00 [39]

GIFTS

English

Carpenter, E., and friends (V,
207)   192.00E

1892

BOOK ORDERS

American

McKay, D. (V, 275)   283.00

---

39 *Lippincott's* paid WW $50.00 for this article on January 6, but in a letter (V, 171) Whitman
reported that he had received $90.00.

A LIST OF WHITMAN'S CORRESPONDENTS

This alphabetical list includes all the recipients of letters printed in this volume. The name is followed by the letter number.

Browne, Francis Fisher, 1350.8

Bucke, Richard Maurice, 892.1, 936.5, 2487.1

Burroughs, John, 758.6, 1208.5, 1486.1

Century Illustrated Monthly Review, 1416.5, 1419.5

Chapin, William E. & Co., 190.7

Child, Josiah, 925

Church, F. P. and W. C., 409.8

Coburn, Mrs. Vine, 1095.3, 1095.6, 1096.1

Costelloe, Mary Smith, 2191.1

The Critic, 1464.1

Eckler, Peter, 162.1

Ford, Isabella O., 1165.5

Forman, H. Buxton, 438.5, 2231.1, 2239.6, 2657.1, 2658.1, 2668.5

Furness, Horace Howard, 1003.5, 1013.5, 2217.5

Garren, Harry, 2722

Gilder, Jeannette L., 901.5

Gridley, C. Oscar, 1437.5, 1449.2

Hoare, C. W., 572.5

Hollyer, Samuel, 1690.5

Huntington, William S., 382.5

Ingram, John H., 766.1

Jenks, John S., 202.5, 203.5

Johnston, Dr. John, 2572.5

Johnston, John H., 1330, 1485.1, 1561.1, 1626.5

Kennedy, William Sloane, 2525.1

Lawrence, Richard Hoe, 1015.5

Linton, William J., 778.1

Lucas, John, 839.1

McKay, David, 2537.1

New York *Herald,* 1639.5

Niemeyer (?), T. W., 1019.1

Noel, Roden, 1393.8, 1397.7, 1411.1

The North American Review, 1113

Price, Helen E., 1694

Ream, Vinnie, 397.05

Redpath, James, 1411

Rhodes, Albert, 2712

Rhys, Ernest, 1401.1, 1481.5, 1481.6, 1497.5, 1499.5, 1514.5, 1541.5, 1547.1, 1557.1, 1572.1, 1577.1, 1581.5, 1603.5, 1604.5, 1614.5, 1650.5, 2179, 2225.7, 2359.1

Sampson, Low, & Company, 652.5

Scott, John A., 998.1

Spofford, Ainsworth R., 758.3

Stanley, Samuel G., 2650.5

Stedman, Edmund Clarence, 735.1

Swinton, John, 733.1

Symonds, John Addington, 1070.5, 2262.1

Toronto *Globe,* 960

Wallace, J. W., 2546

Ward, John Quincy Adams, 749.5

Watson, R. Spence, 760.5, 767.5

White, Stokes & Allen, 1534.1

White, William Hale, 1171.1

Whitman, Louisa Orr, 1350.4

Williams, Talcott, 1595.5, 2375.1

AL	*American Literature*
Allen	Gay Wilson Allen, *The Solitary Singer* (1955)
Allen, Handbook	Gay Wilson Allen, *Walt Whitman Handbook* (1946)
Asselineau	Roger Asselineau, *L'Évolution de Walt Whitman* (1955)
Barrett	Clifton Waller Barrett Literary Manuscripts Collection, University of Virginia
Barrus	Clara Barrus, *Whitman and Burroughs—Comrades* (1931)
Berg	Henry W. and Albert A. Berg Collection, New York Public Library
Blodgett	Harold Blodgett, *Walt Whitman in England* (1934)
Bolton	County Borough of Bolton (England) Public Libraries
Bucke	Richard Maurice Bucke, *Walt Whitman* (1883)
CB	*The Commonplace-Book* (to be published by the New York University Press as *Daybooks and Diaries of Walt Whitman*)
CHAL	*The Cambridge History of American Literature*
Corr.	*The Correspondence of Walt Whitman,* ed. by Edwin Haviland Miller. In Coll W
Coll W	*The Collected Writings of Walt Whitman,* in progress: New York University Press, 1961–
CP	*Prose Works, 1892,* ed. by Floyd Stovall, 2 vols. (1963–1964). In Coll W
CRE	*Leaves of Grass: Comprehensive Reader's Edition* (1965), ed. by Harold W. Blodgett and Sculley Bradley. In Coll W
CT	Complete Text
CW	*The Complete Writings of Walt Whitman* (1902), 10 vols.
DAB	*Dictionary of American Biography*
DNB	*Dictionary of National Biography*
Doheny	Estelle Doheny Collection of the Edward Laurence Doheny Memorial Library, St. John's Seminary
ESQ	*The Emerson Society Quarterly*
Feinberg	Charles E. Feinberg Collection, the Library of Congress
Furness	Clifton Joseph Furness, *Walt Whitman's Workshop* (1928)
Gilchrist	Herbert Harlakenden Gilchrist, *Anne Gilchrist: Her Life and Writings* (1887)
Gohdes and Silver	Clarence Gohdes and Rollo G. Silver, eds., *Faint Clews & Indirections* (1949)

Hanley	T. E. Hanley Collection, University of Texas
Harned	Thomas B. Harned, ed., *The Letters of Anne Gilchrist and Walt Whitman* (1918)
Holloway	Emory Holloway, *Whitman—An Interpretation in Narrative* (1926)
Huntington	Henry E. Huntington Library
Kennedy	William Sloane Kennedy, *Reminiscences of Walt Whitman* (1896)
LC	The Library of Congress
LC #	*Walt Whitman—A Catalog Based Upon the Collections of The Library of Congress* (1955)
Lion	Oscar Lion Collection, New York Public Library
Livezey	Livezey Collection, University of California at Berkeley
McLeod	A. L. McLeod, ed., *Walt Whitman in Australia and New Zealand* (1964)
Manchester	The John Rylands Library, Manchester, England
Morgan	Pierpont Morgan Library
NAR	*The North American Review*
N & Q	*Notes and Queries*
NB	*November Boughs* (1888)
NEQ	*New England Quarterly*
Nonesuch	Emory Holloway, ed., *Walt Whitman—Complete Poetry & Selected Prose and Letters* (1938)
NYPL	New York Public Library
Pennsylvania	University of Pennsylvania
PT	Partial Text
SB	*Studies in Bibliography*
Sup.	*A Supplement to The Correspondence of Walt Whitman*
Syracuse	Syracuse University
Traubel	Horace Traubel, ed., *With Walt Whitman in Camden* (1906–1964), 5 vols.
Trent	Trent Collection, Duke University
UPP	*The Uncollected Poetry and Prose of Walt Whitman* (1921), 2 vols., ed. by Emory Holloway
Visits	John Johnston and J. W. Wallace, *Visits to Walt Whitman in 1890–1891 by Two Lancashire Friends* (1918)
WW	Walt Whitman
WWN	*Walt Whitman Newsletter*
WWR	*Walt Whitman Review*
Yale	Yale Collection of American Literature

ILLUSTRATIONS

Frontispiece: "Walt Whitman at Timber Creek," Drawing by Herbert Gilchrist (1878)
> Henry W. and Albert A. Berg Collection, The New York Public Library, Astor, Lenox and Tilden Foundations

1. William O'Donovan, Bust of Walt Whitman (1891)
> Present location unknown

2. Leonard Baskin, Broadside (1955)
> The Walt Whitman Birthplace, Huntington, Long Island

3. Charles Wells, "Walt Whitman" (1964), Etching
> The Walt Whitman Birthplace, Huntington, Long Island

4. Charles Wells, "Walt Whitman," Etching
> The Walt Whitman Birthplace, Huntington, Long Island

5. Thomas Cornell, "Walt Whitman" (1970), Etching and Colored Aquatint

6. D. Clarke, "Walt Whitman" (1975), Oil Painting
> Collection of Patrick Donovan
> Reproduction copyrighted by the Artist (Courtesy of Bodley Gallery, New York)

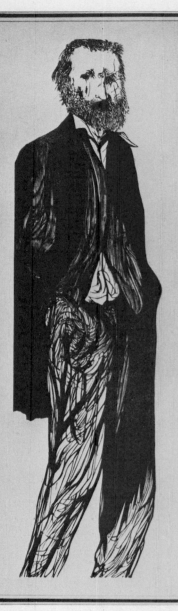

A *Poem*, AS CONSEQUENT, *Etc. written by* WALT WHITMAN
issued to celebrate the publication of LEAVES OF GRASS *in* 1855.

As consequent from store of summer rains,
Or wayward rivulets in autumn flowing,
Or many a herb-lined brook's reticulations,
Or subterranean sea-rills making for the sea,
Songs of continued years I sing.

Life's ever-modern rapids first, soon, (soon to blend,
With the old streams of death.)

Some threading Ohio's farm-fields or the woods,
Some down Colorado's cañons from sources of perpetual snow,
Some half-hid in Oregon, or away southward in Texas,
Some in the north finding their way to Erie, Niagara, Ottawa,
Some to Atlantica's bays, and so to the great salt brine.

In you whoe'er you are my book perusing,
In I myself, in all the world, these currents flowing,
All, all toward the mystic ocean tending.

Currents for starting a continent new,
Overtures sent to the solid out of the liquid,
Fusion of ocean and land, tender and pensive waves,
(Not safe and peaceful only, waves rous'd and ominous too,
Out of the depths the storm's abysmic waves, who knows whence?
Raging over the vast, with many a broken spar and tatter'd sail.)

Or from the sea of Time, collecting vasting all, I bring,
A window-drift of weeds and shells.

O little shells, so curious-convolute, so limpid-cold and voiceless,
Will you not little shells to the tympans of temples held,
Murmurs and echoes still call up, eternity's music faint and far,
Wafted inland, sent from Atlantica's rim, strains for the soul of the prairies,
Whisper'd reverberations, chords for the ear of the West joyously sounding,
Your tidings old, yet ever new and untranslatable,
Infinitesimals out of my life, and many a life,
(For not my life and years alone I give—all, all I give,)
These waifs from the deep, cast high and dry,
Wash'd on America's shores?

Printed by E. & L. Baskin, and R. Warren, at The Gehenna Press, Northampton, Mass.
1955

The Correspondence of Walt Whitman

VOLUME VI: A Supplement *with a* composite Index

0.5   *To an Unidentified Correspondent*   *3.30.* [*1841*]

    Miss Clarissa Lyvere has been assistant teacher in this school for several months past, and I would cheerfully testify to her competence and her general capability as a teacher. Her knowledge of the ordinary branches of a common school education is complete, and I unhesitatingly recommend her to any and all who may desire a good teacher for their children.

                       Walter Whitman

Whitestone School
   March 30

0.5. As John C. Broderick notes in *The Quarterly Journal of the Library of Congress,* 30 (1973), 44–47, this is the earliest extant letter. Nothing is known either of Miss Lyvere or of WW's tenure at this Long Island school during the winter of 1840–41. See Allen, 40.

1865

162.1 *To Peter Eckler*

May 3, 1865.

P. Eckler:

As I remitted $20 May 1st, which I suppose you duly received, I herewith enclose $14.85, as payment in full.

Deliver the sheets to A. Simpson, 8 Spruce street, & send me his receipt. Leave the copy of "Leaves of Grass," with Mrs. Louisa Whitman, Portland av. 4th door north of Myrtle, Brooklyn. If you have the plates of the two cancelled pages, I wish you would take three impressions of each page & enclose to me.

Walt Whitman
Washington
D. C.

I will trouble you also to send me Mr. Alvord's receipt for my plates, in his vault.

162.1. In arranging for the publication of *Drum-Taps* WW had contracts with Peter Eckler, Abraham Simpson, and Coridon A. Alvord. This is the missing letter in answer to Eckler's request of May 1, 1865, that the balance due him be paid. A defailed account of the transactions appears in *Corr.,* I, 260-261n, and in F. DeWolfe Miller's edition of *Drum-Taps* (1959), xxxiv-xlv.

1866

190.7 *To William E. Chapin & Company*

Sept. 24th 1866.

Wm. E. Chapin & Co. please furnish Mr. Ballow with paper for end leaves, &c. similar to that you used for the book.

Walt Whitman

202.5 *To John S. Jenks*

ATTORNEY GENERAL'S OFFICE,

Washington. Nov. 28, 1866.

John S. Jenks,
    Sir,
        In answer to yours of the 27th I reply that no letter from you, of the 17th has come to hand–& of course I have not rec'd $3.

But as I am not willing you should be the loser, in such a manner, I send you my book, by same mail with this.

Walt Whitman

203.5 *To John S. Jenks*

ATTORNEY GENERAL'S OFFICE,

Washington. Dec. 1, 1866.

J. S. Jenks,
    My dear Sir,
        I have rec'd your note of 30th Nov. with $3. Please accept my special acknowledgments. Should the letter of Nov. 17, ever appear, I will return it to you.

Walt Whitman

190.7. William E. Chapin of 24 Beekman Street, New York City, set the type for the 1867 edition of *Leaves of Grass; see Corr.,* I, 284. I have not identified Mr. Ballow.

202.5. When this and the following letter appeared at auction (Henkels #1348, March 21, 1924), they were inserted in an 1867 edition of *Leaves of Grass.* Although WW at this time kept no record of book sales, probably three dollars was the price he expected for this edition.

1868

328.5 *To an Unidentified Printer*

TRANSCRIPT.

November 25, 1868

It suits me first rate the way you have set it up–print 20 copies–give me good clear impressions.

Walt Whitman

328.5. On November 30, 1868, WW informed Ralph Waldo Emerson that "Proud Music of the Storm" was "put in type for my own convenience, and to insure greater correctness" *(Corr.,* II, 72). He asked Emerson to take the poem to James T. Fields, editor of *The Atlantic Monthly,* who promptly accepted it and published it in February, 1869. See *Corr.,* II, 71-73.

1870

382.5 *To William S. Huntington*

ATTORNEY GENERAL'S OFFICE,
Washington. Nov 5 1870

My dear Mr. Huntington:

I write to say I would like to postpone the pleasure of my visit to, & breakfast with, you & Mrs. Huntington till Sunday morning 13th inst. — instead of to-morrow.

Best respects to Mrs. Huntington.

Walt Whitman

I send the Galaxy with one of my last pieces—as I am not certain whether I sent it to you at the time.

382.5. Huntington was employed in the Treasury Department; see *Corr.,* II, 172. "Warble for Lilac-Time" appeared in *The Galaxy* in May, 1870; see *Corr.,* II, 93-94.

1871

397.05 *To Vinnie Ream*   7.17. *[1871?]*

Monday | afternoon | July 17.

Vinnie Ream,
    My dear friend,
        I would like to call on you, with an acquaintance of mine, John Swinton, at about 11 A. M. to morrow, Tuesday.

Walt Whitman

409.   *To an Unidentified Correspondent*

Washington, | Oct. 17, 1871.

Dear Sir:
        In answer to your letter of September 5, (I beg pardon for not replying to it before,) I have to inform you that some time ago Dion Thomas, bookseller, 2d story, Fulton st. north side, about midway bet. Nassau and Broadway, had some copies of 1st edition Leaves of Grass—but whether he still has them to sell I cannot say—
        I can procure you of the artist a good photograph—the price is $1.

Walt Whitman

The last edition of my Poems Complete I publish & sell myself.

397.05. In 1871 WW took his "vacation considerably earlier than usual" *(Corr.,* II, 120). John Swinton (1829–1901), a journalist and friend of Karl Marx, became acquainted with WW during the Civil War; see *Corr.,* I, 74–75n.

Vinnie Ream (1847–1914) made a bust from life of Abraham Lincoln, who agreed to sit weekly for the young sculptor. After his assassination she was commissioned to do a statue for the rotunda in the Capitol. When the work was unveiled in 1871, there was some criticism of the first woman to execute such a commission. Reproductions of her sculpture, as well as a portrait by George Caleb Bingham and a bust by Clark Mills, appear in *Antiques* (November 1976), 1016-1018.

409. In *Corr.,* II, 140, appears a transcription from a catalog of J. Pearson & Company, London, which accurately summarizes the contents of this letter. In 1867 WW informed another correspondent that Dion Dionysus Thomas had copies of the first edition of *Leaves of Grass;* see *Corr.,* I, 336-337.

409.8 *To Messrs. F. P. and W. C. Church*   *11.2. 187[1]*

TRANSCRIPT.

Washington, Nov. 2, 187–

I offer the enclosed Poem "The Mystic Trumpeter" for the January number, 1872, of Galaxy. The price is $40. . . .

Walt Whitman

409.5. F. P. and W. C. Church, editors of *The Galaxy,* printed many of WW's poems beginning in 1867; see *Corr.,* I, 335-336. The first notice of WW to appear in the magazine was John Burroughs' review of *Drum-Taps;* see *Corr.,* I, 285n. Apparently the Churches rejected "The Mystic Trumpeter," which appeared in *The Kansas Magazine* in February, 1872; see *Corr.,* II, 157n.

1872

438.5 *To H. Buxton Forman*

Brooklyn, N. Y. | March 26, 1872.

My dear Mr. Forman,

Your letter & the fine poem of "the Great Peace-Maker" have been rec'd by me, & read with pleasure. With regard to re-printing my book in full in England I can only say that of course it would be gratifying to me—But I should like to be informed in advance of any thing pending that way, as I should like to make one or two suggestions before the book is begun. A preface or introduction mainly of statistical nature (about the book & myself) including a brief syllabus of the plan & idea of "Leaves of Grass" from its own point of view—would be judicious—but I don't think favorably of a literary criticism for preface—

I have an Edition (the sixth) just out—edition 1872—in some respects probably the best—Sampson Low, and Trübner have copies of it.—It looks just now as though some form of international copyright might be legalized here—If so, this might be worth considering in reference to the reprint of my book in England.

If you can get a look at the Danish (Copenhagen) Monthly Magazine *"For Ide og Virkeliged,"* "For Idea & Reality," either of Feb. or March, I am not certain which, I understand it has a criticism on my book, from a believer. I am here on a visit, & return to Washington in a few days. I shall always be happy to hear from you. My address is Solicitor's Office, Treasury, Washington, D. C.—U.S.A.

Walt Whitman

438.5. On February 21, 1872, H. Buxton Forman (1842–1917), later the biographer of Shelley and Keats, sent to WW a copy of R. H. Horne's *The Great Peace-Maker; A Sub-marine Dialogue* (London, 1872). This poetic account of the laying of the Atlantic cable has a foreword written by Forman.

Forman proposed an English edition of WW's writings "verbatim, without any retrenchments," a project of which the poet thoroughly approved (Feinberg; Traubel, II, 265-266).

The 1872 edition is the fifth, not the sixth, edition,

At the conclusion of the second paragraph of the letter is pasted a clipping from the New-York *Tribune* of March 26 in reference to the plans of Senator John Sherman for a new copyright law.

Rudolf Schmidt's laudatory essay appeared in the March issue of *For Ide og Virkelighed;* see *Corr.,* II, 175n.

WW was in Brooklyn at his mother's home from early February until about the tenth of April; see *Corr.,* II, 165-173.

1874

572.5 *To C. W. Hoare*

431 Stevens st | cor West. | Camden | N. Jersey. | January 22, '74
C. W. Hoare,
Dear Sir,
Your note with the $5 enclosed, has safely reached me here.
My books, *Leaves of Grass, Passage to India, Democratic Vistas,* &c. will be duly dispatched to-night or to-morrow, on their way to your brother in Ireland. If convenient, send me word, in due time, about their reaching him— as you will probably hear.
I am laid up here invalided—but expect to get round again—

Walt Whitman

572.5. A year after his "slight stroke of paralysis, on my left side, and especially the leg" *(Corr.,* II, 192), WW was recuperating slowly and was writing occasional articles for magazines as well as handling orders for his books.

1875

652.5 *To Messrs. Sampson, Low & Company*

TRANSCRIPT.

Camden, N.J., February 1, 1875

[WW requests an accounting for the previous year.]

652.5. Sampson, Low, Marston, Low, and Searle, London bookdealers, handled the English distribution of *Leaves of Grass* and *Democratic Vistas;* see *Corr.,* II, 118n, 273n. On February 18, 1876, WW received nine dollars from the firm "closing up acc't" *(CB)*.

According to the auction record (Parke-Bernet, February 7–8, 1944), WW addressed the letter to "Messrs. Samson Low & Co."

1876

733.1   *To John Swinton*   4.12. [1876]

TRANSCRIPT.

431 Stevens St., Camden, N Jersey, April 12

Dear John—

I have adopted your suggestion & written (same mail with this) to Wm. Swinton, Ward, Dr. Seeger, Stedman, [J.] Miller, Mr. Jardine—I am entirely satisfied with your letter, (as with Buchanan's and Rossetti's action in London.) I am pleased well with what you write me in, & are doing by, your letter ... Things go on with me much the same as usual of late ... When you see any thing *notable* or pungent about me or my affairs, send it to me, as I neither see or hear much here.

                                        Walt Whitman

735.5   *To Edmund Clarence Stedman*   [*4.14. 1876*]

TRANSCRIPT.

I send to-day by Adams Express (address same as this card) my Two Vols. new Edition ... will try to write further next week.

                                        Walt Whitman

733.1. In April, 1876, WW, with the assistance of friends here and abroad, began a promotional campaign for the sale of *Leaves of Grass* (sixth edition) and *Two Rivulets*. John Swinton suggested that a circular be sent to his brother William, John Quincy Adams Ward, Dr. Ferdinand Seeger, Edmund Clarence Stedman, Joaquin Miller, and D. Jardine, most of whom ordered copies of the books. See *Corr.*, III, 38–39n.

Swinton reported WW's "penury" in an article in the New York *Herald* on April 1, 1876. Robert Buchanan and William Michael Rossetti made appeals to English admirers to relieve the poet's poverty. The story of the English appeal is recorded in *Corr.*, III.

735.5. This postcard to Stedman has been dated on the basis of an entry in *CB:* "April 13 from E. C. Stedman | 80 Broadway N Y. | sent books, slips photo | &c | $30.00."

749.5 To John Quincy Adams Ward

431 Stevens st. | Camden New Jersey | June 8 '76

My dear Ward,

I have rec'd your friendly & generous subscription, $50, for 5 sets of my Books, & thank you heartily. I send by express to-day prepaid, *three Volumes*—one set complete, & a *Leaves of Grass*—with some other little Vols-slips, duplicate engravings of self—& *a special Photo.* prepared by my own hands (? for your studio)—

As the very limited first issue of my new edition is about exhausted, your other sets will have to be delayed until a further issue, now in press, is ready.

Walt Whitman

Please send me word if the package arrives safely—

758.3 To Ainsworth R. Spofford

Camden N Jersey | July 22 '76

A R Spofford,
  Dear Sir

The editions of my *Leaves of Grass,* as within specified, are the only ones I have published—& *comprise all. (Two Rivulets,* the further Vol. just issued by me, I believe you have.)

Walt Whitman

I write on the letter, & return it so, for greater definiteness.

749.5. WW wrote for the first time to this distinguished American sculptor (1830–1910) on April 12, 1876; see *Corr.,* III, 39, and V, 303. According to entries in *CB* on June 6 and 8, WW sent two copies of *Leaves of Grass* and one copy of *Two Rivulets,* as well as *Memoranda During the War,* John Burroughs's *Notes on Walt Whitman, As a Strong Bird on Pinions Free* (1872), and several photographs taken by Gurney & Son in 1871 and 1872. For the photographs see Henry S. Saunders, *100 Whitman Photographs* (1946), nos. 39 and 40.

758.3. A. R. Spofford (1825–1908) was Librarian of Congress from 1864 to 1897. WW's reply was written on the verso of Spofford's letter of July 21, in which he cited the six editions of *Leaves of Grass* in the Library of Congress.

For other letters to Spofford, see *Corr.,* III, 247, 299.

758.6 *To John Burroughs*   8.1. [1876]

ADDRESS: John Burroughs | Esopus-on-Hudson |
New York. POSTMARK: Camden | Aug | 1 | N.J.

Camden Aug 1

I send a copy of L of G. (same address as this card)—Please let me
know (by postal card will do) if it reaches you safely. Much the same with
me—feel middling fair. Your letter rec'd. Folks well—

W. W.

760.5 *To R. Spence Watson*   [8.30. 1876]

ADDRESS: R Spence Watson | 101 Pilgrim Street |
Newcastle-on-Tyne | England. POSTMARKS:
Camden | Aug | 30 | N.J. ; Philadelphia | Aug |
30 | (?).

431 Stevens street | Camden, N Jersey—U S A

I have to-day forwarded by mail, to same address as this card, my Two
Vols., *L of G.* and *Two Riv[ulets]*—Please let me know, (by postal card will do)
soon as they reach you safely. Another set of same Two Vols. will be sent you
soon.

W W

766.1 *To John H. Ingram*   9.7. [1876]

ADDRESS: J H Ingram | Howard House | Stoke Newington |
London N England. POSTMARKS: Camden | Sep | 7 | N.J.;
Philadelphia, Pa. | Sep | 8 | Paid All.; London (?) |
CA(?) | Sp 19 | 76 | Paid.

Camden, New Jersey—U S America | Sept 7—

I send you to-day by mail, to same address as this card, my Volume,
Two Rivulets. Please let me know (by postal card will do) soon as it reaches
you safely—

W Whitman

758.6. John Burroughs, the naturalist, became acquainted with WW during the Civil War and
remained a steadfast friend; see *Corr.,* I, 14. The transaction referred to in the note was also recorded in
CB. At this time WW lived with George and Louisa Orr Whitman, whose only son, Walter Orr
Whitman, had died on July 12; see *Corr.,* III, 54.

760.5. Watson was apparently one of William Michael Rossetti's friends and among the early
English admirers of *Leaves of Grass.* The transactions mentioned in this and the following letter were
recorded in *CB,* where WW noted receipt of five dollars. On September 29, 1884 (LC), Watson
requested an inscribed copy of *Leaves of Grass.*

766.1. John H. Ingram (1848–1916) edited Poe's writings and wrote critical studies of Chatterton
and Marlowe. WW noted sending the volumes in *CB.*

767.5 *To R. Spence Watson*   9.9. [1876]

ADDRESS: R. Spence Watson | 101 Pilgrim street |
Newcastle-on-Tyne | England. POSTMARK: Camden |
Sep | 9 | N.J.

Camden, N Jersey—U S America | *Sept 9—*
I to-day send you by mail, a *second set,* Two Vols. of my Books. (One
set went nine days ago) Please notify me by postal card soon as you receive
them.

W Whitman

778.1 *To William J. Linton*

Dec 11 '76

My dear Linton
I have been for some weeks down in the country—half moping like—
yet feeling *rather better* these days, upon the whole—
Your note of some weeks since ought to have been answered before. I
have been waiting for the chance to get from the bindery, or from my stack,
(as I unwrap the books) a copy of *Two Rivulets with the dark brown* label you
want—I have it in mind, & shall get it so, & send it you—Meantime, let this
remorseful note be my apology—
My address here is still the same—

Walt Whitman

Camden | New Jersey

778.1. William J. Linton was an engraver and an anthologist; see *Corr.,* II, 171-172; III, 116-117.
According to *CB,* WW was with the Stafford family on November 5-8, 16, and 25-28, and visited
Mrs. Anne Gilchrist in Philadelphia on November 18-20 and 24.

1877

839.1   *To John Lucas*   *11.13.* [*1877*]

Camden N J Nov 13

Mr John Lucas
    Dear Sir
        This is to introduce a young man, a friend of mine, J Horner Stafford,
son of Montgomery Stafford, of Glendale—He has been for some months
studying & practicing Telegraphy—& perhaps you could give him something
to do—At any rate I take the liberty of introducing him to you, to talk it
over. He is a young man of intelligence & first-class integrity.

Walt Whitman

    I want to come down before long, & make you a call or short visit, & see
your works.

839.1. In *Corr.*, III, 102, appears an inadequate summary of this letter based on the catalog of a
sale at the Anderson Galleries on October 18, 1923.
        The Lucas family had a zinc and color works near Kirkwood, New Jersey, where the Staffords
lived; see *Corr.*, III, 103n.
        When WW was recovering from his stroke in the 1870s, he befriended a young man named Harry
Stafford and eventually the Stafford family. For a detailed account of WW's relationship with this
family, see *Corr.*, III, particularly the Introduction.
        Jacob Horner Stafford (1850–1890) was the son of Montgomery (1820–1907), the uncle of Harry
Stafford. The letter followed a visit from "Horner" earlier in the day *(CB)*.

1878

892.1 *To Richard Maurice Bucke*   *10.23.* [*1878*]

ADDRESS: Dr R M Bucke | Asylum for the Insane |
London Ontario | Canada. POSTMARKS: Philadelphia |
Oct | 23 | 5 PM | Pa.; London | Oc 25 | 78 | (?).

Camden New Jersey | U S A Oct 23

My dear friend

Yours of 19th Oct rec'd—(I came up yesterday from the country &
found it)—I return you Forman's letter—am glad you sent it me—but have
nothing decisive to say at present *for myself* about New English edition—

Doctor, I want to come to see you & be with you all, truly—& shall do
so—but havn't felt the spirit move me the past summer—look for me next
summer—

I am well, for me—have had a good summer—

Rec'd a long & kind letter from Tennyson day before yesterday—

As I scribble this (noon) the greatest gale I ever knew seems to be just
subsiding—Our town streets are strewed with wrecks, roofs, timbers, trees
&c—

Love to you & yours
Walt Whitman

892.1. This is the earliest surviving letter to Richard Maurice Bucke, the Canadian physician and
mystic, who became one of the poet's closest friends in the later years and an executor of his literary
effects after his death.

Apparently Bucke sent WW's letter to H. Buxton Forman since it was among letters to Forman
and Ernest Rhys which were recently acquired by the Berg Collection. The letters of Bucke and Forman
are not known. Once again Forman expressed interest in printing an unabridged edition of *Leaves of
Grass* in England; see *Sup.* 438.5.

Tennyson's letter of August 24, 1878, appears in *Corr.,* III, 134-135. WW did not receive it until
October 21 *(CB)*.

In this letter WW enclosed a printed slip of a poem entitled "Thou Who Hast Slept All Night
upon the Storm," with the following notation: "The terrible gale & destruction, here this morning,
brings(?) up this little piece to my mind—let me send it as a souvenir."

901.5   *To Jeannette L. Gilder*

TRANSCRIPT.

Camden New Jersey | Dec 20 '78

My dear Jenny Gilder

Yours of to-day rec'd–(The other also–but I thought you merely contemplated it like, & no hurry)–I only write now in haste to say I will help you to any thing on the subject you desire–Will turn it over in my mind to write more fully Sunday, so you will get it Monday.

Walt Whitman

I have a notion that the raciest part of a fellow's life–mine at any rate–could be told by giving copious strings of characteristic fine *personal anecdotes, incidents–&c–*

Jenny, what is it for?

901.5. Early in December Jeannette L. Gilder wrote to WW, in his words, "that she is going to write my life & asking for items &c" *(Corr.,* III, 141). Although WW complied with her request, nothing came of the proposal. About the same time, in a letter to Burroughs, WW wrote: "(I would like best to be *told about* in strings of continuous anecdotes, incidents, mots, thumbnail personal sketches, characteristic & true–...)"; see *Corr.,* III, 144.

The biographical principle enunciated here was to be followed scrupulously a few years later by Bucke in his biography of the poet.

This letter is known through a transcription prepared by Miss Gilder on May 12, 1902.

1879

925. *To Josiah Child*
TRANSCRIPT.

June 9 '79

My dear Josiah Child

I have only just rec'd yours of April 22d, with $24.50 from Trübner & Co. for which am't see receipt enclosed—

I note the order for nineteen new copies, & as soon as I go back to Camden, (within a week) they shall be carefully forwarded to you. You speak of a remittance for of three guineas, promised to be forwarded by Mr. Fraser for the *Tobacco Plant* piece. *As no such remittance has been rec'd by me, nor heard about,* it has probably been deferred—Mr. F. can address me, & send P O order to Camden—I shall prepare other two pieces & send him for the paper, in response to his kind request.

Thanks for letter enclosures—Mr. Westness's, Mr Walters's & Mr Norman's. Will try to send you photos for him (Thos: Dixon's is not enclosed)—I keep well, for me—have been away from home *gallivanting* around, land & water, & especially this city, the last two months—I send you a paper with this.

Walt Whitman

(I write this from *New York City,* U S A. 1309 Fifth av: near 86th st.: but I return soon to 431 Stevens st: Camden New Jersey—which is my permanent P O address—)

---

925. A summary of this letter from an auction catalog appears in *Corr.*, III, 157–158, 421.

Josiah Child was the agent for Trübner & Company; see *Corr.*, III, 137n, where there is a detailed record of WW's transactions with the English publishing firm.

For "Three Young Men's Deaths," which appeared in *Cope's Tobacco Plant* in April (II, 318-319), WW received $15.30 on June 15 *(CB)*.

In *WWR*, 16 (1970), 56-57, Professor Florence B. Freedman has identified T. D. Westness as an uneducated English admirer; see also Traubel, III, 571-573. She also points out that Walters may be the Frank W. Walters mentioned in William Sloane Kennedy's *The Fight of a Book for the World* (1926), 41.

For Henry Norman of the *Pall Mall Gazette,* see *Corr.*, IV, 62, and for Thomas Dixon, see *Corr.*, II, 99-100.

936.5 *To Richard Maurice Bucke*   [*10.17. 1879*]

TRANSCRIPT by R. M. Bucke.

Have been absent from Camden the last five weeks—been over the Plains & up in the Rocky Mountains—gave out about two weeks ago & have been quite sick ever since (principal trouble with my head) but am recovering—only received yours (of Sept 22) today—will send the book from Camden soon as I get back—shall stay here twelve days—

W W

936.5. Dr. Bucke included this transcription in a letter to his wife. It was discovered in the D. B. Weldon Library of the University of Western Ontario by Artem Lozynsky, who printed it as well as Bucke's letter to WW on November 9, 1879, in *WWR,* 19 (1973), 168–169.

An account of WW's Western trip and his physical collapse appears in *Corr.,* III, 163-171. The poet remained in St. Louis at the home of his brother Jeff until January 3, 1880. On January 7, 1880, he sent ten volumes to Dr. Bucke *(CB).*

1880

960.   *To the Editor,* Toronto Globe

London Ontario Canada | June 17 '80

Editor *Globe:*

Herewith find a letter for the paper. The price is $10—If used *it must be printed in the paper of Tuesday June 22* (or afterward)—The letter is sent to two or three other papers in Canada—(to *you only* in Toronto)—to one each in New York, Washington, Cincinnati &c in the U S on that imperative condition—*this condition a point of honor*—

If used please send me the pay here, also the paper, as this place will be my head-quarters all summer—

Walt Whitman

992.1   *To an Unidentified Correspondent*   [Between 6.4–9.28. 1880]
TRANSCRIPT.

London, Ontario, Canada

. . . I sell them to booksellers at $3.50 a Volume. Should you want any I can send them from here by mail. . . .

Walt Whitman

---

960. This letter replaces the summary derived from the catalog of the Chicago Book and Art Auction on April 29, 1931.

WW sent "Summer Days in Canada," as the letter indicates, to many newspapers; see *Corr.,* III, 181-182. Unless the notation in *CB* refers to the asking price, the *Toronto Globe* printed and paid for the piece.

992.1. In 1880 WW paid his only visit to London, Ontario, where his friend Dr. Richard Maurice Bucke was superintendent of a mental institution. Dr. Bucke accompanied WW from Camden on June 3, and for almost four months, until September 28, the poet vacationed in Canada. See *Corr.,* III, 181-188, *Walt Whitman's Diary in Canada,* and *CB.* The postcard or letter must have been written, then, between June 4 and September 28, 1880.

1881

998.1 *To John A. Scott*

TRANSCRIPT.

431 Stevens Street, Camden,
New Jersey, Jan. 16, 1881.

Dear Sir,
Yours of Dec. 24 rec'd & I have thought the shortest way would be
for me to send the books without further ceremony . . . The price is $10, or its
equivalent in your currency . . .

Walt Whitman

1003.5 *To Horace Howard Furness*

431 Stevens Street | Friday noon Feb 4 '81
Thanks, dear Horace, for the warm affectionate letter & for the $10
just rec'd—
I am kept in by the weather & a special spell of feebleness, but the first
fine day will bring me out—

Walt Whitman

998.1. On January 16, 1881, WW sent the two-volume set of the 1876 edition to John A. Scott,
Pembridge Villa, Southfield, London *(CB);* also see *Corr.,* III, 206, and note 24.
1003.5. According to the entry in *CB,* WW sent *Two Rivulets* to Horace Howard Furness (1833–
1912), the distinguished Shakespearean scholar whom the poet met in 1879; see *Corr.,* III, 150, 175-176,
and Traubel, III, 520.

1013.5 *To Horace Howard Furness*

431 Stevens Street | Camden Jan: 26 | '81

My dear friend

I am sorry to have to send you word that I am not feeling in good trim at all to-day, & shall be unable to meet you & the other friends at dinner—

I send you herewith a couple of pictures (I call it my Quaker picture)—one is for your father—also the books herewith—also my love to you—

Walt Whitman

1015.5 *To Richard Hoe Lawrence*

431 Stevens Street | Camden New Jersey March 8 '81

Dear Sir

Yours of yesterday—in response to which—without a ceremony—I forward you two books by same mail with same address—Please send pay by P O order—

Walt Whitman

1019.1 *To T. W. Niemeyer(?)*   *3.[17?]. 1881*

TRANSCRIPT.

Dear Sir,

Yours of 10th enclosing $10 received Camden, March 1881.

Walt Whitman

1013.5. WW sent *Leaves of Grass* and *Two Rivulets* on the same day, as well as copies of the Gutekunst photograph of 1880; see *Specimen Days* (1971), plate 160, and *WWR,* 18 (1972), 141.

Furness' father, Dr. William Henry Furness, was a minister (Traubel, III, 520).

1015.5. WW sent *Leaves of Grass* and *Two Rivulets* on the same day *(CB)*. Lawrence lived at 81 Park Avenue, New York City.

1019.1. On the basis of an entry in *CB,* on March 17, 1881, it is a reasonable conjecture that WW sent the two volumes published in 1876 to T. W. Niemeyer, 150 Crown Street, New Haven, Connecticut—"for Sarah A Booth" *(CB).*

1070.5 *To John Addington Symonds*   *11.7.* [*1881*]

ADDRESS: J Addington Symonds | Clifton Hill House |
Clifton | Bristol England. POSTMARKS: Camden |
Nov | 7 | 12 M | N.J. ; Philadelphia | Nov | 7 | (?);
(?)ol | (?)B | (?)o 18 | 81.

431 Stevens street | Camden New Jersey U S America

Dear Sir

I send you by same mail with this the circular of my just out
edition—enclosing printed slips of some new pieces not hitherto printed in
book—The Volume is copyrighted in England & published there by Trübner
& Co:—I am well enough in health to go around leisurely & work a little—

Walt Whitman

1070.5. For Symonds, historian, translator, and critic, see *A Century of Whitman Criticism,* ed.
Edwin Haviland Miller (1969), xxx–xxxi. On the same day WW also sent circulars and slips to
William Michael Rossetti and Moncure D. Conway *(CB).*

1882

1095.3 *To Mrs. Vine Coburn*

Camden New Jersey Feb: 9 '82

My dear Madam—

Yours of 9th rec'd—I should be pleased to send you the book—the price is $2—My Photo & auto[graph] are sold by the *Camden Children's Home,* Haddon av: for their benefit, price $1—Or if you desire I can supply you with one for them—

Walt Whitman

If you send to me, please send p o order—

1095.6 *To Mrs. Vine Coburn*   *2.18.* [*1882*]

Feb: 18—Evn'g—

Yours of 15th rec'd, with the $10 for Centennial Edition—2 vols— Sincere thanks—As I am absent from home for a week or so—& shall not be able to send them till I get back (I will see to it immediately then)—thought I would send you this word right away—

Walt Whitman

1096.1 *To Mrs. Vine Coburn*

Camden New Jersey | March 7 '82

Dear Madam

Returning here last evening I have mailed to you the two Volumes of my books. Would you please notify me soon as they reach you safely?

Walt Whitman

1095.3. Mrs. Vine Coburn was a member of a distinguished Maine family; see *WWR,* 15 (1969), 59n. The two-volume set was sent on March 7 after WW's two-week stay with the Staffords *(CB).*

WW began to supply the Children's Home in Camden with signed photographs on November 17, 1876, and also sold them himself "for the benefit of the orphans" *(CB).* The photograph, signed "Walt Whitman 1881," is the 1872 photograph of Frank Pearsall; see frontispiece to *Corr.,* II; *The Artistic Legacy of Walt Whitman* (1970), figure 14; and *Specimen Days* (1971), plate 148.

1113. *To the Editor,* The North American Review

431 Stevens Street | Camden New Jersey | Evn'g May 12 '82

Dear Sir

Yours of yesterday rec'd—I could send the MS of *Carlyle from an American Point of View* by the 20th or 21st—a week from now—It would make about nine or ten pages—

What I said about its being "a candidate for the place of leading paper" &c was meant to be left entirely to the editorial exigencies & judgment—no *condition* at all—

Walt Whitman

1165.5 *To Isabella O. Ford*

ADDRESS: Miss Isabella O Ford | Adel Grange |
Leeds | England. POSTMARKS: Camden | Oct | 11 |
12-M | N.J.; Phila. Paid (?) | Oct | 11 | 1882 | Pa.

431 Stevens street | Camden New Jersey | U S America | Oct 11 '82

Dear Miss Ford

Yours of Sept: 25th rec'd—& accordingly I send you (same mail with this—same address) my two volumes—poetic and prose. The price is one pound sterling (which includes the books, postage, & everything)—send to me here by P. O. order—

When you see Edward Carpenter tell him I am well & hearty (considering) & send him my love—

Walt Whitman

1113. The typescript printed in *Corr.*, III, 277, contains a few minor errors: "Evening" for "Evn'g," "exigencies of" for "exigencies &."

1165.5. Isabella and her sister Elizabeth were intimates of Edward Carpenter; see *Corr.*, III, 400, 402. WW noted the transaction in *CB*.

1171.1 *To William Hale White*

ADDRESS: W Hale White | Park Hill | Carshalton
Surrey | England. POSTMARKS: Camden | May | 6 |
5 PM | N.J.; Phila. Paid | May | 6 | 18(?).

Camden New Jersey | U S America—Nov: 6 '82 | *431 Stevens street—*
In compliance with yours of Oct: 23 I forward the volume "Specimen
Days" special ed'n, same address as this card. The price is $3 (12.s.4.d.) which
please send in p. o. order—thanks for your kindly words & wishes—

Walt Whitman

1171.1. White (1831–1913) published under a pseudonym *The Autobiography of Mark Rutherford*
(1881) and *Mark Rutherford's Deliverance* as well as translations and criticism. WW sent a "Gilt top"
Specimen Days (CB). White's letter to WW is in the Feinberg Collection. For this information I am
indebted to William White's "Some New Whitman Items," in *Prairie Schooner,* 44 (1970), 55.
The translation of dollars into English currency in the note appears to be in a different hand.
According to Kennedy, in *The Fight of a Book for the World* (1926), 41, White wrote about WW
in the *Secular Review,* March 20, 1880.

1883

1208.5 *To John Burroughs*

TRANSCRIPT.

Camden, March 27 1883

... the type-setting on Dr. Bucke's book is about completed.

W. W.

1208.5. In 1883 WW arranged with David McKay, his Philadelphia publisher, to print Bucke's *Walt Whitman* (1883). The poet personally supervised publication, including proofreading; see *Corr.* III, 336-337n.

1885

1313.5 *To Unidentified Correspondents*

328 Mickle st | Camden New Jersey | March 31 '85

Dear Sirs

In answer to yours of March 27 —

Walt Whitman

The first *Leaves of Grass* was printed in 1855 in Brooklyn New York—Small quarto 9 by 12 inches, 95 pages—in the type called "English"—was not stereotyped—800 copies were struck off on a hand press by Andrew Rome, in whose job office the work was all done—the author himself setting some of the type.

2d ed'n, 16 mo was in 1856; 3d, 12 mo. 1860; 4th ditto, 1867; 5th 1871; 6th 1876, two Vols. "Leaves of Grass" and "Two Rivulets"; 7th 1881.

1330. *To John H. Johnston*

ADDRESS: J H Johnston | Jeweler | 150 Bowery |
Cor: Broome | New York City. POSTMARK: Philadelphia |
Pa. | Jul 21 85 | 8 30 PM.

328 Mickle street | Camden New Jersey | July 21 '85 Evn'g

Dear friend

The watch *(a beauty)*—the knives & forks & the china ware all reach'd me safely this afternoon—thanks, thanks & best love—

1313.5. This letter may have been sent to the publishing firm of J. Schabelitz in Zurich, Switzerland. The plans of the publisher to issue German translations of WW's poems by Knortz and Rolleston encountered many delays. See *Corr.*, V, 320-321; IV, 220, 270.

1330. The transcription in *Corr.*, III, 398, derived from the catalog of the sale at the Anderson Galleries on October 18, 1923, includes the substance of the letter, except for the references to Johnston's letter and the weather. WW received the items mentioned in the first sentence on July 19, 1885 *(CB)*.

Of your letter every point & behest shall be obeyed—

Fearfully hot day again—but I am standing it so far—am just going out for my evening sail on the Delaware—God bless you & yours—

Walt Whitman

1350.4 *To Louisa Orr Whitman*   11.16. [*1885*]

328 Mickle street | Camden Nov: 16

Dear Lou

Thanks for the beautiful & costly wolf-skin robe—it is just the thing I wanted most—already comes in first rate—used it yesterday—Ed's stockings came Saturday—I am feeling pretty well—better than three weeks ago—

Walt Whitman

1350.8 *To Francis Fisher Browne*

ADDRESS: F F Browne | Care of Jansen, McClurg & Co: | Chicago Ill:. POSTMARK: [indecipherable].

23d Nov: '85—328 Mickle St: | Camden New Jersey

Dear Sir

I cheerfully give you permission to use in your Volume of War Poetry the pieces specified in your letter to Mr Stedman—or any others of mine you may desire.

Walt Whitman

1350.4. On November 14, 1885, WW noted a "fine wolf-skin lap robe rec'd from Lou" *(CB)*. Louisa Orr Whitman was his sister-in-law, George's wife.

In the last years of his life, particularly in the well-known photographs taken by Thomas Eakins, WW had the wolf-skin about his shoulders. See *Sup.* 2668.5.

The stockings were for Edward Whitman, the feeble-minded brother whose board was paid for by George and Walt.

1350.8. Francis Fisher Browne (1843–1913) was collecting poems of the Civil War; see *Sup.* 1534.1.

Apparently Edmund Clarence Stedman, author and critic, forwarded Browne's request to WW; see *Corr.*, I, 167n and *Sup.* 1534.1.

1886

1393.8 *To Roden Noel*

ADDRESS: Roden Noel | 57 Anesley Park | London
S E | England. POSTMARK: Camden | May | ? |
8 PM | 1886 | N.J.

328 Mickle Street | *Camden New Jersey*
U S America | *May 3 '86*
—Yours of April 22 just rec'd—The book has never reached me—I
have nothing to do with Houghton, Mifflin & Co:—Of course should be glad
to get & read the book, or any of your writings—I am living here well cared
for, but paralyzed in body, & quite unable to walk around—Glad to hear from
you, & would send you my writings, gladly.

Walt Whitman

1397.7 *To Roden Noel*

ADDRESS: Roden Noel | 57 Anesley Park |
London S E | England. POSTMARKS: Camden |
May | 25 | 3 PM | 1886 | N.J.; Philadelphia |
May | 25 | 1886 | (?).

328 Mickle street | Camden New Jersey U S America | *May 25 '86-*
Thanks for the photograph & letter—but the book has not yet reach'd
me—Yes, indeed, I consider you one of my good friends in England.

Walt Whitman

1401.1 *To Ernest Rhys*

ADDRESS: Ernest Rhys | 59 Cheyne Walk | London |
S W | England. POSTMARKS: Camden | Jun | 10 | (?) PM |
1886 | N.J.; Philadelphia | Jun | 10 | 1886 | (?).

Camden New Jersey | U S America | June 10 '86—
Thanks for your handsome little book "King Arthur" wh' has just
reach'd me—In health &c. I remain as of late—

Walt Whitman

1397.7. Noel wrote to WW on May 16, 1886 (Feinberg; Traubel, I, 394), and sent a copy of
Essays on Poetry and Poets (1886); see *Corr.*, II, 162n, and *Sup.* 1411.1. Noel replied to WW's card on
March 30; see Traubel, I, 432-433.
1401.5. *Romance of King Arthur* appeared in Rhys's Camelot Series along with *The Poems of Walt
Whitman* [*Selected*].

1411. *To James Redpath*

TRANSCRIPT.

Camden, N.J. June 29, '86

My Dear friend,

I send you "How I Made a Book—or tried to." If you can use it I think it must be in the Review. It makes 3300 words, & would take from 7 to 8 pages [in] Rev. The price is $80, & I should want 100 proof sets in slips, such as I have had two or three times before from printing office. If usable have it put in type soon, & send me proof here.

Walt Whitman

1411.1 *To Roden Noel*

ADDRESS: Roden Noel | 57 Anesley | Park | London s. e. | England. POSTMARK: Camden (?) | Jun | 29 | 8 PM | (?) | N.J.

328 Mickle Street | Camden New Jersey U S America | *June 29 '86*—
Thanks for your good "Essays" which came safely this forenoon—thanks for your warm & affectionate words ab't me—I am living here quite disabled & paralyzed, but in good heart & able to read & write—Is this the right address?

Walt Whitman

1416.5 *To the Editor,* Century Illustrated Monthly Review

328 Mickle Street | Camden New Jersey | July 25 '86

Dear Sir

I have finished the article

Army Hospitals and Cases
Memoranda of the Time—1863—'6
By Walt Whitman

& will send it on in a couple of days—It will make perhaps six pages—

Walt Whitman

1411. Letter 1411 *(Corr.,* IV, 36) is based on an auction record (S. T. Freeman Company, March 18, 1913), but this appears to be almost a complete transcription of the still unlocated letter.

At this time James Redpath was editor of *The North American Review.* See *Corr.,* IV, 36n, 37, 39.

1411.1. WW struck out the first address on the card: "Mayburg | Woking Station | Surrey." See also *Sup.* 1397.7.

1416.5. This and the following letter refer to "Army and Hospital Cases," which, long delayed, did not appear until October, 1888. WW scrupulously honored his agreement not to publish until after its appearance in the magazine. See *Corr.,* IV, 38, 191-192, 214, 216-217.

1419.5 *To the Editor,* Century Illustrated Monthly Review

328 Mickle street | Camden New Jersey | July 31 '86

Dear Sir

Yours of yesterday rec'd—In answer: Please send me, soon as convenient, a typewritten copy—or, (better still) a good *proof,* of the article, to which I could make additions or emendations—Yes, I "leave its publication to your convenience"—I shall consider your Magazine the owner of the article—I reserving the right to print in future book, but only *after* its publication by you—(some months after at least—probably a year after)—

Walt Whitman

The enclosed slip returned having probably got in your yesterday's letter to me by mistake—

1437.5 *To C. Oscar Gridley*

ADDRESS: C Oscar Gridley | 9 Duke Street |
London Bridge | London | S E | England.
POSTMARKS: Camden | Aug | 30 | 2 30 PM(?) | 1886 |
N.J.; Philadelphia | Aug | 30 | 1886 | Paid(?).

328 Mickle Street | Camden New Jersey | U S America *Aug: 30 '86*

Thanks for "Notes on America"—safely rec'd & read with interest by me. I consider your Carlyle to be as much a democrat as anybody—more than a good many accepted ones—I am much the same as when you saw me last—pulled a little lower down perhaps—

Walt Whitman

1449.2 *To C. Oscar Gridley*

ADDRESS: C Oscar Gridley | 9 Duke Street |
London Bridge | London | SE | England.
POSTMARK: Camden | Sep | 28 | 5(?) PM | 18(?) | N.J.

328 Mickle Street | Camden New Jersey U S America | *Sept. 28 '86-*

Thanks for the package of "Notes" which have reach'd me safely—I shall send most of them to one & another.

I am still here & keeping up ab't the same—good bodily heart, enough, but a prisoner to chair & house—

Walt Whitman

1437.5. Gridley, who was the secretary of the Carlyle Society in England, visited WW in April, 1884 *(CB).* He was one of the contributors to a Whitman fund in 1885; see *Corr.,* III, 405; Traubel, IV, 210.

1463.1 *To an Unidentified Correspondent*

TRANSCRIPT.

Camden, Dec. 13, 1886

I did not know of any "pirated edition" in Chicago. Do you mean that some one has printed the book surreptitiously there—& is or has been selling it?

Walt Whitman

1464.1 *To the Editor,* The Critic

328 Mickle Street | Camden New Jersey | Dec. 17 '86—Evn'g

I send the Tennyson piece—in hopes it will suit you [&] in hopes you will have it put in type to-day, so you can send me a proof this evening—which I will get to-morrow Sunday & return in the evening—Any how at the worst you would get it not later than Tuesday forenoon. The price of the piece is $10—

Walt Whitman

1463.1. In *CB,* opposite the entry for December, 1886, appears the name of "S E Gross. . . . Chicago Ill," who apparently had written to WW on November 30, 1886. Gross may have been the recipient of this letter, but identification must remain tentative.

1464.1. "A Word about Tennyson" appeared in *The Critic* on January 1, 1887; see *Corr.,* IV, 58 and 61.

The appearance of this note makes it clear that Letter 1472 *(Corr.,* IV, 61), dated December? 1886, should be renumbered 1464.2, since it was written shortly after 1464.1.

1887

1481.5

ADDRESS: Ernest Rhys | 59 Cheyne Walk |
Chelsea | London | England. POSTMARKS: Camden |
Feb | 2 | 6 PM | 1887 | N.J.; Philadelphia | Feb |
2 | 1887 | Paid; London S.W. | 0 (?) | Fe 14 | 87.

            328 Mickle St–Camden New Jersey | U S America Feb. 2 '87
Dear friend
    Yours rec'd & welcomed, as always–I send Vol. of "Specimen Days
and Collect," with emendations–My notion would be for you to print a Vol.
including all to page 200, and call it *"Specimen Days in America–By Walt
Whitman"* for title page, & then another Vol. of the matter from page 203 to
338 (including "My Book & I" which I send) & call it *"Democratic Vistas and
other papers" by Walt Whitman* for title page–*making two books*–
    But I leave the thing, (after having expressed my suggestion, & sent you
the copy) in your & the publisher's hands, with full authority from me to do
what the exigencies require, & what you think best–should I feel like writing
a few lines for Preface, I will send you within ten days–but if not, not–It is
not certain–If you don't get such lines from me go on without them when
you are ready–Should you wish the print facing page 222 I can get it for you,
printed here in Philadelphia by the 100 or 1000– (I think it is ab't 3cts a
piece, but am not certain)–or I will send you the photo & you can have one
made there, if you prefer to have your own as you may–Write me often as
you can–I am tied up in my corner by paralysis, & welcome friends' letters–
bad cold raw weather–my bird is singing furiously–I am ab't as usual–
                                  Walt Whitman
    I have put a couple of photos in the book, at page 122–one is for *you*–the
other I think you can *transfer* & make for yourself a good plate for picture for
the book–I like it better to go in the vol. of the book off against the scene in

---

1481.5. WW gave Rhys permission to print *Specimen Days* on October 13, 1886; see *Corr.,* IV, 52.
The arrangements for English publications are documented in the notes to *Corr.,* IV, 52 and 66.
    Through the recent acquisition by the Berg Collection of WW's letters to Rhys, it is now possible
to follow in detail Rhys's publication of WW's writings. See below 1481.6, 1497.5, 1499.5, 1514.5,
1541.5, 1547.1, 1557.1, 1572.1, 1577.1, 1581.5, 1603.5, 1604.5, and 1614.5.
    Rhys quickly introduced himself to the Costelloes and became an admirer of Mary Smith
Costelloe, who was later to become Mrs. Bernard Berenson; see *Corr.,* IV, 98–99n.

the text described (as at p. 122)—tell the pub. when he sends me my 10 guineas to send (if convenient) in P.O. order, (or orders) to me at 328 Mickle st. Camden New Jersey—

Write soon, & specifically, & copiously—I will send you the lith. portraits you request—If you want another copy of "Spe. Days," to make proper printer's copy, get one of Wilson's Glasgow Ed'n—it is correct—mind my emendations—Go & see B F C Costelloe, 40 Grosvenor Road, the embankment, & ask to be introduced to his wife, Mrs. C. She is an American, & my best friend—

1481.6 *To Ernest Rhys*

ADDRESS: Ernest Rhys | 59 Cheyne Walk | Chelsea | London England. POSTMARKS: (?) | Feb | 3 | (?); Philadelphia, Pa. | Feb | 3 | 4 PM | 1887 | Transit.

Camden New Jersey U S America | Feb. 3 '87—

I yesterday sent you as copy, a volume of *Spec. Days,* & a letter—please notify me if they both come safely—I don't think of any thing I want to add to the suggestions in the letter—If any thing further occurs to me, I will write to you—It strikes me that from a business & publisher's point of view your folks w'd do well to have the *three volumes* viz: L of G as you already have it & then the two prose books "Spec: Days" & "Democratic Vistas"—

W W

1485.1 *To John H. Johnston*

ADDRESS: J H Johnston | Jeweler | 150 Bowery Cor: Broome | New York City. POSTMARKS: Camden | Feb | (?) | (?)87; (?) | 2-14-87 | 5-(?).

328 Mickle street | Camden New Jersey Sunday noon | Feb 14 '87 Still here in the land of the living—in pretty good heart most of the

---

1485.1. This postcard poses problems in dating: there is an ink smudge where WW apparently changed *12* to *14;* one legible postmark is clearly "2-14-87." In 1887, however, February 14 fell on Monday, not on Sunday. According to *CB,* the Johnstons had visited WW on February 6, a fact (if correct) which makes some of the comments in the note superfluous. Since the poet was "half sick (or more than half) most of the month" *(CB),* he could have erred in dating the card either as to the day of the week or the date, or have forgotten the recent visit.

time, & comfortable enough, but horribly crippled & banged up–Spirit moved me to write you a line & send my love to Alma and Al and all–I am just going out for an hour's midday drive.

Walt Whitman

1486.1 *To John Burroughs*

ADDRESS: John Burroughs | West Park | Ulster County | New York. POSTMARKS: Camden | Feb | 17 | 1887 | N.J.; New York | Feb 17 | 4 P M | 87 | Transit.

328 Mickle Street | Camden New Jersey Feb. 17 '87

Every thing very much the same with me–quite completely disabled in my locomotion–O'Connor has gone to Southern California (to Dr Channings's,) Eldridge has gone with him–(I fear O'C is in a bad plight)– J B Marvin is in Wash'ton 1121 I street *out* of office–Dr Bucke is well & writes often–I have been out two hours midday to-day, driving in the sun–

Walt Whitman

1497.5 *To Ernest Rhys*

ADDRESS: Ernest Rhys | 59 Cheyne Walk | Chelsea | London | England. POSTMARKS: Camden | Mar | 8 | 6 PM | 1887 | N.J.; London S.W. | (?) | Mr 18 (?) | 87.

Camden America | March 8 '87

Have rec'd to-day yours of Feb. 21. Send you herewith a little Preface to "Specimen Days"–it might make two pages–Send me three or four slip impressions when in type–Yes, you can retain the Edgar Poe lines on p 17 as you wish–& in brief (having no doubt you will remember what I have said or suggested) I hereby empower you to make any arrangements or ways the publishing exigencies there or your own judgment require–

I will probably send a short MS to be added on p 199 or p 200 to bring my diary up (or nearly up) to date–Something possibly also to the 2d Vol.– giving both books a touch (at any rate) of *original identity* & fulness–

Walt Whitman

1486.1. For an account of the illness of WW's old friend William D. O'Connor, see *Corr.,* IV, 68–69.

1497.5. See *Corr.,* IV, 66, n. 11. Included with this letter is the Preface, reprinted in *November Boughs* (1888), 93–94.

According to a letter dated May 23, 1889 (Berg), Rhys offered Forman a number of Whitman manuscripts including " 'Specimen Days & Collect' with WW's corrections in ink-pencil"; the price was £2.2s.

1499.5 *To Ernest Rhys*

ADDRESS: Ernest Rhys | 59 Cheyne Walk | Chelsea | London |
England. POSTMARKS: Camden | Mar 15 | 6 PM | 1887;
Philadelphia, Pa. | Mar 15 | 1887 | Paid; London (?) |
7 T | Mr 2(?) | 87.

Camden New Jersey America | March 15 1887

My dear Ernest Rhys

Here is for your edition, a special concluding note to "Specimen
Days"—a short Preface for it I have already sent you—also I suppose you have
rec'd the parcel of pictures I sent you—Nothing very new with me—I have
been lately ab't the same as usual, but am quite unwell to-day—I shall send an
additional paper or so to eke out the "Democratic Vistas" volume—I told you
in the former note that I gave you power to decide in such exigencies as
always occur in book publishing, & I confirm it—

Walt Whitman

1514.5 *To Ernest Rhys*

ADDRESS: Ernest Rhys | Care of Walter Scott,
Publisher | 24 Warwick Lane | London England | EC.
POSTMARKS: Camden, N.J. | Apr 11 | 12 M | 87;
London | (?) | Ap 22 | AH.

Camden New Jersey U S America | April 11 '87—

Yours of March 29 rec'd & welcomed—I sent you a request for two or
three printed slips of the Preface, when in type—also some of the "additional
note"—Keep your eyes open sharp to any little technical or *sentence* alterations
of the text of "Spec: Days in America" for your Ed'n—as the book was
printed rather hurriedly here for the American area, without tho't of foreign
reprint—If you have any frontispiece portrait, try to have a good one—else
none at all w'd be best—the one in y'r little L of G is bad—I go on to New
York (if I can get there) to deliver my "Death of Lincoln" lecture—

W W

1499.5. Included is an "Additional Note," which WW reprinted in *November Boughs* (1888), 94–
95. According to *CB*, WW enclosed a receipt for "10 guineas," which he had received on the previous
day. He made no mention of his health in *CB* on this date.

1514.5. For Rhys's letter (Barrett), see *Corr.*, IV, 80–81n. An account of what was to be WW's
last reading of his Lincoln lecture appears in *Corr.*, IV, 82–83n.

1534.1 *To White, Stokes & Allen*

ADDRESS: White, Stokes & Allen | Publishers |
New York City. POSTMARKS: Camden, N.J. | Apr 29 |
12 M | 87; C | 4-29-87 | 6 P | N.Y.

328 Mickle Street | Camden New Jersey | April 29 | '87

Thank you for your beautiful & interesting *Bugle Echoes* which has just reached me—Please send this to F F Browne with my best respects—

Walt Whitman

1541.5 *To Ernest Rhys*

ADDRESS: Ernest Rhys | Care Walter Scott,
Publisher | 24 Warwick Lane | London EC England.
POSTMARK: Camden, N.J. | May 11 | 4 30 PM |
87.

328 Mickle St: Camden New Jersey | U S America May 11 '87

Y'rs of April 28 rec'd—but no slips of printed Preface or Additional Note yet—the P[all] M[all] Gazette rec'd—If convenient, & as soon as convenient, I want y'r publishers to send me over fifty (50) copies of "Specimen Days"—(two or three of them in y'r good leather binding)—direct the package to me *care David McKay 23 South 9th St. Philadelphia*—I will soon send some add'l papers for the *Dem: Vistas* Vol.

Walt Whitman

1534.1. Browne (see *Sup.* 1350.5) was the compiler of *Bugle-Echoes: A Collection of the Poetry of the Civil War, Northern and Southern* (New York: Frederick A. Stokes Company, [1886]). The volume was copyrighted by White, Stokes, & Allen. Six of WW's poems appear in the work: "Beat! Beat! Beat!" (1-2); "Come Up from the Fields, Father" (133-135); "Bivouac on a Mountain Side" (241); "Ethiopia Saluting the Colors" (270-271); "When Lilacs Last in the Dooryard Bloom'd" (287-291, abridged); and "O Captain! My Captain!" (291-292).

On April 30, 1887, Frederick A. Stokes informed WW that he was forwarding the note to Browne, and that he would "feel honored if you will allow me to send [another copy] to you with my compliments" (Feinberg).

1541.5. *Pall Mall Gazette* on April 27 quoted from WW's "Additional Note"; see *Corr.,* IV, 63n, and Traubel, IV, 487-488.

David McKay was WW's Philadelphia publisher.

1547.1 *To Ernest Rhys*

ADDRESS: Ernest Rhys | Care Walter Scott Co: |
Publishers | 24 Warwick Lane–Paternoster |
Row | London England. POSTMARKS: Camden, N.J. |
May 25 | 6 PM | 87; London E(?) | A | Ju 6 87 |
AG.

May 25 '87–328 Mickle Street | Camden New Jersey U S America
I am ab't as usual in health–*minus* perhaps a little, as the heat of the
weather here is great & a little premature–But I am getting along well–tho'
the letter some four weeks ago ab't me & "millionaires" in the "P[all] M[all]
Gaz:" (or was it "Athenaeum") was mostly *lollipop* streak'd with *falsehood*–
but I have several beloved & staunch friends here in America, men &
women–I wish you to give my love to Addington Symonds–no slips of
Preface or additional note yet–no H Gilchrist yet–

Walt Whitman

1557.1 *To Ernest Rhys*

ADDRESS: Ernest Rhys | Care Walter Scott Publishing
Co: | 24 Warwick Lane Paternoster | row | London
England. POSTMARKS: Camden, N.J. | Jun 3 | 9 PM |
87; London | A | (?) 87 | (?).

Camden New Jersey U S America | June 3 '87–
No slips of the printed Preface or "additional note" have arrived yet–
I would like three or four of each of them–fine weather this forenoon, as I
write, sunny & "growing"–rec'd last even'g a kind complimentary greeting
by cable from Henry Irving–I remain much as usual–bodily disabled,
however, & a prisoner to the house–I expect to see Herbert Gilchrist to-day
(from N[ew] York)–send me a copy of *Spec: Days* soon as it is out–

Walt Whitman

1547.1. On May 6, 1887, William T. Stead, editor of the *Pall Mall Gazette,* printed an excerpt
from a private correspondent (probably Moncure D. Conway) alleging that Americans were niggardly
in their gifts to WW; see *Corr.,* IV, 116-117n.

Herbert Gilchrist, the son of Anne Gilchrist and an artist of sorts, arrived in New York on May
27 (Feinberg), and appeared in Camden on June 3 *(Corr.,* IV, 98, and Sup. 1557.5). For the next several
months Gilchrist worked on the portrait now in the Rare Book Department of the University of
Pennsylvania. It is reproduced in *CRE* and *The Artistic Legacy of Walt Whitman* (1970), figure 25.

1557.1. Henry Irving, the actor, and others congratulated WW on his 68th birthday on May 31.

1561.1 *To John H. Johnston*

TRANSCRIPT.

Camden, June 13, 1887

[Refers to the cottage subscription undertaken by Boston friends.] Noble and generous to me & I appreciate & shall accept it—I chafe here the hot weather—

Walt Whitman

1572.1 *To Ernest Rhys*

ADDRESS: Ernest Rhys | Care Walter Scott Publisher | 24 Warwick Lane Paternoster | Row | London | England. POSTMARKS: Camden, (?) | Jun 28 | 10 AM | 87; Philadelphia | Jun | 28 | 1887 | Paid; London E.C. | A | Jy 8 87 | AB.

Camden New Jersey U S America | June 26 '87—3 ½ P M—

Edith & another girl have been to see me to-day—nearly two hours—a nice visit—they are well—appear to be enjoying their trip—we all liked them much—they have been to Niagarà—I wrote you a while ago that the books had come, & that I liked the get up of them—I will send very soon some more stuff for the "Democratic Vistas, &c. &c." Vol. Fine summer weather—

Walt Whitman

1577.1 *To Ernest Rhys*   7.9. [1887]

ADDRESS: Ernest Rhys | Care Walter Scott | 24 Warwick Lane Paternoster | Row | London England. POSTMARKS: Camden, N.J. | Jul 9 | 4 30 PM | 87; London E.C. | M | Jy 21 87 | (?).

Camden N.J. U S America July 9

Yours of June 28 just rec'd, & welcomed. I forgot what I wrote ab't the P[all] M[all] Gaz.

—but it was *not* for publication, (& especially not as coming from me.) I

1561.1. Boston admirers of WW, including William Sloane Kennedy and Sylvester Baxter, solicited funds in 1887 for the purchase of a summer cottage. See *Corr.*, IV, 93–114, and Kennedy, 10–11.

1572.1. I have not been able to identify Edith or her companion; perhaps she was Rhys's sister.

1577.1. Rhys's letter is apparently not extant.

For the *Pall Mall Gazette*, see *Sup.* 1547.1.

consider myself as most handsomely treated all round, by friends & upholders in Britain & in America—We are having fearfully hot weather here & I am suffering from it—Just at this moment it is clouded—a great relief—H Gilchrist is here finishing his portrait of me to take back to England—it is mighty good both as likeness & work—I am writing a little—small bits—will post them to you, when printed—

Walt Whitman

1581.5 *To Ernest Rhys*

ADDRESS: Ernest Rhys | Care Walter Scott Publisher |
24 Warwick Lane Paternoster Row | London England.
POSTMARK: Camden, N.J. | Jul 2(?) | 4 30 PM | 87.

Camden New Jersey U S America | July 20 '87—
A fearfully hot month here but I am getting along with it pretty well—H Gilchrist is still here—he is well—Still painting my portrait & succeeding—you will see it as it is for London he is working—A sculptor (Sidney Morse) is also here—has made a good head of me & I want you to have one—I am well pleased with the bookmaking of your edn "Spec: Days"— shall soon send you more stuff for "Democratic Vistas"—I wish you send me the next "Fortnightly," if Swinburne's piece ab't me is in it—

Walt Whitman

1595.5 *To Talcott Williams*

TRANSCRIPT.

Camden, Aug. 11, 1887
Davis's report of me and my talk, in re the Swinburne article, is very cute and is satisfactory to me every way.

Walt Whitman

1581.5. For Sidney H. Morse, see *Corr.,* IV, 92–93n. Morse's bust of the poet is reproduced in *Corr.,* IV, following 278, and in *The Artistic Legacy of Walt Whitman* (1970), figure 24. The work of a sculptor with perhaps more enthusiasm than talent, it, like Herbert Gilchrist's portrait, is not one of the successful studies of WW, who, however, admired it; see *Corr.,* IV, 124.

1595.5. In the August issue of *The Fortnightly Review.* Swinburne repudiated his earlier praise of WW. John Addington Symonds and the *Pall Mall Gazette* came to WW's defense. See *Corr.,* IV, 63n., 119n, and Harold Blodgett, *Walt Whitman in England* (1934), 112-121. Apparently a reporter named Davis from the Philadelphia *Press,* of which Talcott Williams was the editor, questioned WW on his reactions. The interview evidently appeared in the *Press* on August 3, 1887; see *Corr.,* IV, 115.

1603.5 *To Ernest Rhys*

ADDRESS: Ernest Rhys | Care of Walter Scott
Publisher | 24 Warwick Lane Paternoster | row |
London England. POSTMARKS: Camden, N.J. | Sep 8 |
8 PM | 87; Philadelphia, Pa. | (?) | 1887 | Paid;
London E.C. | (?) | Sp 19 87 | AF.

Camden New Jersey U S America | Sept. 8 '87—
I send you some additional newer matter for the "Democratic Vistas"
volume—will write you further anent of the Vol. soon—(will write a little
Preface)—Do not bother or think any thing further of the Swinburne article—
we do not *here*—send me word if the new matter now sent reaches you safely—
I am ab't as usual—

Walt Whitman

1604.5 *To Ernest Rhys*

ADDRESS: Ernest Rhys | Care Walter Scott, Publisher, |
24 Warwick Lane Paternoster | row | London | England.
POSTMARKS: Camden, N.J. | Sep 11 | 5 PM | 87; London E C |
(?) | Sp 23 87 | (?).

328 Mickle street | Camden New Jersey U S America | Sept: 11 '87
My dear Rhys
I suppose you got the copy I mail'd you some three or four days ago—
the additional matter (27 printed pages) for "Democratic Vistas"—I enclose
herewith the MS of a little Preface. The title page ought to be

Democratic Vistas
and other Pieces
By Walt Whitman

Leave out "Two Letters" (p 315 and partly on p 316)—Leave out altogether
the Appendix pieces (pp 339 to 374 inclusive)—And I should suggest to have
"Notes left over" (pp 317 to 338) come last in the volume, & *finishing it.*
Finally I give you the same general privilege over the putting together of this,
as my other volumes. (Is there any probability of a second edition of "Spec:
Days"? Is it stereotyped?)
To the Publisher—For this Volume, the Preface, &c. I shall expect £10:10s
(same as my other vols) and also 10 copies of the "Vistas" *bound in roan.* I

1603.5. The new material for *Democratic Vistas* which WW enclosed was reprinted in *November Boughs* (1888), 95–96.

1604.5. This letter illustrates WW's careful, almost obsessive, supervision of every detail of publication. Although he granted Rhys authority to make adjustments as needs arose, in actuality he restricted Rhys's freedom.

wish the am't of the bill for the 50 copies "Spec: Days" (sent me three months ago,) deducted from the £10:10s and when you send the balance, send in P.O. order.

Respects & good will to all

Walt Whitman

1614.5 *To Ernest Rhys* *10.1-2. 1887*

ADDRESS: Ernest Rhys | Care Walter Scott Publisher |
24 Warwick Lane | Paternoster | row | London England.
POSTMARKS: Camden, N.J. | Oct 2 | 5 PM | 87;
Philadelphia, Pa. | (?) | 2 | 1887 | Paid; London
E.C. | A | Oc 14 87 | AB.

Camden New Jersey U S America '87 | Saturday Evn'g Oct. 1–

I remain ab't as usual in health–you probably have seen Herbert Gilchrist, & rec'd y'r picture I sent you of myself (as the "laughing philosopher")–Suppose you rec'd the add'l copy I sent (by mail) to "Demo: Vistas," & the brief preface (in letter)–It is near sundown & I am sitting here by the open window, temperature moist & pleasant, & I feeling comfortable– Our "Indian Summer" now–

Sunday mn'g Oct. 2–Fine sunny mn'g–I have had a bit of mutton chop & some coffee–relish'd well–am going out for a drive in the country–am feeling comfortable–love to you and H G.

Walt Whitman

1626.5 *To John H. Johnston* *11.10. [1887]*

ADDRESS: J H Johnston | Diamond Merchant | 150
Bowery cor: Broome St: | New York City. POSTMARK:
Camden, N.J. | Nov 10 | 4 30 PM | 87.

Camden Nov: 10 P M

The "Fusiyama" has come all right & I have no doubt will be

1614.5. Herbert Gilchrist sailed for England on September 21, 1887; see *Corr.,* IV, 123.

"The Laughing Philosopher," one of the most famous photographs of WW, was taken by G. C. Cox in 1887. It is reproduced in *Corr.,* IV, following 278, *The Artistic Legacy of Walt Whitman* (1970), figure 19, and *Specimen Days* (1971), plate 174.

WW noted receiving photographs from Cox on September 13, 1887 *(CB);* he signed and sent them back to New York.

1626.5. J. H. Johnston, the New York jeweler, visited WW on November 2, at which time the poet paid Morse, presumably for one of his busts, "30 & 10–$40" *(CB).* On November 15 WW noted receipt of ten dollars from Johnston "(wh' I had paid to M)" *(CB).* See also *Corr.,* IV, 120-121n.

On November 12, 1887, Conway proposed taking WW to visit Robert Pearsall Smith in Philadelphia for a few days, an invitation which he declined *(CB).*

beneficial–best thanks–I am under a cloud to-day physically–& the weather is dark & rainy–but no doubt a change for the better soon–

I saw Morse ab't an hour after you left & paid him the $10–next forenoon rec'd your card countermanding–Conway has been here lecturing ag't the President–as he did ag't the Devil–Probably both are indispensable & immovable–

Walt Whitman

1639.5 *To the Editor,* New York Herald   [*12.14(?). 1887*]
TRANSCRIPT.

328 Mickle St., Camden, New Jersey

I send the lines on Whittier–wh' I suppose are to be printed in paper of Dec. 18–The price is $20, which please send me here by p. o. order–

Walt Whitman

1639.5. On December 11, 1887, Julius Chambers of the New York *Herald* asked WW to write a poem to commemorate John Greenleaf Whittier's eightieth birthday. The poet replied on December 12 *(Corr.,* IV, 136), and on December 14 *(CB)* sent "As the Greek's Signal Flame. [For Whittier's eightieth birthday, December 17, 1887]," which was printed in the *Herald* on the following day. Although WW asked twenty dollars, he was paid twenty-five *(CB).*

1888

1650.5 *To Ernest Rhys*

ADDRESS: Ernest Rhys | Care W S Kennedy | Belmont |
Mass:. POSTMARKS: Camden (?) | Jan (?) | 8 PM | 88;
Philadelphia, Pa. | Jan | 17 | 12 M | 1888 | Transit.

Camden | P M Jan. 17 '88

Yours of 16th rec'd. Also Kennedy's card the day before—thanks for
both. Nothing notable with me—Still sort o' moping.—I am sitting here in
the little front room—it is snowing roundly outside & wind east—Just got a
letter from Morse—he seems to be all right—he is in Richmond Indiana yet—

I am not doing any thing particular—idly eking out the time—I send some
letters that have come & the "Preface" proof—but not papers or books—cold,
cold here—

Walt Whitman

1690.5 *To Samuel Hollyer*

328 Mickle street | Camden New Jersey | April 3 '88

Thank you for the handsome etchings—which reach'd me safely. I
send you herewith a picture of myself wh' I think might be better for your
purposes than the Sarony one—

Walt Whitman

1650.5. Rhys arrived in the United States early in December, 1887 and apparently spent most of
the month in or near Camden. He was with WW at a Christmas dinner at the home of Mr. and Mrs.
Thomas B. Harned. In *CB* WW noted: "Ernest Rhys here daily—his talks &c. ab't English matters &
people."

On December 22 Morse, "who has been here the last seven or eight months, started this evn'g by
western RR. for Richmond Indiana" *(CB)*. At this time Thomas Eakins was doing his famous portrait
of the poet.

1690.5. Samuel Hollyer (1826–1919), an etcher and engraver, emigrated to the United States in
1851. His engraving of WW as a laborer appears in the first edition of *Leaves of Grass*.

WW sent Hollyer the photograph called "Lear" (reproduced in *Corr.,* IV, following 278, and in
Specimen Days [1971], plate 180). WW referred favorably to the finished etching on August 4, 1888
(Corr., IV, 197), and in *CB* on the preceding day. For WW's reservations later, see Traubel, II, 131, 144.

Several of Sarony's photographs, taken in 1879, appear in *Specimen Days* (1971), plates 154 and 155.

1694. *To Helen E. Price*

ADDRESS: Miss Helen E Price | Woodside |
Queens county | New York. POSTMARKS: Camden (?) |
Apr 12 | 4 30 PM | 88; Woodside | Apr | 13 | 188(?) |
N.Y.

                                  328 Mickle street | Camden New Jersey | April 11 '88
Dear friend Helen Price
    Yours rec'd—Yes, I will sit to Warren Davis the painter—w'd like to
have it over with in five or six sittings—In May w'd suit me, as far as I see at
present—W'd probably accept any time that might suit W D who had better
write to me a little in advance—
    I am still living here & comfortable & in good spirits enough but
probably near the end of my rope—badly paralyzed & do not go out at all,
except by being *toted*—Am real glad to hear from you once more—Wish you
had told ab't y'r brother & sister, & the latter's children.
    Best love & remembrances to you & them—I hear from Dr Bucke often—
he is well—Still Superintendant in Canada—

                                                              Walt Whitman

    1694. A brief version of this letter appears in *Corr.*, IV, 161-162, based on *The Autograph*, I
(November, 1911), 14.
    Helen E. Price was the daughter of Mrs. Abby H. Price, an old Brooklyn friend of WW's mother.
The poet wrote to her brother Arthur on January 25, 1887 *(Corr.*, IV, 65), but there are no extant
letters to her sister Emily, who apparently in 1869 married a man named Law, "an artist in the cheap
picture line," according to WW's mother *(Corr.*, II, 81n). Emily may have named one of her sons
Walter Whitman; see *Corr.*, III, 222n.
    A reminiscence by Helen appeared in Bucke's *Walt Whitman* (1883), 26-32.

1890

2179   *To Ernest Rhys*

ADDRESS: Ernest Rhys | Care Walter Scott 24 Warwick
Lane | Paternoster Row | London | England. POSTMARKS:
Camden, N.J. | Jan 23 | 6 AM | 90; London E.C. | C |
Fe 3 90 | AK.

Camden New Jersey U S America | January 22 1890

My dear E R

Y'rs regularly rec'd & welcom'd (I often send them afterward to Dr
Bucke, Canada)—

I am still here, no very mark'd or significant change or happening—fairly
buoyant spirits &c—but surely slowly *ebbing*—at this moment sitting here in
my den Mickle Street by the oak wood fire, in the big strong old chair with
wolf-skin spread over back—bright sun, cold, dry winter day—America
continues generally busy enough all over her vast demesnes *(intestinal
agitation* I call it)—talking, plodding, *making money*, every one trying to get
on—perhaps to get toward the top—but no special individual signalism—(just
as well I guess)—I write without any particular purpose, but I tho't I w'd
show you I appreciate y'r kindness & remembrance—The two slips enclosed
you are at liberty to do what you like with—affectionate remembrance to the
dear sister—

Walt Whitman

2179. The transcription of this letter in *Corr.*, V, 22, is based on the version published in *Pall
Mall Gazette,* which WW himself used in *Good-bye My Fancy* (1890), 47. With the appearance of the
manuscript it is now possible to add the first sentence and the last few lines beginning "I write without
any particular purpose."

In the sentence beginning "America continues generally," "is" appears directly below "continues."

2191.1 *To Mary Smith Costelloe*

ADDRESS: Mrs: Mary Whitall Costelloe | 40 Grosvenor
Road | the Embankment | London England. POSTMARKS:
Camden, N.J. | Mr 2 | 5 P M | 90(?); Paid |
Liverpool | U S Packet | (?) Mr 90 | 5.

Camden N J U S America | Sunday aft'n – March 2 '90

Only a line to say I am here yet & in buoyant spirits enough. Every
thing much the same, allowing for wear & inevitable decay –

America is probably "taking stock" as the storekeepers call it – resting –
having a lull (perhaps dull) time – but every thing here inwardly active –
laying a good foundation for better (moral & mental – physicall too I hope)
races and times – Love to you, to parents, husband & children –

Walt Whitman

Love to dear boy Logan –

2217.5 *To Horace Howard Furness*   4.27. 1890

with best respects & love
Walt Whitman

April 27 1890

2225.7 *To Ernest Rhys*

ADDRESS: Ernest Rhys | Care Walter Scott | Publisher
Warwick Lane | Paternoster Row | London | England.
POSTMARKS: Camden, N.J. | May 11 | 5 PM | 90; Philadelphia |
May 11 | 9 PM | (?); London E. C. | 7 |
My 23 | 90 | (?).

Camden New Jersey U S America | May 11 '90

Still hold the fort (sort o' yet) – have had another bad attack of *the
grip,* but am easier to-day. Send you some slips enclosed wh' I am willing (&

2191.1. WW became acquainted with the family of Robert Pearsall Smith in the early 1880s; see
Corr., III, 320-321n.

Logan Pearsall Smith (1865–1946) was an adolescent when he met WW for the first time. After
1888 he lived in England and in Europe. The author of many collections of essays, he recalled his early
meetings with the poet in his autobiography, *Unforgotten Years* (1938).

2217.5. This correspondence card apparently accompanied a transcription of "O Captain! My
Captain!" which WW sent to Furness on April 27, 1890 *(CB).* Furness and his father visited the poet
on April 10; see *Corr.,* V, 35 and note.

2225.7. Enclosed in the letter were printed slips of "A Twilight Song" and "For Queen Victoria's

even hopeful) sh'd be pub'd in any London or other British papers mn'g of May 24th—*Have also sent some slips to R Pearsall Smith & you might see him if convenient*—

Y'r letter rec'd—always thanks—Dr Bucke will be here next week— Herbert Gilchrist has gone to fine summer quarters—His address is Centreport, Suffolk Co: New York—I enclose "Twilight Song," one of my last.

Kennedy remains as proofreader for Boston Transcript—I am writing this in my den in Mickle st. seated in the strong old chair with wolf-skin on back (as it is rather chilly weather & I have wood fire)—Best wishes & love—

Walt Whitman

2231.1 *To H. Buxton Forman*

> ADDRESS: H Buxton Forman | 46 Marlborough Hill |
> St John's wood | London n w | England. POSTMARKS:
> Camden, N.J. | May 22 | 6 PM | 90; London N.W. | Z A |
> Ju 2 | 90.

Camden New Jersey U S America | May 22 1890

My dear Forman

Y'r good letter with the £5 has reach'd me, & I have sent off to-day the books & pictures by the International Express (Adams's) address'd the same as this letter, (as the package was too big for mail)—Send me word when it reaches you in good order—also what the expressage freight charge was—

I am feeling pretty well at present, but have had a bad winter—have had *the grip* & a second attack—was out yesterday four or five miles, to the bay shore & linger'd some time by the water side— eat & sleep middling well—in good spirits—

Dr Bucke is here temporarily—is well—shall probably get out this fine

---

Birthday." The latter was published in the following English journals: *Pall Mall Gazette* on May 24, *The Observer* (London), on May 25, *The Star* on May 27, and *The Home News* on May 30.

On May 25, 1890, Rhys wrote to Forman about the slips: "Not being a Royalist, I did not much relish having to make a midnight pilgrimage from here to Fleet St. on Friday night with the slips in question (for they only reached me that evening); but I felt compelled to honour the old fellow's wish. I enclose one of the slips, as it has his own autograph, & may fit in to your collection of odds & ends" (Berg).

WW wrote to Robert Pearsall Smith on May 10; see *Corr.,* V, 45–46.

2231.1. For Forman, see *Sup.* 438.5. WW noted the shipment of books and receipt of payment in *CB.* On June 16 (Feinberg) Forman informed WW that the books had arrived in London.

Bucke arrived in Camden about this time, and was one of the speakers honoring WW on his 71st birthday on May 31. Ingersoll delivered a "grand speech, never to be forgotten by me," WW wrote in *CB.* See also *Corr.,* V, 50–51.

afternoon in wheel-chair—have kind attention—I send you my last piece—
Love to you & best wishes & remembrances to British friends—

Walt Whitman

2239.6 *To H. Buxton Forman*

ADDRESS: H Buxton Forman | 46 Marlborough Hill |
St John's Wood | London England. POSTMARK:
Camden | Ju 17 | 6 PM | 90.

328 Mickle Street—June 16 '90 | Camden New Jersey—U S America
Yours of June 4 rec'd & welcomed—There is no other ed'n of *Specimen
Days* (that I know) but the one I believe you have—the "Celebrities"
pamphlet rec'd safely with thanks—
I am keeping on fairly—have been out in wheel chair to the river side
(Delaware) to-day—pleasant weather here—

Walt Whitman

2262.1 *To John Addington Symonds*

ADDRESS: John Addington Symonds | Davos Platz |
Switzerland. POSTMARKS: Camden | Jul (?) | 6 AM |
90; Davos | 1.VIII(?)0.—7 | Platz.

328 Mickle st—Camden New Jersey | U S America July 20 1890
Y'r fine "Essays Speculative & Suggestive" two vols: have just come—
thank you—I shall write soon ab't them more at length—Have you rec'd my
Complete Works in one big vol: 900 pp? sent by mail to you—Also the L of G.

2239.6. In his letter of June 4 (Feinberg), Forman acknowledged receipt of the books and
photographs mentioned above in 2231.1. On the day the books arrived in London, on June 2, Forman
attended a lecture on WW given by an unidentified lady to "some thirty or forty people, mostly ladies.
After the paper, which was very sympathetic & intelligently done, I read the people your letter . . . and
that message to 'British friends' fitted several. I have sent that to the Athenaeum, so that all may know
how you are going on."
Forman requested a copy of what he described as " 'The Family Edition' " of *Specimen Days*. He
sent to WW a copy of *Celebrities of the Century,* to which he had contributed "the notice of you &
several others on the distinct understanding that I should say what I pleased."
2262.1. *Essays Speculative & Suggestive* (1890) contains an essay on WW, on which the poet

latest ed'n (in pocket b'k binding?)–also the portraits in large envelope?–Say in y'r next if so or no.

I keep up yet–paralyzed almost completely–get out in wheel chair–sleep & appetite fair–my N[orth] A[merican] Rev: piece is in "Spec: Days" call'd "Poetry to-day in America"–Y'r letter three months ago rec'd–

Walt Whitman

2359.1 *To Ernest Rhys*

ADDRESS: Ernest Rhys | Care Walter Scott Pub'r | Warwick Lane | Paternoster row | London England. [Readdressed in another hand: Mr E. Rhys | 1 Mount Vernon | Hampstead.] POSTMARKS: Camden, N.J. | Nov 19 | 6 AM | 90; London E C | A | No 28 90 | A(?).

Camden N J, U S America | Nov: 18 '90–

Nothing particular to write but tho't I w'd send a word. Still here in same spot (holding out the fort sort o')–Still grip & bladder trouble on me badly–writing a little–I believe I sent you Ingersoll's lecture–A visitor to-day f'm England Mr Aidé (with Stanley)–I am sitting here by oak wood fire–

Walt Whitman

---

commented acidly in letters to Bucke *(Corr.,* V, 63–64) and to Kennedy (V, 68–69). He answered Symonds publicly in "An Old Man's Rejoinder," in *The Critic* on August 16, 1890; see *Corr.,* V, 67–68. WW's essay appears in *Prose Works 1892* (1964), 655-658.

"Poetry To-day in America–Shakspere–The Future" also appears in *Prose Works 1892,* 474-490. On its first appearance in *The North American Review* in 1881 the title was "The Poetry of the Future"; see *Corr.,* III, 204-205.

The date of this postcard, which has been twice misdated recently, is established by Symonds' reply on August 3, 1890 to "your card of July 20" *(The Letters of John Addington Symonds* [1969], III, 481) and by WW's reference to Symonds' book in his letter to Bucke on July 18-19 *(Corr.,* V, 63–64).

On August 3 Symonds inquired about the secret meaning of the Calamus poems, which WW answered with a monumental fib; see *Corr.,* V, 72-73, and *The Letters of John Addington Symonds,* III, 481-486, 489-490, 492-494. In a letter on August 27, 1890, to Rhys, Symonds was glad to note "that you substantially take the same view as I do about Whitman's attitude toward what he calls Comradeship" (III, 489).

2359.5. Robert G. Ingersoll, the celebrated freethinker, delivered an address entitled "Liberty and Literature" in Philadelphia on October 21, 1890. It was issued in the following month as a pamphlet; see *Corr.,* V, 102, 103-104, 118.

Charles Hamilton Aidé (1826-1906), a poet and a British army officer, was the companion and secretary of Sir Henry Morton Stanley (1841-1904); see *Corr.,* V, 118.

2375.1 To Talcott Williams

ADDRESS: Talcott Williams | Office *Press*
newspaper | Chestnut Street | Philadelphia.
POSTMARKS: Camden, (?) | Dec 2(?) | 8 PM | 90; Received | Dec | 2 | 9 30 PM |
1890 | Phila.

Camden P M Dec: 2 '90

Dear T W

W'd you do me the favor to have the accompanying sheets as
corrected, carefully type written (carefully correctly done) & let me have half
a dozen (6) copies—It will be either the verbatim or substantial report of the
conversation—I don't think it is sufficiently whole to Col: I[ngersoll]'s side—
but as what I said (& think) is what we are now after, let it go so.

With best wishes & respects
Walt Whitman

2375.1 On May 31, 1889, at WW's seventieth birthday celebration in Philadelphia, a reporter
from the Philadelphia *Press* "took down the conversation bet'n Ingersoll and self (ab't immortality
&c)"; see *Corr.,* V, 130 and n. 37.

1891

2487.1 *To Richard Maurice Bucke*

ADDRESS: Dr Bucke | Asylum | London | Ontario Canada.
POSTMARKS: Camden, N.J. | Mar 22 | 5 P M | 91;
(?) | Mr 23 | 91 | Canada.

Camden 3 p m March 21 '91

Ab't same—badly enough—no worse—am sitting here—H[orace]
T[raubel] goes to N Y this evn'g for two days—am looking for the Doctor—
ate a roasted apple for breakfast—printing gets on very slowly—

Walt Whitman

2525.1 *To William Sloane Kennedy*

Camden P M Apr: 30 '91

Dr B[ucke] has been quite under the weather & this is the just rec'd
note of recovery—Bad days with me have been specially the past ten—at this

2487.1. In the late 1880s WW and Dr. Bucke wrote to each other almost daily. Although these
letters individually are often pedestrian, in total they provide a detailed account of the poet's physical
and emotional state in his twilight days. Dr. Bucke was a shrewdly supportive friend and physician.

2525.1. The transcription in *Corr.*, V, 196, derived from a catalog of the Rains Galleries, March
25–26, 1936, includes only the references to the printing of *Good-bye My Fancy*.

The letter was written on the verso of one from Dr. Bucke dated April 28, 1891, in which he
referred to his illness of seventeen days.

Horace Traubel wrote "Walt Whitman at Date" for *The New England Magazine* in May, 1891; see
Corr., V, 194n. It was included in *In Re Walt Whitman*, 109-147.

In the following month WW had stationery printed with the following inscription:

From the Boston Eve'g Transcript, May 7, '91.
    —The Epictetus saying, as given by Walt Whitman in his own quite utterly
    dilapidated physical case, is, a "little spark of soul dragging a great lummux of corpse-body
    clumsily to and fro around."

In the last sentence of the letter, above "understood" WW wrote "realize," apparently intending
to strike the former.

moment sitting alone here a little chilly—have just had a cup of hot cocoa—the proofs of little "Good-Bye" are done, (66) and the pages cast—(if you like careless touches you'll be satisfied with it)—20 pp: go into L of G. as concluding annex—the rest is melanged prose "as if haul'd in by some old fisherman's seine, & disburs'd at that"—It will, after the first specific ed'n, be bound as latter part of "November Boughs" & go with that—I hear that May N[ew] E[ngland] Magazine has a piece ab't me, with pictures—havn't yet seen—H[orace] L T[raubel] is well & faithful as ever—as things are I understand [realize] perfectly well that definition Epictetus gives—of the living personality & body "a corpse, dragging a soul hither & thither"—

Walt Whitman

2537.1 *To David McKay* [5.19(?). 1891]

ADDRESS: David McKay.

Have printed
    1000 copies "Good-Bye my Fancy"
    400   "   "Nov: Boughs"
             paper &c: to match
Out of these I want to reserve to myself
    50 "Good-Bye" in sheets
    & 100 bound
    —also 100 the little double vol:
    N B & G B bound (as to be made)
Leaving to you in sheets
      450 G B
      & 300 the double little vol: N B & G B
You to pay me   30cts set sheets G B
        & 40 cts "   "   N B & G B
  135 }
  120 } $255
the retail price G-B $1
  "   "   " N B 1.50

2537.1. This note to WW's Philadelphia publisher was probably sent on May 19, 1891.

WW applied for the copyright of *Good-bye My Fancy* on May 18 *(CB)*. On the envelope as well as on the letter itself Horace Traubel has written "see notes May 19 1891." (This part of Traubel's Boswellian account of WW's last years has not been published.) Probably Traubel delivered the note to McKay.

For WW's change of plans about publication, see *Corr.*, V, 202.

deduct f'm these (& f'm above bill) 25 copies each book
    for free press copies
you to pay the whole binders' bill

I have taken out the copyright f'm Wash'n

2546. *To J. W. Wallace*

ADDRESS: J W Wallace | Anderton near Chorley | Lancashire |
England. POSTMARK: Camden (?) | May 28 | 8 P M | 91.

                    Camden New Jersey—U S America | May 28 '91
    Still badly prostrated—horrible torpidity—Y'rs & Dr [Johnston]'s
letters rec'd, & cheer me much—am sitting here in big chair at this moment
    I guess I have a good deal of the feeling of Epictetus & stoicism or tried
to have—they are specially needed in a rich & luxurious & even scientific age—
But I am clear that I include & allow & probably teach some things stoicism
would frown upon & discard—One's pulses & marrow are not *democratic* &
natural for nothing—Let Plato's steeds prance & curvet & drive at their
utmost, but the master's gripe & eyes & brain must retain the ultimate power
for all, or things are lost—Give my loving compliments to all the boys, & give
this scrawl to Wentworth Dixon to keep if he cares for it—
                                            Walt Whitman

2572.5 *To Dr. John Johnston*

ADDRESS: Dr Johnston | 54 Manchester road | Bolton
Lancashire | England. POSTMARKS: Camden, N.J. | Jun
23 | 8 P M | 91; Philadelphia, Pa. | Jun 23 | 11 P M | Paid.

                    Camden N J—U S America | June 23 '91—
    Tolerably fairly—(free from mark'd pain or bother)—b'kfast of
raspberries, b'd & coffee—warm weather—Dr Bucke leaves here July 8 on the
S S Britannic—look out for July *Lippincott's* (I will send you one to make

---

2546. The transcription in *Corr.,* V, 205, is based on the version in John Johnston and J. W.
Wallace's *Visits to Walt Whitman in 1890–91* (1917), 256, where it is misdated May 29. Differences in
punctuation, spelling, and paragraphing are minor.
    2572.5. "Walt Whitman's Last" appeared in *Lippincott's Monthly Magazine* in August, 1891 (not
in July); see *Corr.,* V, 211-212, *and Prose Works 1892,* 739-740.
    Warren Fritzinger was WW's nurse and companion in the closing years of his life. His picture
appears in *Corr.,* V, following 212, and in *Specimen Days* (1971), plate 183.
    J. W. Wallace wrote to WW on June 11, 1891 (Feinberg), and Dixon on June 13 (Feinberg).

sure)—H[orace] T[raubel] is well & flourishing—Warry ditto—Wallace's and W[entworth] Dixon's good letters rec'd—my love to both—

Walt Whitman

2650.5 *To Samuel G. Stanley*

Camden N J—Oct: 13 '91

Dear Sam

    Y'r note rec'd & welcom'd—My dear brother Jeff is dead—died over a year ago at St: Louis—his remaining child a young woman Jessie now lives there—I believe I wrote to you of my bad paralysis (f'm the war & hospital excitements & overdoings of 27 or '8 y'rs ago) & I am now laid up here completely wreck'd—now in my 73d year—but pretty fair spirits—

    Where is Jo Hyer?—I send best remembrances & loving regards to you & him & all inquiring friends.

Walt Whitman

2657.1 *To H. Buxton Forman*

ADDRESS: H Buxton Forman | 46 Marlborough Street | St: John's Wood | London N W | England. POSTMARKS: Philadelphia | Oct 18 | 8 PM | Paid; (?) | 91 | (?); London N.W. | (?) | 91.

Camden N J—328 Mickle Street | U S America Oct: 18 '91

    Wonder if you could help me in a matter of publishing negotiations &c: in England. Have rec'd the enc'd letter wh' with proposal, address &c: explains itself—My wish w'd be *to put the whole matter with absolute powers in y'r hands to see the pub'r's & make the contract* wh' of course I w'd sign—

    2650.1. Samuel G. Stanley, according to a letter he wrote to WW on July 13, 1886, was an old friend from Brooklyn. Apparently he was in Washington during the War years, for he recalled standing near Secretary Chase's residence as Abraham Lincoln passed (Feinberg; *Prairie Schooner,* 44 [1970], 50). In 1886 he was a manufacturer of doors, and Joe Hyer, another old friend of the poet and his brother Jeff, was employed by the firm.

    On October 12, 1891, Stanley, now living at 323 Macon Street, Brooklyn, again wrote to WW after reading "an interesting account of a birthday meeting of your friends: "May the good 'Lord' give you continued life & loving friends to cheer you on your journey" (Feinberg; *Prairie Schooner,* 44 [1970], 51).

    Thomas Jefferson Whitman, the poet's favorite brother, had died on November 25, 1890, while his daughter Jessie Louisa was in Camden. WW was not able to attend the funeral in St. Louis because of his health; see *Corr.,* V, 122–126.

    In his reply on October 25, 1891, Stanley did not answer WW's query about Joe Hyer (Feinberg; *Prairie Schooner,* 44 [1970], 52).

    2657.1. This and the following two letters clarify a publishing scheme which WW discussed in

I w'd like a lump-sum down better than a royalty—w'd give the pub'rs complete & exclusive right in the British islands & (as far as my word w'd do) in the English-reading market of continental Europe—I have two books, the completed *Leaves of Grass* (my main book now just finished) 438 pp—& *Complete Works,* a big vol: poems & prose, ab't 1000 pp:—w'd furnish the revised copy to them these vols: & plate or copy for frontispiece portrait—you may show them this letter—

for your own eye   Walt Whitman

If you can do this for me, I will not make a parade of thanks here—If not, return me Gilder's letter, & let all drop—

My own impromptu tho't of terms suggests 200 pounds down cash—& 100 pounds in ab't a year f'm now—300 pounds altogether—but I leave all to you—their lawyer to draw up the contract, holding every thing right & tight *to give them all the power & security I can give them.*—(One great point with me in this opportunity is to give an absolutely correct & authentic text & typography—wh is already beginning to be vitiated here & abroad)—

Nothing very different with my health—only waning slowly, doubtless surely—gastric, bladder & catarrhal troubles—Dr Bucke is well—I suppose you rec'd the *Complete Works, Good Bye* sheets, *Dem: Vistas,* German *Grashelme,* Burroughs's *Notes* &c I sent Sept: 28—

2658.1 *To H. Buxton Forman*

ADDRESS: H Buxton Forman | 46 Marlborough Street | St John's Wood | London n w | England. POSTMARKS: Camden, N.J. | Oct 19 | 6 PM | 91; Philadelphia, Pa. | Oct 19 | 9 PM | Paid; London N.W. | (?)A | Oc 28 | 91.

328 Mickle Street | Camden N J—U S America | Oct: 19 '91
My dear Sir
      You have rec'd (perhaps will rec[eive] by same mail with this) my

letters to friends beginning on October 14, 1891; see *Corr.,* V, 253, 257, 267, 272.

On October 13 (Berg) Joseph B. Gilder, the editor of *The Critic,* informed WW that Balestier would like to open negotiations for the publication of his writings and proposed a royalty or lump sum for "absolute permission."

On October 29 (Berg) Balestier, after reading WW's letter of October 18, wrote to Forman to clarify that he was not primarily interested in the rights for publication in England or on the continent, but in the American copyright for publication in the United States.

Arthur Waugh, a member of Balestier's firm, notified Forman on November 26 (Berg) that Balestier was ill, and that Heineman was interested in publication on the continent, but primarily in America.

Charles Wolcott Balestier (1861–1891), an American novelist and collaborator on *The Naulahka* with his brother-in-law Rudyard Kipling, died of typhoid in Dresden early in December.

With Balestier's death and the poet's declining health, nothing came of the negotiations, and Forman kept Gilder's letter.

request including the proposition of Heinemann, Balestier & Lovell, Publishers, 2 Deans yard, Westminster Abbey, London, ab't bringing out my books for the British market & English speaking Europe.

Instead of *two vols:* as in my yesterday's letter, perhaps the issue had better be in *three vols.* (Copy furnished with latest revisions by me)

one *Leaves of Grass*

(the poems—the main vol:)

one *Specimen Days*

(prose)

& one *November Days* (in Prose)

including "Good-Bye my Fancy"

Show this if you desire to pub'rs:

Walt Whitman

2668.5 *To H. Buxton Forman*

ADDRESS: H Buxton Forman | 46 Marlborough Street | St John's wood | London N W | England. POSTMARKS: Camden, N.J. | Oct 29 | 6 PM | 91; Philadelphia, Pa. | Oct 29 | 11 PM | Paid; London N.(?) | M Z | No 7 | 91.

Camden N J—U S America | Oct: 29 '91

Dear H B F

Y'rs of 17th Sept: rec'd, with 3 pounds enc'd, and acknowledging books &c: and specifying more, wh' of course shall all be duly sent (you have sent plenty of money)—

Suppose you have the letters I sent ab't the Heinemann & Ballestier propositions (or *feeler)* to publish my books, copy authenticated by me—wh' I wish, if you are willing, (the inquiry, negotiation, bargain &c) to place quite wholly & absolutely in y'r hands—one point is to get a genuine text (3 vols.)—& the other is to get as much & fair money, lump down as may be— Things physical move on with me much the same—I am sitting here alone in big chair (with wolf-skin spread back)—cold sunny bright weather out.

Walt Whitman

2668.5. In the closing years of his life WW was frequently photographed with his "wolf-skin"; see Eakins's photographs in *Specimen* Days (1971), plates 184, 186–188, and Gordon Hendricks, *The Photographs of Thomas Eakins* (1972), 109–114.

Undated Post Cards and Letters

2712. *To Albert Rhodes*   8.8. [?]

431 Stevens street | cor West | Camden N Jersey | Aug 8

Glad to get living sign from you again, my dear Albert Rhodes—
Should be gladder still to have you come in & bless me with one of your
cheery talks, as of old. Would accept with thanks *"the French at Home"*—

I am hauled up here like an old hulk, the voyaging done, but the timbers
may (or may not) hold together yet awhile—maintain good heart & spirits
most of the time—

Walt Whitman

2722. *To Harry Garren*

ADDRESS: Harry Garren.

Harry, if convenient bring me around 20 or 25 good oysters—At any
rate bring around a few the best you can—by ¼ to 1—

Whitman

2712. In *Corr.,* V, 279, one line of this letter appears, from an auction record. The letter was
written between 1876 and 1884, while WW lived with his brother and sister-in-law on Stevens Street in
Camden.

Rhodes (1840-?) had been in the consular service and, perhaps after retirement, wrote a chatty
account of his experiences in *The French at Home* (New York: Dodd & Mead, 1875). According to the
preface, some of the chapters had appeared earlier in *The Galaxy.*

2722. Garren was evidently a Camden or Philadelphia fisherman or delivery boy. Charles E.
Feinberg has recently acquired a copy of the 1876 edition of *Leaves of Grass* with the following
inscription in WW's hand: "Harry Garren | for a birth-day gift | from a friend."

2723. *To Unidentified Printer*

Camden, New Jersey

If convenient pull two sets of proofs (slips like these) & send me, address'd as below. I will keep them in my hands & of course will prevent any publication or extract until after issued by the magazine.

Walt Whitman

2724. *To an Unidentified Correspondent*

Letter of July 25 rec'd. No copies of original (1855) edition in my possession.

Respectfully,
W. W.

2723. This note was probably at one time attached to proof sheets. Since the sheets were not with the letter when it came up for auction, there appears to be no way of establishing date or recipient.

2724. According to the auction record (American Art Association, May 4–5, 1925), this letter or postcard was laid into a facsimile edition of the first edition of *Leaves of Grass* along with the following note: "To Mr. H. P. Main, with the Regard of Tho. Donaldson, Feb. 7/97." Possibly WW's letter was addressed to Donaldson.

Appendix A

A LIST OF MANUSCRIPT SOURCES AND PRINTED APPEARANCES

The locations of the manuscripts transcribed in this volume appear in the following list, through an abbreviation explained in the list of abbreviations in the Introduction. If the version in this edition is based upon a printed source, or is derived from an auction record, the fact is indicated by the word TEXT. Unless otherwise indicated, the manuscripts have not previously appeared in print. I record all earlier printed appearances through the abbreviations CT (Complete Text) and PT (Partial Text). The locations and printed appearances, if any, of draft letters are also noted. Some of the letters in the Supplement were cited in earlier volumes in an Appendix, "A Check List of Whitman's Lost Letters."

This list is followed by a list of the institutions and individuals whose manuscripts are represented in this volume, in order that scholars may readily tell which letters are to be found in a given collection.

Letters

0.5 Feinberg. CT and Facsimile: *The Quarterly Journal of the Library of Congress*, 30 (1973), 44–47.

162.1 Feinberg.

190.7 Feinberg.

202.5 Feinberg.

203.5 Feinberg.

328.5 TEXT: Merwin-Clayton, January 12, 1906.

382.5 Feinberg.

397.05 Feinberg.

409. Southern Illinois University. CT: *ICarbS*, 1 (Spring-Summer 1974), 141-144.

409.8 TEXT: Anderson Galleries, May 1–3, 1916.

438.5 Berg.

572.5 Feinberg.

652.5 TEXT: Parke-Bernet, February 7–8, 1944.

733.1 TEXT: Hamilton Sale #23, December 12, 1967.

735.5 TEXT: Rains Galleries, November 20–21, 1935.

749.5 Feinberg. CT and Facsimile: *WWR*, 21 (1975), 131-132.

758.3 Library of Congress (Ainsworth R. Spofford Papers). FACSIMILE: *The Quarterly Journal of the Library of Congress*, 28 (1971), 123.

758.6 Feinberg. CT: *Prairie Schooner*, 44 (1970), 54.

760.5 Feinberg.

766.1 Feinberg.

767.5 Feinberg.

778.1 Feinberg.

839.1 Feinberg.

892.1 Berg.

901.5 Feinberg. Cited in "Lost Letters," *Corr.*, III, 432.

925. Mrs. Pearl Stone. CT: *WWR*, 16 (1970), 55.

936.5 TEXT: Transcription in D. B. Weldon Library, University of Western Ontario, London, Ontario. CT: *WWR*, 19 (1973), 168.

960. Feinberg.

992.1 TEXT: Libbie, April 26–27, 1904.

998.1 TEXT: Parke-Bernet, December 11, 1940.

999.1 Feinberg. FACSIMILE: *WWR*, 18 (1972), 142.

1003.5 Feinberg.

1015.5 Feinberg.

1019.1 TEXT: Swann, May 26, 1949.

1070.1 Professor Richard F. Giles. CT and Facsimile: *WWR*, 21 (1975), 168.

1095.3 Mrs. Roy L. Marston, Sr. CT: *WWR*, 15 (1969), 60. Cited in "Lost Letters," *Corr.*, III, 437.

1095.6 Mrs. Roy L. Marston, Sr. CT: *WWR*, 15 (1969), 60.

1096.1 Mrs. Roy L. Marston, Sr. CT: *WWR*, 15 (1969), 60.

1113. Feinberg.

1165.5 Feinberg.

1171.1 Feinberg. CT: *Prairie Schooner*, 41 (1970), 55.

1208.5 TEXT: Parke-Bernet, February 15–16, 1943. Cited in "Lost Letters," *Corr.*, III, 438.

1313.5 Feinberg.

1330. Feinberg.

1350.8 Feinberg.

1393.8 Feinberg

1397.7 Feinberg. Cited in "Lost Letters" as "About May 15," *Corr.*, IV, 424.

1401.5 Feinberg.

1411. TEXT: Swann #844, March 18, 1971.

1411.1 Feinberg. CT and FACSIMILE: *WWR*, 20 (1974), 117-118.

1416.5 Feinberg. CT: *WWR*, 19 (1973), 118.

1419.5 Feinberg.

1437.5 Feinberg. CT: *WWR*, 20 (1974), 74.

1449.2 Feinberg.

1463.1 TEXT: Chicago Book and Art Auctions, December 11, 1935.

1464.5 Feinberg.

1481.5 Berg. Cited in "Lost Letters," *Corr.*, IV, 425.

1481.6 Berg. Cited in "Lost Letters," *Corr.*, IV, 425.

1485.1 Feinberg. CT: *American Notes & Queries*, 10 (1971), 3.

1486.1 Feinberg.

1497.5 Berg. Cited in "Lost Letters," *Corr.*, IV, 425.

1499.5 Berg. Cited in "Lost Letters," *Corr.*, IV, 425.

1514.1 Berg.

1534.1 Feinberg. Cited in "Lost Letters" as addressed to Frederick A. Stokes, *Corr.*, IV, 425.

1541.5 Berg. Cited in "Lost Letters," *Corr.*, IV, 425.

1547.1 Berg.

1557.1 Berg.

1561.1 TEXT: Anderson Galleries #1583, May 9–11, 1921.

1572.1 Berg.

1577.1 Berg.

1581.5 Berg.

1595.5 TEXT: Anderson Galleries, May 20, 1915.

1603.5 Berg.

1604.5 Berg.

1614.5 Berg.

1626.5 Pennsylvania.

1639.5 TEXT: Chicago Book and Art Auctions, November 27, 1934.

1650.5 Berg.

1690.5 Feinberg. Cited in "Lost Letters," *Corr.*, IV, 426.

1694. Feinberg.

2179. Berg.

2191.1 Feinberg. CT: *WWR*, 22 (1976), 42–43. Cited in "Lost Letters," *Corr.*, V, 331.

2217.5 Feinberg.

2225.7 Berg. Cited in "Lost Letters," *Corr.*, V, 331.

2231.1 Berg. PT: *The Athenaeum* (London), June 7, 1890; *The Home News*, June 13, 1890. Cited in "Lost Letters," *Corr.*, V, 331.

2239.6 Berg.

2262.1 Feinberg. CT: *The Letters of John Addington Symonds, 1885–1893,* ed. Herbert M. Schueller and Robert L. Peters (1969), III, 484n; *Prairie Schooner*, 44 (1970), 54.

2359.1 Berg.

2487.1 Feinberg. Cited in "Lost Letters," *Corr.*, V, 332.

2525.1 Feinberg.

2537.1 Feinberg.

2546. Feinberg.

2572.5 Feinberg. CT: *American Notes & Queries*, 10 (1971), 3.

2650.5 Feinberg. CT: *Prairie Schooner*, 44 (1970), 51–52. Cited in "Lost Letters," *Corr.*, V, 332.

2657.1 Berg. Cited in "Lost Letters," *Corr.*, V, 332.

2658.1 Berg. Cited in "Lost Letters," *Corr.*, V, 332.

2668.5 Berg.

2712. Feinberg.

2722. Feinberg.

2723. TEXT: American Art Association, February 14–16, 1927.

2724. TEXT: American Art Association, May 4–5, 1925.

Collections

Henry W. and Albert A. Berg Collection, New York Public Library, 438.5, 892.1, 1481.5, 1481.6, 1497.5, 1499.5, 1514.5, 1541.5, 1547.1, 1557.1, 1572.1, 1577.1, 1581.5, 1603.5, 1604.5, 1614.5, 1650.5, 2179, 2225.7, 2231.1, 2239.6, 2359.1, 2657.1, 2658.1, 2668.5.

Charles E. Feinberg Collection, The Library of Congress, 0.5, 162.1, 190.7, 202.5, 203.5, 382.5, 397.05, 572.5, 749.5, 758.6, 760.5, 766.1, 767.5, 778.1, 839.1, 901.5, 960, 999.1, 1003.5, 1015.5, 1113, 1165.5, 1171.1, 1313.5, 1330, 1350.4, 1350.8, 1393.8, 1401.1, 1411.1, 1416.5, 1419.5, 1437.5, 1449.2, 1464.5, 1485.1, 1486.1, 1534.1, 1690.5, 1694, 2191.1, 2217.5, 2262.1, 2487.1, 2525.1, 2537.1, 2546, 2572.5, 2650.5, 2712, 2722.

Professor Richard F. Giles, 1070.5.

Library of Congress, 758.3.

Mrs. Roy L. Marston, Sr., 1095.3, 1095.6, 1096.1.

University of Pennsylvania, 1626.5.

University of Southern Illinois, 409.

Mrs. Pearl Stone, 925.

Appendix B

A CHECK LIST OF WHITMAN'S LOST LETTERS

It is sometimes of importance to biographers and critics to know about letters WW wrote, even though the letters themselves are not extant. The entries in this check list include (1) the date, (2) the name of the recipient of WW's letter, and (3) the source of information that makes possible the reconstruction. Many of the dates are approximate because the information is based upon a letter addressed to WW, which simply informs us that the poet had written before the correspondent had replied. I have indicated the date and present location of correspondence addressed to WW. Allusions to lost letters in WW's own correspondence are designated WW and followed by the appropriate letter number. Auction records that contained no text are incorporated into this list, since the letters as of the moment are "lost." The abbreviations are explained in the table of abbreviations in the Introduction.

1867

About August 10. To Martha Whitman. Letter from Martha Whitman, August 11 (Ohio Wesleyan University).

1868

Early March. To Martha Whitman. Letter from Martha Whitman to Louisa Van Velsor Whitman, March 20 (Ohio Wesleyan University).

Early June. To Thomas Jefferson Whitman(?). Letter from Martha Whitman to Louisa Van Velsor Whitman, June 8 (Ohio Wesleyan University).

Late July. To Thomas Jefferson Whitman(?). Letter from Martha Whitman to Louisa Van Velsor Whitman, August 4 (Ohio Wesleyan University).

1870

February 28(?). To Louisa Van Velsor Whit-man(?). Letter from Martha Whitman, March 1 (Ohio Wesleyan University).

1872

March 16(?). To Thomas Jefferson Whitman(?). Letter from Martha Whitman to Louisa Van Velsor Whitman, March 17 (Ohio Wesleyan University).

1875

December 19. To John H. Johnston. Henkels #1177, November 3, 1916.

1876

July 13. To William Michael Rossetti. Parke-Bernet, April 30–May 1, 1951.

1881

March 3. To an unknown correspondent. Henkels #1137, May 13–14, 1915.

July 7. To Joseph B. Gilder. Anderson Galleries #1669, October 16–19, 1922.

August 21. To John Burroughs. Merwin Sales Company, April 14, 1914.

1891

June 29. To an unknown correspondent. Anderson Galleries #1709, February 13–14, 1923.

Appendix C

A CALENDAR OF LETTERS WRITTEN TO WHITMAN

This Calendar includes extant letters written to WW. The following information appears in the entries: (1) the date; (2) the name of the correspondent, sometimes with a brief identification in order to indicate the nature of the correspondence; (3) the location of the letter, if known; and (4) appearance in print, if applicable. The letters to WW which are reproduced in this volume are marked WW with the appropriate letter number. Excerpts from many of these letters appear in the notes. Abbreviations are explained in the table of abbreviations in the Introduction.

1850

July 2. From H. Onderdonk, Jr. Feinberg.

1856

April 21(?). From Fanny Fern (Mrs. James Parton). Feinberg. CT: *The American Book Collector,* 11 (May 1961), 8-9.

1860

May 12. From Henry Clapp, Jr. Location unknown. CT: Traubel, IV, 195-196.

1862

May 26. From James Redpath. Feinberg.

1863

December 21-23. From Martha Whitman. Ohio Wesleyan University.

1864

December 25. From Lieutenant William E. Babcock. Berg.

1867

August 11. From Martha Whitman. Ohio Wesleyan University.

1869

August 10. From Dr. William A. Hawley. Syracuse. CT: Traubel, IV, 365.

1870

February 27. From Martha Whitman. Ohio Wesleyan University.

March 30. From Martha Whitman. Ohio Wesleyan University.

November 20. From Ellen M. O'Connor. Feinberg. CT: *The Long-Islander,* May 25, 1967.

1872

October 28. From Martha Whitman. Ohio Wesleyan University.

1874

July 16. From Colonel John R. Johnston. Fragment in Barrett.

1875

December 12. From Richard J. Hinton. Livezey.

1876

February 17. From E. A. Ellsworth, an

admirer. Feinberg (verso of draft letter to Abraham Stoker, March 6, 1876).

July 21. From Ainsworth R. Spofford. Library of Congress (Ainsworth R. Spofford Papers). CT: *The Quarterly Journal of the Library of Congress,* 28 (1971), 130.

1877

1877?. Friday. From Frederick Wedmore. Feinberg.

1879

July 3. From Horace L. Traubel. L.C.

July 5. From the Office of the Recorder, Katonah, N. H. (ordering a book). Livezey.

July 16. From an unidentified correspondent (requesting an autograph). Livezey.

[Before 1880]. From A. B. Ashley (requesting an autograph). Fragment in Livezey.

[Before 1880]. From J. L. Smith (requesting an autograph). Livezey.

1883

February 23. From Robert Pearsall Smith (presenting WW with 200 shares of Sierra Grande Mining stock). Feinberg.

1884

March 12. From Allen Upward. Syracuse. CT: Traubel, IV, 212-217.

1885

[November (?)]. From Karl Knortz. Feinberg. CT: Traubel, III, 488-489 (undated).

1886

July 13. From Samuel G. Stanley. Feinberg. CT: *Prairie Schooner,* 44 (1970), 50–51. See *Sup.* 2650.1.

1889

October 18. From Dr. W. H. Raymenton. Princeton. CT and FACSIMILE: *WWR,* 19 (1973), 171-172.

1891

April 28. From Richard Maurice Bucke. Feinberg.

October 12. From Samuel G. Stanley. Feinberg. CT: *Prairie Schooner,* 44 (1970), 51. See *Sup.* 2650.1.

October 13. From Joseph B. Gilder. Berg. See *Sup.* 2657.1.

October 25. From Samuel G. Stanley. Feinberg. CT: *Prairie Schooner,* 44 (1970), 52. See *Sup.* 2650.1.

Appendix D

1819	Born May 31 at West Hills, near Huntington, Long Island.
1823	May 27, Whitman family moves to Brooklyn.
1825–30	Attends public school in Brooklyn.
1830	Office boy for doctor, lawyer.
1830–34	Learns printing trade.
1835	Printer in New York City until great fire August 12.
1836–38	Summer of 1836, begins teaching at East Norwich, Long Island; by winter 1837–38 has taught at Hempstead, Babylon, Long Swamp, and Smithtown.
1838–39	Edits weekly newspaper, the *Long Islander,* at Huntington.
1840–41	Autumn, 1840, campaigns for Van Buren; then teaches school at Trimming Square, Woodbury, Dix Hills, and Whitestone.
1841	May, goes to New York City to work as printer in *New World* office; begins writing for the *Democratic Review.*
1842	Spring, edits a daily newspaper in New York City, the *Aurora;* edits *Evening Tattler* for short time.
1845–46	August, returns to Brooklyn, writes for *Long Island Star* from September until March.
1846–48	From March, 1846, until January, 1848, edits Brooklyn *Daily Eagle;* February, 1848, goes to New Orleans to work on the *Crescent;* leaves May 27 and returns via Mississippi and Great Lakes.
1848–49	September 9, 1848, to September 11, 1849, edits a "free soil" newspaper, the Brooklyn *Freeman.*
1850–54	Operates printing office and stationery store; does free-lance journalism; builds and speculates in houses.
1855	Early July, *Leaves of Grass* is printed by Rome Brothers in Brooklyn; father dies July 11; Emerson writes to poet on July 21.
1856	Writes for *Life Illustrated;* publishes second edition of *Leaves of Grass* in summer and writes "The Eighteenth Presidency!"
1857–59	From spring of 1857 until about summer of 1859 edits the Brooklyn *Times;* unemployed winter of 1859–60; frequents Pfaff's bohemian restaurant.
1860	March, goes to Boston to see third edition of *Leaves of Grass* through the press.
1861	April 12, Civil War begins; George Whitman enlists.
1862	December, goes to Fredericksburg, Virginia, scene of recent battle in which George was wounded, stays in camp two weeks.

1863	Remains in Washington, D.C., working part-time in Army Paymaster's office; visits soldiers in hospitals.
1864	June 22, returns to Brooklyn because of illness.
1865	January 24, appointed clerk in Department of Interior, returns to Washington; meets Peter Doyle; witnesses Lincoln's second inauguration; Lincoln assassinated, April 14; May, *Drum-Taps* is printed; June 30, is discharged from position by Secretary James Harlan but re-employed next day in Attorney General's office; autumn, prints *Drum-Taps and Sequel,* containing "When Lilacs Last in the Dooryard Bloom'd."
1866	William D. O'Connor publishes *The Good Gray Poet.*
1867	John Burroughs publishes *Notes on Walt Whitman as Poet and Person;* July 6, William Michael Rossetti publishes article on Whitman's poetry in London *Chronicle;* "Democracy" (part of *Democratic Vistas)* published in December *Galaxy.*
1868	Rossetti's *Poems of Walt Whitman* (selected and expurgated) published in England; "Personalism" (second part of *Democratic Vistas)* in May *Galaxy;* second issue of fourth edition of *Leaves of Grass,* with *Drum-Taps and Sequel* added.
1869	Mrs. Anne Gilchrist reads Rossetti edition and falls in love with the poet.
1870	July, is very depressed for unknown reasons; prints fifth edition of *Leaves of Grass,* and *Democratic Vistas* and *Passage to India,* all dated 1871.
1871	September 3, Mrs. Gilchrist's first love letter; September 7, reads "After All Not to Create Only" at opening of American Institute Exhibition in New York.
1872	June 26, reads "As a Strong Bird on Pinions Free" at Dartmouth College commencement.
1873	January 23, suffers paralytic stroke; mother dies May 23; unable to work, stays with brother George in Camden, New Jersey.
1874	"Song of the Redwood-Tree" and "Prayer of Columbus."
1875	Prepares Centennial Edition of *Leaves of Grass* and *Two Rivulets* (dated 1876).
1876	Controversy in British and American press over America's neglect of Whitman; spring, meets Harry Stafford, and begins recuperation at Stafford farm, at Timber Creek; September, Mrs. Gilchrist arrives and rents house in Philadelphia.
1877	January 28, gives lecture on Tom Paine in Philadelphia; goes to New York in March and is painted by George W. Waters; during summer gains strength by sun-bathing at Timber Creek.
1878	Spring, too weak to give projected Lincoln lecture, but in June visits J. H. Johnston and John Burroughs in New York.
1879	April to June, in New York, where he gives first Lincoln lecture, and says farewell to Mrs. Gilchrist, who returns to England; September, goes to the West for the first time and visits Colorado; because of illness remains in St. Louis with his brother Jeff from October to January.
1880	Gives Lincoln lecture in Philadelphia; summer, visits Dr. R. M. Bucke in London, Ontario.

1881   April 15, gives Lincoln lecture in Boston; returns to Boston in August to read proof of *Leaves of Grass,* being published by James R. Osgood; poems receive final arrangement in this edition.

1882   Meets Oscar Wilde; Osgood ceases to distribute *Leaves of Grass* because District Attorney threatens prosecution unless the book is expurgated; publication is resumed in June by Rees Welsh in Philadelphia, who also publishes *Specimen Days and Collect;* both books transferred to David McKay, Philadelphia.

1883   Dr. Bucke publishes *Walt Whitman,* a critical study closely "edited" by the poet.

1884   Buys house on Mickle Street, Camden, New Jersey.

1885   In poor health; friends buy a horse and phaeton so that the poet will not be "house-tied"; November 29, Mrs. Gilchrist dies.

1886   Gives Lincoln lecture four times in Elkton, Maryland; Camden; Philadelphia; and Haddonfield, New Jersey; is painted by John White Alexander.

1887   Gives Lincoln lecture in New York; is sculptured by Sidney Morse, painted by Thomas Eakins.

1888   Horace Traubel raises funds for doctors and nurses; *November Boughs* printed; money sent from England.

1889   Last birthday dinner, proceedings published in *Camden's Compliments.*

1890   Writes angry letter to J. A. Symonds, dated August 19, denouncing Symonds's interpretation of "Calamus" poems, claims six illegitimate children.

1891   *Good-Bye My Fancy* is printed, and the "death-bed edition" of *Leaves of Grass* (dated 1891-92).

1892   Dies March 26, buried in Harleigh Cemetery, Camden, New Jersey.

Appendix E

A LIST OF CORRECTIONS AND ADDITIONS TO VOLUMES I-V

The list that follows corrects all factual and typographical errors which other scholars and the editor have discovered in the past fifteen years. Many changes are attributable to the appearance of letters which were printed in earlier volumes from unreliable sources, such as auction records, or were listed in the various Check Lists of Whitman's Lost Letters. Occasionally letters have had to be renumbered. Letters have also changed hands, and envelopes to known letters have appeared; this information has been included.

Errors in the indices to the five volumes have not been corrected in the list below; these changes have been made in the Composite Index at the conclusion of this volume.

Volume I

I, 19b. Add: Ryder, Jr., Anson, 160, 179

I, 25, letter 2. Add: ENDORSED: Ans. June 23, '42 | Wishes Manuscript | [*stricken:* Messrs Bradbury, Sodeis(?) & Co"] | N. Hale Jr. | Boston | Mass.

I, 32, note 18. Delete and read: "and found," room and board.

I, 91, note 89. Add: Sholes (1843-1889) was wounded at Fredericksburg on December 13, 1862, and had his leg amputated before he was transferred to Armory Square Hospital. He was discharged on June 9, 1863.

I, 119, note 71. Read: Brown had written from Elkton, Maryland, on July 10 and 27 (Hanley).

I, 131, note 99. Read: The letter referred to appears in *Corr.,* V, 283-284, number 59.1.

I, 145, note 34. Read: A poet of sorts and a contributor to the Brooklyn *Daily Eagle*

during WW's editorship. He apparently went to New Orleans for reasons of health in 1846. See *WWN,* III (1957), 24-25.

I, 160, note 73. Add: For WW's comment on Miss Stevenson after her death, see Traubel, V, 199-200.

I, 170, note 10. After "Hurly-burly House.") read: In his reply of October 27 Redpath said that there was "this lion in the way — $. I cd easily publish a small Book, but the one you propose ... implies an expenditure that may be beyond my means" (Syracuse; Traubel, IV, 418).

I, 252-253, note 23. For a correction of this note see *Civil War Letters of George Washington Whitman,* ed. Jerome M. Loring (1975), 22n.

I, 258, letter 160. Read: To Anson Ryder, Jr.

I, 262-263, note 48. Add: See Jerome M. Loving, "Whitman and Harlan: New Evidence," *AL,* 48 (1976), 219-222.

I, 270-271. Delete letter 170 and see 164.1.1 (*Corr.*, V, 285-286).

I, 272. Delete letter 171 and see 207.1 (*Corr.*, V, 290-291).

I, 276, letter 179. Read: To Anson Ryder, Jr.

I, 285. Delete letter 189 and see *Corr.*, V, 287-288.

I, 294, letter 198. Add: ADDRESS: To | Mrs. Louisa Whitman, | P. O. Box 218, | Brooklyn New York. POSTMARK: Washington, D. C. | Nov | 16 | FREE.

I, 298. Delete letter 203 and see 164.1.1 and 207.1 (*Corr.*, V, 285-286, 290-291).

I, 338, note 5. According to Professor Randall Waldron, Martha Whitman and her children boarded with friends in Towanda, Pennsylvania (not in New Jersey).

I, 357a, letter 2. Add: Arizona State University.

I, 357a, letter 9.1. Add: CT: *NEQ*, 34 (1961), 239-242.

I, 361b, letter 198. Read: Feinberg.

I, 369a. Delete August 16 and see 164.1.1 (*Corr.*, V, 285-286).

I, 370a. Delete About February 23 and see 207.1 (*Corr.*, V, 290-291).

I, 370a. Delete About July 18 and see 238.1 (*Corr.*, V, 291).

I, 373b, August 27. Read: Formerly in Hanley.

I, 374a. Delete October 28 and read: October 27. From James Redpath. Syracuse. CT: Traubel, IV, 418 (misdated October 27).

I, 377a [1866] February 21. Delete "Location unknown" and read: Gay Wilson Allen.

Volume 2

II, 8a. Read: Botta, Anne C. L., 387, 388.1. (See 388 [*Corr.*, V, 293]).

II, 9a. Read: Redpath, James S., 384 (renumbered 425.5).

II, 9b. Add: Ryder, Jr., Anson, 336.

II, 18, letter 272, lines 10-11. Read: "225 sheets" and "325 sheets."

II, 64, note 9. Add: Miss Perry published a qualified defense of WW entitled "A Few Words About Walt Whitman" in *Appleton's Journal*, 15 (April 22, 1876), 531-533. She was a friend of William D. O'Connor; see his letter to John Burroughs on May 4, 1876, in which he called her "a perfect pussy-cat" (Doheny; Barrus, 130).

II, 76, letter 36. Read: To Anson Ryder, Jr.

II, 76, note 45. Read: See 164.1.1 (*Corr.*, V, 285-286).

II, 79, note 9. Read: Alexander Gardner.

II, 99, note 20. Read: Samuel H. Morse.

II, 102, note 32. Read: see 341.

II, 106, note 44. Delete second sentence and read: Pleasants resigned as chief clerk in the Pardons Office in 1871. According to Charles W. Eldridge's letter to Burroughs on June 26, 1902, Pleasants was "now, as he has been for many years," clerk of the United States Circuit Court at Richmond, Va. (Berg).

II, 108, note 52. Read: February 25.

II, 111, note 59. Read: Lawrence Barrett.

II, 118, letter 384. This letter should be renumbered 425.5. WW went to the Solicitor's Office in the Treasury about January 5-9, 1872. (This correction was pointed out by Professor F. DeWolfe Miller.)

II, 118, note 4 (second last line). Read: J. S. R.

II, 121. Delete letter 388 and see *Corr.*, V, 293.

II, 130, note 43. Professor Randall Waldron's research indicates that Martha Whitman visited her mother-in-law in the spring or early summer (not the fall) of 1871.

II, 140. Delete letter 409 and see *Sup.* 409.

II, 146, note 87. Add: According to a letter sent in 1928 to Harry Hanson, of the New York *World*, which he in turn transmitted to Professor Emory Holloway, Mrs. Elizabeth Stanton was the daughter of an editorial writer on the New York *News*. Her daughter described WW as a "rude and rough" man who enjoyed sitting in the Stanton kitchen as he recited his poetry.

II, 162. The original of this draft letter appears in *Corr.*, V, 294-295.

II, 168-169, note 79. Delete the first sentence and read: Mrs. Gilchrist referred to reading *Wake-Robin* (1871) in a letter to Burroughs on October 19, 1875 (Barrus, 115).

II, 210, note 52. Read: Sarah Mead.

II, 224, note 92 (second last line). Read: February 28, 1876.

II, 257, letter 556. Add: ADDRESS: Peter Doyle, | M street south | bet 4½ & 6th | Washington | D. C. POSTMARKS: Camden | Nov | 21 | N.J.; Carrier | 22 | Nov | 8 AM(?). (This addition was supplied by Edward A. Martin.)

II, 264, letter 565, line 5. Read: & my confidence remains (still unaffected, etc.

II, 275, letter 579. For the conclusion of this letter, see *Corr.*, V, 297.

II, 280-281. Delete letter 586 and see *Corr.*, V, 297-298.

II, 315, note 51. Read: Henry Lummis Bonsall.

II, 330. Delete letters 671-672 and see *Corr.*, V, 300-301.

II, 330, note 30. Delete and see *Corr.*, V, 300-301.

II, 345, letter 698. Read: To Jeannette L. Gilder. (This correction was pointed out by Professor F. DeWolfe Miller.)

II, 345, note 79. Delete and read: In the New York *Herald* on January 2, 1876, "Literary Chit-Chat" announced the publication of the two-volume edition: "His mind, however, is as brilliant as ever, and his spirits good. He is poor in purse, but not in actual want."

II, 350a, letter 272. Read: Barrett.

II, 352a, letter 359. Add: Manuscript in possession of Witter Bynner.

II, 352b, letter 388. Delete and see *Corr.*, V, 293.

II, 354b, letter 499. Add: Manuscript in possession of M. I. D. Einstein.

II, 354b, letter 500. Add: Manuscript in possession of M. I. D. Einstein.

II, 355a, letter 527. Add: Manuscript in New York University.

II, 355b, letter 556. Add: (Envelope in Abernethy Collection, Middlebury College.)

II, 355b, letter 565. Add: Manuscript in Feinberg. (The transcription in *Corr.*, II, 264, is correct except for minor differences in punctuation.)

II, 357a, letter 671. Delete and see 672 *(Corr., V, 300-301)*.

II, 357a, letter 672. See 672 *(Corr., V, 300-301)*.

II, 357a, letter 674. Add: Manuscript in possession of Edward Orlandini.

II, 361a. Delete November 25 and see *Sup.* 328.5.

II, 361b. Delete January 7 and see 336.1 *(Corr., V, 292)*.

II, 363a. Delete April 11. To William Michael Rossetti, and see 495.1 *(Corr., V, 296)*.

II, 363b. Add: [1874] About April 1. To Trübner & Company. WW 601.1 *(Corr., V, 298)*.

II, 364a. Delete About December 14 and see 639.1 *(Corr., V, 298-299)*.

II, 364b. Delete October 19 and see 691.1 *(Corr., V, 302)*.

II, 364b. Add: [Undated] February 12. To Edward C. Stewart. WW's notation on letter from Stewart, [undated] February 25 (Feinberg).

II, 366a, October 1. Add: Manuscript in Barrett.

II, 366b, After November 10. Add: Formerly in Hanley.

II, 367b, March 1. Read: Manuscript in Feinberg.

II, 369a, September 6. Add: Formerly in Hanley.

II, 369b, February 18. Add: Manuscript in Syracuse.

II, 370a, February 24. Read: Manuscript in Feinberg.

II, 370b, November 10. Delete and read: From Jessie Louisa Whitman. Feinberg.

II, 371a, December 12. Add: CT: *Transatlantic Dialogue—Selected American Correspondence of Edmund Gosse*, ed. Paul F. Mattheisen and Michael Millgate (1965), 59-60.

II, 371b, July 12. Read: Edward Carpenter.

II, 371b, December 10. Read: Mrs. Marian Smith.

II, 372a, March 16. Delete entry and see [1878] March 16. *(Corr.,* III, 443a).

II, 373a, Undated Letters. Read: February 25. From Edward C. Stewart.

Volume III

III, 10b. Read: Eldridge, Charles W., 1272, 1343.1

III, 11a. Read: Holland, Josiah, 780 (renumbered 695.5)

III, 21, note 8. Read: *Littell's Living Age.*

III, 39, letter 734. Delete and see *Corr.,* V, 303.

III, 43, note 98. Read: Four poems—"As in a Swoon," "The Beauty of the Ship," "When the Full-Grown Poet Came," and "After an Interval"—were pasted into the first printing of the 1876 edition; they were placed in the text in the second printing.

III, 49, note 23. Add: Italicized passages in this letter are in WW's hand; the rest is a printed form. The *s* in "Volumes" should be italicized.

III, 66, letter 780. This letter should be dated [1875?] and renumbered 695.5. See *AL,* 44 (1972), 227. If "Eidólons" was one of the two poems sent to Holland, the letter was probably written in 1875 since the poem appeared in the New York *Tribune* on February 19, 1876.

III, 83, note 31. Delete the clause after "(see 803)."

III, 102, letter 839.1. Delete and see *Sup.* 839.1.

III, 112, letter 854. Delete and see *Corr.,* V, 304-305.

III, 139, note 32. Read: "Roaming in Thought."

III, 140, note 40. Read: (Barrus, 178).

III, 154, letter 919. Add: ADDRESS: Harry L Stafford | Kirkwood | (Glendale) | Camden County | New Jersey. POSTMARK: New York | May 13 | 6 PM | 79.

III, 150, note 25. Read: Pennsylvania Academy of the Fine Arts.

III, 159, note 69. Read: James W. Thompson.

III, 173, note 5. Read: Linton J. Usher, the son of Judge Usher. See Robert R. Hibach, *Kansas Historical Quarterly,* 10.

III, 182, letter 960. Delete and see *Sup.* 960.

III, 183, letter 963. Add: ADDRESS: George and Susan Stafford | Kirkwood (Glendale) | New Jersey | U S A. POSTMARK: London | PM | Jy 13 | 80 |On(?).

III, 183, note 38. Add: On May 12, 1889 (Feinberg), Bucke informed WW that he had seen McKenzie, now a law student in Toronto.

III, 209, letter 1003. Read: To Ellen Louise Chandler Moulton.

III, 248, letter 1065. Read: To Alma Calder Johnston.

III, 255. Delete letter 1077 and see *Corr.,* V, 314-315.

III, 280, note 64 (last line). Read: Crosby Stuart Noyes.

III, 289, letter 1128. Add: Sylvester Baxter | Daily *Herald* office | Boston Mass:. POSTMARKS: Philadelphia | Jun | 2 | 4 PM | Pa.; Boston (?) | Jun | 3 | 7 AM | Rec'd.

III, 304, letter 1158. Read: To Helen E. Price.

III, 349, letter 1233. Add: ADDRESS: Thomas Nicholson | City Arms Hotel | London | Ontario | Canada. POSTMARKS: Philadelphia | Pa. | Sep 6 83 | (?) AM; | 5 | PM Sp | 7.

III, 355, letter 1243. Read: 10.26. [1883].

III, 362, letter 1259. Add: ADDRESS: Dr Karl Knortz | Cor: Morris Avenue | & 155th Street | New York City. POSTMARK: Philadelphia | Pa. | Jan 11 84 | 5 30 PM.

III, 365, note 18. Add: Excerpts from Dowe's manuscript appear in *WWR,* 13 (1967), 73-79. The picture, a pen and ink drawing, is now in the Feinberg Collection; it is reproduced in *WWR,* 11 (1965), 105-106.

III, 365, note 23. Read: The son of Francis H. Williams. See Harrison S. Morris, *Walt Whitman* (1929), 79.

III, 373, note 46. Read: "Army and Hospital Cases."

III, 380, note 66. Add: Clifford's drawing is in the Hanley Collection.

III, 382, letter 1302. Add: ADDRESS: J H Johnston | Jeweler | 150 Bowery Cor: Broome St: | New York City. POSTMARK: Philadelphia | Pa. | Nov 18 84 | 7 PM.

III, 398, letter 1330. Delete and see *Sup.* 1330.

III, 403, letter 1343. Read: To an Unidentified Correspondent.

III, 404, note 72. Delete the last sentence and add: For Knortz's reply see Traubel, III, 488-489.

III, 418a, letter 721. Read: DRAFT LETTER (in Feinberg).

III, 418b, letter 734. Delete and read: University of Tulsa. See 734 *(Corr.,* V, 303).

III, 419a, letter 750. Read: Feinberg.

III, 419a, letter 757. Read: Feinberg.

III, 421a, letter 909. Add: CT: *The Illustrated American,* 3 (August 30, 1890), 351 (undated).

III, 421a, letter 910. Add: (Envelope in Feinberg).

III, 422b, letter 1006. Add: (Envelope in Feinberg).

III, 423b, letter 1077. Read: Feinberg. See 1077 *(Corr.,* V, 314-315).

III, 424a, letter 1113. Add: Manuscript in Feinberg.

III, 424b, letter 1128. Add: (Envelope in Feinberg).

III, 425b, letter 1229. Read: Feinberg.

III, 425b, letter 1233. Add: (Envelope in Feinberg).

III, 425b, letter 1243. Add: Anderson Galleries, November 21-22, 1923.

III, 426a, letter 1259. Add: (Envelope in Feinberg).

III, 426a, letter 1280. Read: Feinberg.

III, 426b, letter 1302. Add: (Envelope in Iowa State Educational Association).

III, 426b, letter 1304. Read: Feinberg.

III, 427a, letter 1337. Read: Feinberg. PT: *Pall Mall Gazette,* December 23, 1886 (dated August 1886).

III, 432b, November 27. To John Fraser. Delete and see 895.1 *(Corr.,* V, 305-306).

III, 432b, December 20. To Jeannette L. Gilder. Delete and see *Sup.* 901.5.

III, 434b, March 18. Read: James W. Thompson.

III, 434b, June 9. To C. H. Sholes. Delete and see 957.1 *(Corr.,* III, 181).

III, 434b, June 10. To George and Susan Stafford. Delete and see 957.2 *(Corr.,* V, 307).

III, 435a, June 20. To George and Susan Stafford. Delete and see 962.1 *(Corr.,* V, 308).

III, 436a, January 2. Delete and see 994.1 *(Corr.,* V, 310-311).

III, 436a, May 6. To Susan Stafford. Delete and see 1026.1 *(Corr.,* V, 312-313).

III, 436b, June 2. Delete and see 1034.1 *(Corr.,* V, 313-314).

III, 437a, November 7. To John Addington Symonds. Delete and see *Sup.* 1070.5.

III, 437b, February 3. Delete and see 1094.1 *(Corr.,* V, 315).

III, 437b, February 9. Delete and see *Sup.* 1095.3.

III, 438a, March 27. Delete and see *Sup.* 1208.5.

III, 439a. Add: [1885] May 13. To John Boyle O'Reilly. Envelope in Feinberg.

III, 441a, April 24. From John Swinton. Add: CT: *AL,* 39 (1968), 549.

III, 442b, September 24. From Annie Talman Smith. Add: CT: *AL,* 39 (1968), 550n.

III, 442b, [September 24]. From John Swinton. Add: CT: *AL,* 39 (1968), 549.

III, 444b, December 29. Add: CT: *Emerson Society Quarterly,* 43 (II Quarter 1966), 67-68.

III, 444b, January 20. Read: James W. Thompson.

III, 444b, January 31. Read: Feinberg.

III, 448b, 1882?. Delete and see [1888] May
(*Corr.*, IV, 432b).

III, 449b, July 20. From John Swinton. Add:
CT *AL*, 39 (1968), 550.

Volume IV

IV, 8, *Critic, The.* Read: 1472 (renumbered
1464.2).

IV, 61. Letter 1472 should be renumbered
1464.2. See *Sup.* 1464.1.

IV, 116, letter 1596. Delete: TRANSCRIPT.

IV, 161-162, letter 1694. Delete and see *Sup.*
1694.

IV, 355, note 55. Read: *Henri-Frédéric Amiel.*

IV, 412a, letter 1412. Read: Feinberg.

IV, 415a, letter 1607. Read: Feinberg.

IV, 417b, letter 1819. Read: *The Personalist,*
xxxvi (1955), 373-374.

IV, 424a, About May 15. Delete and see *Sup.*
1397.7.

IV, 425a, February 2. Delete and see *Sup.*
1481.5.

IV, 425a, February 3. Delete and see *Sup.*
1481.6.

IV, 425a, March 8. To Ernest Rhys. Delete
and see *Sup.* 1497.5.

IV, 425a, March 15. Delete and see *Sup.*
1499.5.

IV, 425b, April 29. Delete and see *Sup.*
1534.1.

IV, 425b, May 11. Delete and see *Sup.*
1541.5.

IV, 426a, April 3. Delete and see *Sup.* 1690.5.

Volume V

V, ix, line 9. Read: Ernest Kroll.

V, 22. Delete letter 2179 and see *Sup.* 2179.

V, 196. Delete letter 2525.1 and see *Sup.*
2525.1.

V, 205. Delete letter 2546 and see *Sup.* 2546.

V, 279. Delete letter 2712 and see *Sup.* 2712.

V, 297, note 31. Add: CT: *WWR,* 13 (1967),
60-61.

V, 302, note 41.1. Read: MS: Feinberg.

V, 304, note 42.3. Read: MS: Feinberg.

V, 325b, letter 2416. Add: Draft Letter in
Feinberg.

V, 327a, letter 2546. Read: Feinberg.

V, 329b, letter 2720. Read: Ernest Kroll.

V, 330a. Read: Kroll, Ernest.

V, 331a, March 2. Delete and see *Sup.* 2191.1.

V, 331b, May 11. Delete and see *Sup.* 2225.7.

V, 331b, May 22. Delete and see *Sup.* 2231.1.

V, 332b, March 21. Delete and see *Sup.*
2487.1.

V, 332b, October 13. Delete and see *Sup.*
2650.5.

V, 332b, October 18. Delete and see *Sup.*
2657.1.

V, 332b, October 19. Delete and see *Sup.*
2658.1.

Composite Index To Volumes I-VI

Abbott, Edward, 3. 178-79
Abdy-Williams, Ellen M., 3. 452. Letter to, 3. 385
Abbey, Henry, 3. 440
"Abraham Lincoln," 3. 309n, 412; 4. 21; 5, 320n
Academia, 2. 29
Academy (London), 2. 314, 318, 327n, 330n, 332n, 337n, 344n; 3. 20, 23, 48n, 313, 319, 341n, 355, 404; 4. 18n, 103; 5. 299
Achilles, 4. 341
Adams, 1. 51
Adams, Henry, 5. 289n
Adams, Robert. Letters to, 5. 66, 106, 112
Adams, Dr. William, 2. 247
Addams, Jane, 3. 191n
Adler, Felix, 4. 166
Ady, Julia, 4. 234n
Aesop, 4. 393
"After All, Not to Create Only," 2. 139, 151, 156, 244, 274; 3. 45n, 46; 5. 294n
"After an Interval," 3. 43n
"After the Argument," 5. 41n, 121n
"After the Dazzle of Day," 4. 144n
"After the Supper and the Talk," 3. 387n
Agassiz, Alexander, 2. 14
Agassiz, Louis, 1. 77n
"Ah, Not This Granite, Dead and Cold," *see* "Washington's Monument, February, 1885"
Aïdé, Charles Hamilton, 5. 118, 121; 6. 53
Akerman, Amos Tappan. Letter to, 2. 117
Albany (N.Y.) *Evening Times*, 3. 284n
Alcott, A. Bronson, 1. 10, 14, 42n, 74n; 2. 16, 19n, 30, 99n, 139n, 365, 366; 3. 40n, 171, 244. Letter to, 2. 29
Alcott, John, 3. 436, 446
Alcott, Louisa May, 1. 170n; 2. 139n; 3. 244n
Alcott, William, 2. 314-15; 316, 318
Alden, Agnes Margaret. Letter to, 4. 38
Alden, Henry M., 2. 370, 371; 3. 357n, 387n, 392n, 402n, 432, 450, 451, 452; 4. 48n, 119n, 122, 368n, 376, 384n, 425, 427, 429, 439, 440; 5. 340. Letters to, 2, 255, 259
Alden, John, 4. vii
Alden, John B., 4. 32n
Alden, William Livingston, 1. 124n, 356n, 370, 378. Letter to, 2. 40

Aldrich, Charles, 3. 452; 4. 230n, 440; 5. 57
Aldrich, Thomas Bailey, 1. 339; 4. 309, 310, 318, 341, 437. Letter to, 4. 309
"Aleck." Letter to, 5. 318
Alexander, Mr. (an actor), 5. 349
Alexander, Mrs. J., 5. 306
Alexander, John White, 3. 391n; 4. 20, 369n; 5. 193, 341. Letter to, 4. 20
Allen, 2. 114-15
Allen, Elizabeth Chase (Florence Percy), 1. 303
Allen, E. M., 1. 303n
Allen, Gay Wilson, 1. viii, 296n; 2. v, 5; 3. vii; 4. vii, viii; 5. viii
Allen, George, 2. 236
Allen, Henry Stanley, 1. 329-30
Allen, Joe, 3. 371, 431
Almeida, Charles d', *see* d'Almeida
Almy, Frederic, 3. 445. Letter to, 3. 190-91
Alvord, Coridon A., 1. 260; 6. 4
"Ambition," 5. 333
"America," 4. 144n
American, The, 3. 204n, 208n, 214n, 223n, 225n, 263n, 344; 4. 401, 409n; 5. 106, 109
American Bookmaker, The, 3. 448; 4. 432
American House (Denver), 3. 165
American Institute, 2. 5, 138n; 5. 294. Letter to, 2. 132
American Literature, 1. vi
American Mercury, The, 1. vi
"American National Literature," 5. 109, 113, 114, 115, 116, 120, 132, 150, 153, 154, 158, 169, 173
American Naturalist, 4. 403n
American News Company, 1. 354
American Phrenological Journal, The, 1. 44n
American Poems, 5. 296
"American War, The" 3. 23, 52
Amerikanische Anthologie, 3. 351n
Amicis, Edmondo de, 5. 178n
Amiel, Henri Frédéric, 4. 355
Anders (father), 3. 324
Anders (son), 3. 324, 438
Andersen, Hans Christian, 2. 144
Anderson, Prof. R. B., 3. 442
Anderson & Archer, 1. 350. Letter to, 2. 18
Andrews, Stephen Pearl, 1. 184, 301n
Andrews, Mrs. Stephen Pearl, 1. 184, 301

"Angel of Tears, The," *1.* 9, 25

Angus, W.C., *4.* 435

Anne Gilchrist, 4. 44*n,* 57*n,* 65*n,* 79, 82, 85, 88, 91, 101, 139*n,* 265

Antietam, *1.* 82

Appleton, Messrs., *4.* 57

Appleton, Prof. W., *4.* 151*n*

Appleton's Encyclopedia, 4. 474*n*

Appleton's Journal, 2. 127*n,* 191

Archer, Mrs., *3.* 99

Arctander, Emil, *2.* 369

Arena, The, 5. 118, 120, 128

Argus, 5. 112*n*

Armáchalain, P., *3.* 433, 444

Armory Square Hospital, *1.* 12, 89, 90, 91, 93-94, 96, 99-100, 106, 112, 118, 119, 122, 125, 127, 128, 139, 149, 153, 162, 175-82, 184, 191, 218*n,* 224, 230, 231, 242, 250, 264, 280*n,* 311, 331; *2.* 96*n*; *4.* 346*n*; *5.* 286

Armstrong, Prof. Edward, *3.* 59

Armstrong, Henry W., *5.* 348

Armstrong, John, *3.* 127*n*

Armstrong, Rodney, *3.* vii

"Army and Hospitals Cases," *3.* 373-74; *4.* 38, 40-41, 42, 43, 51, 191-92, 194*n,* 214, 216, 217; *6.* 33, 34

Army of the Potomac, *1.* 67, 90, 92, 99, 180, 204, 212, 214, 215, 216, 218

Arnold, Sir Edwin, *4.* 373, 374, 385-86, 440; *5.* 260, 261, 262, 345, 346

Arnold, George B.(?), *1.* 45*n*

Arnold, James, *3.* 280*n,* 435, 441, 448

Arnold, John, *1.* 42, 43, 161, 292, 301, 319, 335; *2.* 26, 49, 81, 123, 200

Arnold, Matthew, *3.* 171*n,* 397; *4.* 229-30

Arthur, Chester Alan, *3.* 63*n*

"As A Strong Bird on Pinions Free," *2.* 118*n,* 171*n,* 175*n,* 176, 177, 179, 180, 184, 190, 244, 273, 274, 275; *3.* 42; *4.* 41*n*; *5.* 247*n,* 295, 297

"As I Ebb'd with the Ocean of Life," *1.* 47*n*; *4.* 5, 6

"As in a Swoon," *3.* 43*n*

"As I Sit Waiting Here," *4.* 145*n*

"As One by One Withdraw the Lofty Actors," *see* "Death of General Grant"

"As the Greek's Signal Flame," *4.* 136, 426; *6.* 46

Ashbee, C. R., *4.* 29

Ashby, Gen. Turner, *1.* 196

Ashby, Mrs. Hannah R., *1.* 196

Ashe, Thomas, *3.* 56*n*

Ashley, A. B., *6.* 69

Ashley, Mary, *4.* 436

Ashton, J. Hubley, *1.* 235, 236, 237, 239, 242, 246, 248, 263*n,* 268, 270, 289, 309-10, 311*n,* 312, 317, 320, 322, 368; *2.* 38, 39, 40, 41, 43, 49, 54, 64, 79, 117, 146, 193, 221*n,* 222, 224,

225, 292, 293, 296, 363; *3.* 315; *5.* 288

Ashton, Kitty, *2.* 292

Asselineau, Roger, *4.* 273*n*; *5.* 296*n,* 302*n*

Associated Press, *3.* 30, 296

Athenaeum, The, 2. 28*n,* 30*n*; *3.* 20*n,* 23*n,* 29*n,* 52, 56, 174*n,* 398*n,* 399*n*; *4.* 18*n,* 425; *6.* 41

Atkinson, Prof. Robert, *3.* 26*n,* 59

Atlantic Monthly, The, 1. 48, 57, 281, 336*n,* 339*n*; *2.* 72, 86, 157; *4.* 287, 399; *5.* 78, 82, 83, 183, 188, 293; *6.* 6*n.* Letter to, *1.* 48

Attila, *2.* 288

Audubon County (Iowa) *Sentinel,* 3. 281*n*

Aurelius, Marcus, *4.* 207; *5.* 38

Aurora, The, 1. 9, 25

Avery, John, *2.* 215*n*; *5.* 210

Avery, Jr., Llewellyn. Letter to, *1.* 314

Avery, Sarah, *2.* 215, 370

Avery, Margaret, *2.* 188; *4.* 437; *5.* 344, 348

Avery, William A., *5.* 344, 348

Babbitt, Caleb, *1.* 141, 175, 191, 196, 366, 367, 373, 374

Babbitt, Mary A., *1.* 373. Letter to, *1.* 141

Babcock, Lt. William E., *1.* 243*n,* 249, 368, 376; *6.* 68

"Backward Glance O'er Travel'd Roads, A," *4.* 36*n,* 222

"Backward Glance on my Own Road, A," *3.* 362; *4.* 36*n*

Bacon, Sir Francis, *3.* 351*n,* 377*n,* 394; *4.* 25*n,* 29, 118, 169*n,* 186*n,* 295, 357*n*; *5.* 263*n,* 266

Bacon, George, *2.* 304

Bailey, O.J., *5.* 171*n*

Baillie, Edmund J., *5.* 336, 337, 339

Bainbridge, Thomas F., *1.* 369

Bainbridge, William F., *1.,* 377

Baiugrim, F., *5.* 338

Baker, Dr. Frank, *2.* 193*n.* Letter to, *5.* 299-300

Baker, Frederick, *1.* 372. Letters to, *1.* 51, 286

Baker, Isaac N., *5.* 97, 118*n,* 120, 129, 263, 332

Baker, John, *4.* 433

Baker, Gen. Lafayette C., *1.* 94*n,* 278*n*

Baker, Mary (Mrs. Frank). Letter to, *5.* 299-300

Baker, Nathan M., *4.* 173*n,* 174, 180*n,* 182, 212, 328-29

Baker, Portia, *1.* 46*n*

Balch, W. R., *3.* 223*n,* 435, 436

Baldwin, Joseph C., *2.* 372; *3.* 431, 432, 435, 442

Baldwin, O. S., *3.* 439; *4.* 425. Letter to, *3.* 358-59

Baldwin, Capt. William M., *1.* 230

Baldwin's Monthly, 3. 358*n,* 360; *4.* 48*n*

Balestier, Charles Wolcott, *5.* 253*n,* 257, 267, 272; *6.* 60

Balfour, Sir Graham, *3.* 406*n*

Ballow, Mr., 6. 5
Ballou, Mrs. Eveline, *1.* 366
Ballou, William Hosen, *3.* 398*n*; *4.* 432
Baltimore *American*, *2.* 150*n*
Baltimore *Sun*, *4.* 19*n*
Banfield, Mrs., *2.* 276
Bangs & Stetson, *3.* 213*n*
Barber, Mr., *3.* 94
"Bardic Symbols," *1.* 47; *2.* 72*n*
Barkeloo, Josephine, *2.* 209; *3.* 450
Barkeloo, Tunis S., *2.* 209*n*
Barker, John J., *1.* 101*n*, 107, 147-48, 366, 373
Barnes, William, *2.* 260-61
Barnett, Rev. S. A., *3.* 396*n*; *5.* 320
Barnhill, John B., *4.* 438
Barnum, Phineas Taylor, *4.* 328
Baron, Joseph, *3.* 436
Barrett, Charles E., *5.* 158*n*
Barrett, Clifton Waller, *1.* vii; *2.* v; *3.* viii, 428; *4.* vii
Barrett, Dennis, *1.* 96, 104
Barrett, Lawrence, *2.* 111*n*; *3.* 364, 407
Barrett, Roger W., *4.* viii
Barrett, Wilson, *4.* 73
Barrus, Clara, *1.* vi; *2.* 237*n*; *3.* 162*n*, 170*n*; *5.* 28*n*
Barry, Mrs., *3.* 147
Bartlett, Adrian, *1.* 238, 331
Bartlett, Dr. J. W., *3.* 450. Letter to, *3.* 372
Bartlett, John, *1.* 280*n*
Bartlett, Truman Howe, *3.* 450; *4.* 57*n*. Letter to, *3.* 354
Barton, Fred B., *2.* vi
Barton, William E., *1.* 81; *3.* viii, 428; *4.* viii
Barton, William Gardner, *3.* 441
"Base of All Metaphysics, The," *5.* 176*n*
Bates, Charlotte Fiske, *3.* 435; *4.* 192, 426, 433
Bates, Edward, *1.* 310
Bates, James, *1.* 291*n*
Bates, Pedelia (?), *2.* 369
Bates, William R., *5.* 333
Bathgate, Herbert J., *3.* 174*n*, 305*n*, 405, 434, 444, 445
Batters, Edward, *3.* 190
Baxter, Sylvester, *2.* 126*n*; *3.* 249*n*, 262, 315, 340*n*, 436, 437; *4.* 65-66, 94, 97, 100, 103, 105, 106, 114, 131, 132, 136, 182, 242, 252, 253, 256, 258, 262, 263, 268, 269, 289, 352, 373, 378*n*, 382, 425, 426, 429, 430, 431, 433, 436; *5.* 21, 68, 110, 236, 316, 335. Letters to, *3.* 236-37, 251-52, 289, 308-9, 391-92, 394; *4.* 56, 93, 102, 110, 114, 125, 262; *5.* 235
Bayley, William D., *1.* vii
Bayne, Peter, *3.* 21, 27
Beach, Alfred E. Letter to, *5.* 282-83
Beach, Mrs. Juliette H., *1.* 55*n*, 236*n*
Beach, Moses S. Letter to, *5.* 282-83

Beare, J. I., *4.* 159*n*
"Beat! Beat! Drums!" 6. 40*n*
Beatty, Samuel A., *1.* 95, 201
Beauregard, Gen. Pierre Gustave Toutant de, *5.* 289
"Beauty of a Ship, The," *3.* 43*n*
Beckett, Katie E., *4.* 432
Beckett, Reginald A., *4.* 189*n*, 432
Beecher, Henry Ward, *1.* 42, 309; *2.* 104, 219; *3.* 249; *4.* 430
Beecher, Lyman, *1.* 42
Beemer, Dr., *4.* 387, 389; *5.* 104, 162
Beers, Mr., *5.* 130*n*
Beers, Henry A., *3.* 446. Letter to, *3.* 225
Behrens, Otto, *2.* 315
Belghannie, Miss, *5.* 341
Belisle, D. W., *3.* 146*n*
Bell, George, *2.* 103, 113
Bell, Horace ("Pensey"), *2.* 103, 113
Bell, R(?). H., *5.* 85*n*
Bella (Louisa Whitman's servant), *3.* 114, 115
Bellamy, Edward, *4.* 256*n*, 379*n*
Bellini, Fernando, *1.* 185*n*, 307*n*
Bellini, Vincenzo, *1.* 86, 183
Bellows, Edward D., *3.* 442. Letter to, *3.* 102-3
Bendz, Waldemar E., *2.* 185
Benedict, A.C., *5.* 347
Benedict, Mr. & Mrs. Newton, *1.* 312, 322, 345, 351; *2.* 42, 71. Letter to, *2.* 69
Benjamin, Dr. Dowling, *3.* 311, 312
Benner, Mr., *3.* 417
Bennerman, Mr. Letter to, *4.* 171
Bennett, Mr., *4.* 20*n*
Bennett, George C., *3.* 386
Bennett, James Gordon, *4.* 143-44, 183, 431, 432, 434, 438. Letter to, *4.* 181
Bensel, James Berry, *3.* 370*n*, 444
Benson, Eugene, *3.* 441
Benson, Lillian R., *3.* vii, 180*n*
Bentley, Richard, *3.* 56
Benton, Joel, *1.* 280*n*; *3.* 111, 113
Berdoe, Edward, *5.* 102*n*
Berenson, Bernard, *3.* 327*n*; *5.* 225*n*
Bergazzi's, *2.* 257
Bergen, Tunis G., *1.* 38, 308*n*; *2.* 52*n*. Letter to, *1.* 36-37
Bergen, Van Brunt, *1.* 308
Bertz, Eduard, *4.* 353, 362, 394, 427, 439; *5.* 36
"Bervance; or Father and Son," *1.* 26*n*
Bethel, Emma(?), *3.* 127
Bey, Emin, *4.* 391*n*
Biachi, *1.* 183
Bible, *4.* 86*n*, 239; *5.* 149*n*
"Bible as Poetry, The," *3.* 322, 324*n*, 329
Biddle, Mrs. Noble T., *5.* 335, 342. Letter to, *4.* 62
Bielby, Dr. Letter to, *5.* 296

Bigelow, Blake, 5. 348
Bigelow, John, 3. 121
Bilstein, Mr., 4. 280n
Binckley, John M., 2. 37, 365. Letters to, 1. 337; 2. 24-25
Bingham, Dr. L. M., 5. 215n, 232, 248, 255, 264, 332, 343, 344, 346
Bingham's School, 3. 94
Binns, Henry B., 1. viii; 5. 4-5, 340
Birds and Poets, 5. 318
Birss, John H., 5. ix
Bismarck, Prince Otto Eduard Leopold von, 2. 288; 3. 335n
"Bivouac on a Mountain Side," 6. 40n
Björnson, Björnstjerne, 2. 144, 164, 175, 270, 283, 288, 295n; 3. 257
Black, Mrs., 1. 161
Black, William, 2. 368
Black Crook, 2. 50
Blaine, James Gillespie, 3. 379, 380n; 4. 178
Blair, Montgomery, 1. 292n; 2. 36, 51
Blake, Rev., 4. 312
Blake, Dr. E. Tucker, 2. 236
Blake, Edmund, 4. 432
Blake, J.V., 5. 22n
Blake, William, 2. 1, 49; 3. 169n, 208; 4. 5; 5. 66, 310
Blamire, J. L., 2. 19
Blanch, Charles F. Letters to, 2. 77, 81
Blasius, 5. 104
Blathwayt, Raymond, 5. 341
Blauvelt, William H., 4. 239n, 426, 435
Bliss, Dr. D. W., 1. 91, 94, 106-7, 132, 133, 134, 154, 191n, 259, 331
Bliss, L. O., 3. 317n
Blodgett, Harold W., 2. v, 318n; 4. 119n; 5. 288n
Bloom, Nathaniel, 1. 11, 13, 123, 125, 126, 158-59, 343. Letters to, 1. 80-85, 135, 141-43
Bloomfield, Ben, 3. viii, 428
Bloor, Alfred Janson, 3. 433, 444, 447. Letter to, 3. 155
Boccaccio, Giuseppi, 5. 102n
Bogue, David, 3. 34n, 255, 258, 272; 5. 314-15. Letter to, 3. 257
Bok, Edward W., 4. 430
Bolger, Peter. Letter to, 3. 371
Bond(?), A. W., 5. 348
Bonner, Robert, 1. 52n
Bonsall, Bartram, 3. 133, 432
Bonsall, Sr., Henry L., 3. 133n, 215n
Bonsall, Henry (Harry) L., 2. 315n; 3. 170n, 215, 372n, 433, 434, 436; 4. 282, 336n, 343
Book News, 4. 329
Booth, Edwin, 3. 405n, 451; 4. 125n. Letter to, 3. 376
Booth, John Wilkes, 1. 315n

Booth, Junius Brutus, 3. 376
Booth, Sarah A., 6. 24n
"Booth and 'The Bowery,' " 3. 376n, 403, 409n; 5. 320n
Borley, Pleasant, 1. 177, 181, 184
Borody (or Boroday), Alexander, 3. 147
Borton, Walter, 4. 32
Bosis, Adolfo de, 4. 38
Boston, 3. 220-21, 231, 237-48
Boston Advertizer, 4. 109n, 137n
Boston Athenaeum, 1. 49n
Boston Commonwealth, 3. 40n
Boston Courier, 1. 46n; 5. 300
Boston Daily Advertiser(?), 3. 249n, 281n. Letter to, 2. 179
Boston Evening Transcript, 1. 160n, 188n; 2. 31n; 3. 282n, 344; 4. 1, 68, 112, 155, 157, 158, 169, 203, 223, 224, 230, 234, 243, 261, 263, 268n, 279, 338, 339, 340n, 362n, 384, 391, 401; 5. 19, 21n, 22, 37, 41, 44n, 58, 71, 74, 76, 79n, 94, 97n, 107, 110, 115, 136n, 171, 202n, 222, 236, 263, 272n; 6. 51
Boston Globe, 3. 232n, 239, 241n, 280n, 295, 314n, 340n, 437
Boston Herald, 3. 181n, 221n, 237n, 250n, 262, 280n, 281n, 283, 289, 295, 308, 311, 315, 340n, 434, 437; 4. 1, 85, 101n, 109n, 131, 132, 169, 262, 263, 266, 267, 269, 352, 382n; 5. 64n, 68n, 71, 74, 235, 236
Boston Liberty, 3. 281n
Boston Miscellany, 1. 9, 25
Boston Pilot, 3. 224n
Boston Post, 1. 191n; 3. 280n, 437
Boston Postmaster, 3. 437
Boston Public Library, 5. 93n
Boston Record, 4. 109
Boston Saturday Evening Gazette, 1. 254n
Boston Traveller, 4. 372n
Boswell, James, 4. 165, 170, 239; 5. 5, 195n
Botsfor(?), Charles, 1. 365
Botta, Anne C. L., 3. 162; 5. 293n. Letter to, 2. 121
Boucicault, Dion, 2. 124n
Boutelle, Harry E., 5. 347
Bowen, Dr. Charles H., 1. 331; 2. 79n, 84n
Bowen (or Brown), Sarah E., 3. 442
Bowen, Sayles J., 2. 34
Bowers, Fredson, 1. 45n
Bowles, Samuel, 3. 39n
Bownes, Mrs. Walter, 3. 443
Boyd, Justus F., 1. 372, 373, 375
Boyden, William A,, 2. 242n
Boyle, Arthur, 3. 449
Boyle, E. Mell, 3. 440
Boyle, Rev. F.E. (or A.F.), 1. 149; 2. 113
Braddon, Mary Elizabeth, 1. 297n
Bradley, Joseph H., 1. 334n

Bradley, Sculley, *2.* v; *5.* viii

Bradley, Thomas, *3.* 190, 201, 248

Bradshaw, Claudius W., *3.* 371*n*

Bradstreet & Son, J. M., *1.* 260, 330*n*

Brady, Mathew B., *2.* 122, 304

Brainerd, Erastus, *3.* 170*n,* 433. Letters to, *4.* 113, 115

"Bravest Soldiers, The," *4.* 145*n*

"Bravo, Paris Exposition!" *4.* 376, 380, 394, 427

Brazen Android and Other Tales, The, 5. 65, 70, 90, 91, 92, 93, 94, 95, 96, 100, 101, 122, 132*n,* 140, 144, 145, 146, 183, 188, 189, 239, 258, 260, 263, 265

Bremer, Fredrika, *5.* 283

Briggs, Mrs. George W., *1.* 375

Bright, John, *4.* 312

Brignoli, Pasquale, *1.* 324; *2.* 169; *3.* 69*n,* 382

Brinton, Dr. Daniel Garrison, *3.* 437; *4.* 67*n,* 377, 430; *5.* 33, 36, 38, 50*n,* 210-11, 334

Brisbane, R., *4.* 425, 430

Bristow, Benjamin H., *1.* 329*n*; *2.* 342*n*

Broadbent & Taylor, *3.* 432

"Broadway," *4.* 145*n*

Broadway, The, 1. 355; *2.* 14, 24*n,* 26, 44, 46, 47, 50*n*

"Broadway Pageant, A," *2.* 40*n*

"Broadway Revisited," *3.* 153, 157*n*

Brockie, W. Letter to, *3.* 57

Broderick, John C., *5.* 292*n*

Broido, Mrs. Louis, *4.* viii

Brooke, W. G., *3.* 159*n*

Brookfield, Meredith, *2.* 367

Brooklyn *Daily Advertizer, 1.* 37*n,* 43*n*

Brooklyn *Daily Eagle, 1.* 9, 27*n,* 28, 30, 32, 35, 57, 62, 79, 87*n,* 95, 97, 105, 138, 140, 148, 190, 217, 245*n*; *2.* 42*n*; *3.* 386; *5.* 283*n*

Brooklyn *Daily Freeman, 1.* 10, 37*n*

Brooklyn *Daily Times, 1.* 10, 87*n*; *3.* 385-86

Brooklyn *Daily Union, 1.* 95*n,* 100*n,* 105*n,* 151, 157, 165, 167, 172

Brooklyn *Evening Star, 1.* 35

Brooklyn *Standard-Union, 1.* 148*n*; *2.* 132*n,* 139

Brooks, Livingston, *1.* 111-12, 367, 374

Brooks, Phillips, *5.* 229

Brother Jonathan, 5. 333, 344

"Brother of All, with Generous Hand," *2.* 90-91

Brown, Alice G., *3.* 450

Brown, Arthur Newton. Letters to, *4.* 305, 310

Brown, Charles, *3.* 436

Brown, Emily Louisa (Mrs. Charles W. Eldridge), *4.* 406

Brown, Henry(?), *1.* 29, 33

Brown, Isabel Yeomans, *5.* 347

Brown, Sgt. James C., *1.* 222

Brown, John, *1.* 51*n,* 96, 105, 132, 136, 158,

203-4; *2.* 30*n*; *3.* 40*n*

Brown, Leonard M., *4.* 57*n,* 156*n*; *5.* 341. Letters to, *4.* 132-33; *5.* 25

Brown, Lewis K., *1.* 3, 4, 91, 93-94, 106, 184, 192, 194, 195, 201, 207, 242, 311, 331, 332, 373, 374, 375. Letters to *1.* 119-21, 132-34, 175-82, 237-38

Brown, Martina A., *3.* vii, 334*n*

Brown, Dr. Morgan, *4.* 127, 325, 332

Brown, Teresa B. H., *5.* 341

Brown, William A., *1.* 96, 132, 158

Brown Brothers & Co., *3.* 36; *5.* 298

Browne, Francis Fisher, *6.* 40. Letter to, *6.* 31

Browne, Mrs. Walter, *4.* 425

Brownell, Mrs., *2.* 276, 289, 304; *3.* 25

Browning, C. H., *4.* 155, 205, 345*n,* 433

Browning, Deborah, *see* Deborah Stafford

Browning, Howard, *3.* 278

Browning, Joseph L., *3.* 115*n,* 126*n,* 131, 139, 189, 203, 208, 238, 261, 278, 307; *4.* 78, 146, 163, 167, 191, 282, 361; *5.* 17, 126, 309

Browning, Orville Hickman, *2.* 24*n,* 25, 26, 37, 74*n,* 117. Letter to, *2.* 25

Browning, Robert, *3.* 57*n*; *4.* 330, 405, 406, 407; *5.* 20, 102

Browning, Susan, *5.* 17

Browning Society, *5.* 20*n*

Bruce, Mrs., *2.* 149*n,* 156

Bruce, Thomas, Earl of Elgin, *4.* 319

Bruno, Giordano, *5.* 33, 36

Bruns, Werner, *5.* 345

Brush, Conklin, *1.* 105

Brush, Hannah, *3.* 157

Bryant, Carolan O'Brien, *3.* 452

Bryant, William C., *3.* 439, 451. Letter to, *3.* 380

Bryant, William Cullen, *1.* 26*n*; *2.* 30*n,* 171*n*; *3.* 110*n,* 120-21, 124, 132, 136*n,* 144*n,* 167*n,* 406; *5.* 206

Bryce, Mr., *5.* 99

Bryn Mawr College, *4.* 39*n,* 323*n*; *5.* 56*n*

Buchan, Peter, *4.* 98*n*

Buchanan, Robert, *1.* 355*n*; *2.* 152, 321; *3.* 21*n,* 30, 35, 36, 38*n,* 39*n,* 44, 52, 60, 133, 431, 441; *4.* 75; *5.* 305; *6.* 13. Letters to, *3.* 36-37, 47-48, 56, 64

Buchanan, Capt. "Tim," *2.* 329

Buck, Jerome, *4.* 434

Bucke, Charles H., *4.* 431

Bucke, Clare, *5.* 159

Bucke, E. Pardee, *4.* 387, 389; *5.* 47, 107

Bucke, Ina, *5.* 107*n*

Bucke, Dr. Richard Maurice, *1.* v; *2.* 47*n,* 84*n,* 232*n,* 244*n,* 329*n,* 368; *3.* 9, 49*n,* 60*n,* 142, 172*n,* 174, 175*n,* 178, 181, 183, 184, 187, 189*n,* 190*n,* 191*n,* 193, 196*n,* 199*n,* 200-201, 209, 212*n,* 218, 221, 223, 231*n,* 234*n,* 235, 237, 238*n,* 247*n,* 249, 251, 258, 268-69, 274*n,*

237, 238n, 247n, 249, 251, 258, 268-69, 274n, 275, 283, 291, 292, 293, 294, 301, 305, 309, 310, 315, 317, 319, 320, 325, 328, 329, 330n, 332, 336n, 337, 338, 339, 340, 341n, 342, 343, 344, 347n, 349, 350, 351, 352, 356n, 357, 361, 363n, 364, 366n, 383n, 387, 389, 393, 394, 397, 404, 410, 414, 430, 431, 432, 433, 434, 435, 436, 437, 438, 439, 442, 444, 446, 447, 448, 449, 452, 453; 4. 2, 4, 18, 24, 25, 26, 28, 31, 32n, 34, 35n, 36, 39, 41, 42, 44, 49, 53, 55, 59, 65n, 68n, 69, 74, 77, 80, 87, 91, 100, 103, 110, 114, 116, 117, 119, 120, 121, 122, 125, 126, 128, 129, 132, 137, 138, 140, 141, 143, 144, 146, 149, 150, 151, 152, 157, 159, 162, 167, 168, 173, 176, 177, 186, 189, 190, 203, 212, 214, 218, 219, 220, 224, 226, 227, 233, 234, 235n, 238, 249, 252, 254, 258, 263, 273, 274, 275, 276, 277, 278, 279, 282, 284, 288, 289, 291, 292, 293, 294, 295, 296, 297, 298, 299, 300, 301, 302, 303, 304, 305, 306, 307, 308, 317, 319, 320, 321, 323, 324, 326, 330, 334, 340, 343, 349, 350, 355, 358, 361, 367, 368, 371, 372, 374, 380, 382, 395, 396, 401, 406, 410, 424-41; 5. vii, 1-2, 3, 4, 5, 6, 7, 22, 26n, 28n, 41, 43, 44, 45, 46, 48, 50, 51, 53, 54, 68, 71, 77, 78, 82, 85, 90, 93, 96, 98, 108, 110, 111, 112, 114, 119, 121, 125, 136, 139-40, 145, 146, 148, 154, 159, 160, 162, 163, 164, 184, 189, 196, 198, 200, 202n, 203, 206, 207, 208, 211, 216, 219, 220, 221, 223, 224, 226, 227, 228, 231, 232, 233, 234, 236, 237, 238, 239, 240, 241, 242, 244, 248, 250, 251, 254, 256, 263, 264, 267, 269, 273n, 275, 314, 316, 319, 332-47; 6. 19n, 22n, 29, 38, 48, 49, 51-52, 53n, 55, 57, 59, 69.

Letters to, 3. 266-67; 4. 70-71, 75, 80-81, 87, 91, 107, 112, 118, 134-35, 139, 142-44, 146-47, 150-54, 156-58, 160-61, 163-65, 168, 171-84, 186-208, 210-12, 214-19, 221-25, 227-34, 237-81, 283-85, 287-89, 292-93, 304, 306-9, 311-14, 316-25, 327-29, 331-77, 379-405, 407-9; 5. 17-21, 23-25, 27-43, 45-49, 51-54, 56-61, 63-66, 68, 70-75, 77-79, 81, 83-84, 87-88, 90-92, 94-95, 97-109, 114-25, 127-34, 137, 139-40, 142, 144, 146-47, 149-66, 168-71, 173-74, 177-81, 183-200, 202-4, 206-23, 225-27, 229-35, 240-46, 250, 252-55, 257-63, 265-72, 274-77; 6. 18, 21, 55

Bucke, Mrs. Richard Maurice, 4. 80, 307, 329, 346, 356, 387, 403, 407; 5. 307
Buckle, Henry Thomas, 2. 174
Buckley, Mr. & Mrs., 2. 205, 207, 211
Buckley, G. Swayne, 2. 113n
Buckley, Theodore Alois, 1. 262n
Buckny, Mrs. Talbot, 5. 346
Buckwalter, Geoffrey, 4. 336n, 343, 364n; 5. 209

Buel, C. C., 4. 40
Bugle-Echoes, 6. 40
Bull, George W., 3. 443
Bullard, Laura Curtis, 3. 430, 441
Bulwer-Lytton, Edward George Earle, 2. 224; 5. 293n
"Bumble-Bees and Bird Music," 3. 223n
Bunce & Huntington, 1. 270n, 340n
"Buntline, Ned," *see* Edward Z. C. Judson
Burbank, Alfred P., 5. 171n
Burd, Charles E., 2. 132, 368
Burgh, A. C.(?) de, 3. 59
Burke, John F., 5. 332
Burkhardt, Charles A., 5. 335
Burlingame, Anson, 2. 35
Burnham, Carrie S., 3. 61n
Burns, Mr., 1. 178
Burns, Robert, 2. 327n; 3. 318, 320; 4. 55, 325n, 396, 399; 5. 339
Burnside, Gen. Ambrose Everett, 1. 85, 92n, 103, 138-39, 146, 151, 156, 212, 213, 215, 216, 217, 218, 222, 230, 232
Burr, Mr., 3. 223
Burr, Aaron, 4. 396
Burr, Celie M., 1. 376
Burritt, Ira N.(?). Letter to, 2. 189
Burroughs, John, 1. 6, 8, 11, 14, 157n, 200n, 237n, 238n, 285, 294n, 297, 298n, 303n, 329n, 333n, 335n, 340, 343, 351, 354, 368, 375; 2. 3, 14, 32, 34n, 36, 37, 41, 43, 48, 54, 76n, 80n, 81, 96n, 127, 131, 133n, 139, 150, 153, 155, 159, 162n, 183, 184, 185n, 191, 194, 204, 206, 208, 221, 222n, 227, 230, 233, 240, 242-43, 249, 279, 293, 295, 304, 305, 309, 322, 328, 330n, 337n, 341n, 369, 370, 371, 372; 3. 2, 4, 7, 19, 20, 22, 42, 62n, 78, 80, 81, 84, 85, 91, 96, 99, 100, 103, 120-21, 122-25, 139, 144, 147, 151, 152n, 153n, 156, 171, 174n, 183n, 193, 196, 214n, 220, 251, 264n, 283, 288n, 299n, 302, 313, 315n, 316, 317, 319, 329, 338, 339n, 349, 353, 361n, 383n, 385n, 386n, 388, 393, 394, 397, 405n, 410, 431, 432, 433, 435, 437, 438, 442, 443, 444, 445, 446, 447, 448, 449, 450, 452, 453; 4. 18, 20n, 26, 28, 36, 45, 82n, 87, 91, 116n, 117, 128, 129, 141, 142, 150, 162, 187, 188, 203, 214, 224, 234, 255, 263, 271, 280, 294, 305, 314, 315, 341, 347, 353, 356, 358, 359, 365, 369, 376, 377, 378, 406, 407, 424, 427, 428, 429, 431, 432, 433, 434, 436, 437, 438, 439, 441; 5. 3, 6, 28, 36, 38, 45, 77, 81, 83, 94, 95, 96, 97, 99, 103n, 273n, 279n, 301, 304, 318, 334, 340, 347; 6. 9n, 14n, 19n, 59, 67. Letters to, 1. 281, 285, 340-41; 2. 66, 168-69, 178, 216-17, 225-26, 237-38, 241, 278, 299-300, 302, 312-13, 317-18, 325, 327, 331-32, 344-45; 3. 39-40, 50-51, 71, 74, 76, 77-78, 78-79, 79-80, 83, 89, 108, 109,

110-11, 112, 113-14, 126, 127-28, 136, 141-42, 143-44, 146, 149-50, 158, 159-60, 162-63, 170-71, 172, 173-74, 178-79, 198, 199-200, 208-9, 217-18, 230-31, 235, 244-45, 245-46, 274, 301, 302, 324-25, 328, 331, 334-35, 347, 355, 367-68, 390, 395-96, 413-14; *4.* 21-22, 26, 53, 59, 70-71, 75, 80-81, 82, 87, 91, 110, 118, 128, 139, 149, 167-68, 185-86, 195, 202, 219, 222-23, 226-27, 241-42, 283-84, 294, 297, 335, 338, 357, 368, 377-78; *5.* 29, 36, 92, 287-88, 301-2, 304-5; *6.* 15, 29, 38

Burroughs, Julian, *3.* 127, 141, 149, 153, 158, 159, 170, 179, 274, 301, 414; *4.* 140, 141, 186, 280, 284, 294, 315, 357, 377, 378, 406; *5.* 45, 92, 96

Burroughs, Ursula, *1.* 281, 341; *2.* 36, 41, 168, 191, 202, 206, 208, 216, 221, 226, 295, 318, 332, 344; *3.* 51, 71, 74, 80, 89, 122, 123-25, 141, 143, 144, 149, 158, 160, 162, 170, 171, 179, 274, 301, 414; *4.* 22, 140, 186, 280, 284, 294, 315, 357, 377, 378, 406; *5.* 29*n*, 45, 92, 96, 288. Letter to, *3.* 127-28

Burton, Robert, *4.* 357*n*

Bury, Thomas, *5.* 62, 113, 138, 168, 176

Bush, Alonzo S., *1.* 176*n*, 177*n*, 332*n*, 367, 374, 375

Bush, Harry D., *5.* 347

Bush, Mrs. Harry D., *5.* 241

Bushell, W., *4.* 25

Butler, Dr., *1.* 134

Butler, Gen. Benjamin Franklin, *1.* 219, 245*n*, 252

Butler, Samuel, *3.* 116*n*

Butterworth, Hezekiah, *5.* 335

Butts, Asa K., *2.* 144*n*, 244*n*, 277*n*, 294, 345*n*; *3.* 42*n*, 430. Letters to, *2.* 263-64, 273-74, 275; *5.* 297

"By Blue Ontario's Shore," *3.* 270*n*

"By Emerson's Grave," *3.* 274*n*

Byron, George Gordon, *2.* 86, 162*n*

C., V. S. Letter to, *4.* 172

Cabot, James Elliot, *4.* 208

"Calamus," *3.* 53*n*; *5.* 72, 167*n*

Calder, Albert L., *5.* 264*n*

Caldwell, Capt. William, *1.* 249, 262

Calhoon, Philo, *2.* vi

Calhoun, Pete, *2.* 57, 122*n*

Californian, The, 3. 214*n*, 260*n*

Callicot, T.C. Letter to, *3.* 284

"Calming Thought of All, The," *4.* 145*n*

Cambridge (Mass.) *Chronicle, 3.* 281*n*, 295; *5.* 316

Camden & Atlantic Railroad, *3.* 199, 207*n*, 434, 446

Camden *County Courier, 3.* 341*n*, 416*n*; *4.* 94*n*, 348; *5.* 129*n*

Camden *Daily Post, 3.* 63*n*, 81*n*, 90*n*, 133*n*, 149*n*, 170*n*, 176*n*, 178*n*, 181*n*, 184*n*, 188*n*, 204*n*, 281*n*, 313*n*, 349*n*, 372*n*, 389, 398*n*, 434; *4.* 150, 256, 258, 409*n*, *5.* 40*n*, 51*n*, 70*n*, 192*n*, 222*n*, 231*n*

Camden *Democrat, 3.* 87*n*, 210*n*

Camden *Morning News, 5.* 30, 71*n*

Camden *New Republic, 2.* 303*n*, 306*n*, 309*n*, 315*n*, 338*n*; *3.* 3, 36*n*, 94*n*, 133*n*

Camden Postmaster, *3.* 433, 436

Camden *Press, 3.* 234. Letter to, *3.* 177

Camden's Compliment to Walt Whitman, 4. 343, 344, 345, 352, 354, 355, 356, 360, 368, 370, 372, 375, 379, 380, 381, 382-83, 390, 391, 393, 394, 395, 401, 404*n*; *5.* 30

Camelot Classics, The, *4.* 23*n*

Campbell, Charles B., *5.* 335

Campbell Hospital, *1.* 63, 68, 71, 106, 116

Canniff, Gomley, *3.* 190

Canning, George, *4.* 18

Cannon, William, *3.* 433

Canterbury Poet Series, The, 3. 407*n*; *4.* 22*n*

Captain Lobe, 5. 164*n*

Carey, William, *4.* 123, 124, 430, 433, 439; *5.* 271*n*, 347. Letters to, *4.* 122, 124, 130, 351

Carleton, George W., *1.* 329*n*

Carleton, Will, *4.* 438; *5.* 341

"Carlyle from American Points of View," *3.* 277; *6.* 27

Carlyle, Jane, *3.* 334*n*; *4.* 216, 221, 224

Carlyle, Luther, *5.* 337

Carlyle, Thomas, *1.* 2, 3, 188*n*, 338, 342; *2.* 1, 30*n*, 100, 300; *3.* 210, 211, 214, 218, 277, 302, 316, 326-27, 329, 334-35, 344, 405*n*; *4.* 207, 208, 210, 216, 223, 224, 260, 263, 370; *5.* 62*n*, 118*n*, 163*n*; *6.* 34. Letter to, *2.* 185

Carnegie, Andrew, *4.* 83*n*, 85, 86, 87, 88, 116*n*, 147, 161, 173*n*. Letter to, *4.* 146

"Carol Closing Sixty-Nine, A," *4.* 145*n*, 161, 426

"Carol of Harvest for 1867, A," *see* "Return of the Heroes, The"

"Carpenter, The," *4.* 24*n*, 398*n*; *5.* 239

Carpenter, Alfred, *5.* 335

Carpenter, Edmund, *2.* 371

Carpenter, Edward, *3.* 58*n*, 83, 85, 86, 87, 88, 89, 95, 98, 135, 159, 214, 265, 363, 373*n*, 400, 402, 404, 409*n*, 410, 440, 441, 442, 443, 444, 445, 446, 447, 450, 452, 453; *4.* 17, 21, 23, 27*n*, 31, 90, 244, 271, 277, 278, 280, 282, 346, 383, 402, 428, 430, 436, 438; *5.* 55, 74, 127, 207, 211, 223, 233, 239, 305, 308, 314, 315, 334, 338, 342, 346, 347; *6.* 27. Letters to, *3.* 41, 43, 100, 101, 103, 135-36, 186-87, 227, 253, 299, 399-400; *4.* 29-30, 77, 89-90, 244-45, 266-67, 269-70, 341-42; *5.* 50, 111, 207-8, 255-

56

Carpenter, Francis B., *5.* 256, 257
Carpenter, Frank, *5.* 334
Carpenter, Matt H., *2.* 369
Carpenter, Mrs. Mollie W., *3.* 446
Carpet Bag, 1. 191*n*
Carson, Hampton L., *4.* 431
Carson, Thomas J., *1.* 176, 184
Carter, Robert. Letter to, *2.* 332
Carver, Mrs., *4.* 362*n*
Carver Hospital, *1.* 223, 230
Cary, Anne Louise, *2.* 191*n*
Case, Mrs. Leslie V., *3.* vii, 178*n*
Case, Marie, *5.* 348
Caswell, Charles, *3.* 141*n*
Caswell, Smith, *3.* 141, 144, 149, 158, 160, 162,
　170, 173, 179, 432, 433, 435
Cate, Mr., *5.* 30*n*
Cate, Charles, *1.* 176, 332
Cathcart, G. L., *3.* 59
Catlin, George, *5.* 341
Cattell, Edward, *3.* 3, 71*n,* 108*n,* 431, 433, 435,
　436, 443. Letter to, *3.* 77
Cattell, James McKeen, *5.* 87-88
Cattell, Jonas, *3.* 76*n*
Catton, Bruce, *1.* 68*n,* 74*n*
Cavanaugh, James Michael, *2.* 25
Cave, Oswald, *5.* 348
"Cedar-Plums Like," *3.* 203
Celebrities of the Century, 6. 52
"Central Park Jottings," *see* "These May
　Afternoons"
Century Club, *3.* 436; *4.* 141, 142, 147, 150
Century Guild Hobby Horse, The, 4. 271*n*
Century Illustrated Monthly Review, The, 3. 66*n,*
　110*n,* 167*n,* 263*n,* 328, 329, 334*n,* 373, 375,
　378, 397*n*; *4.* 1, 20, 21, 41, 42, 43, 51, 55, 86,
　108, 118, 124, 161, 191-92, 194*n,* 204, 214,
　217, 261, 262, 267, 329, 347*n,* 362, 363, 370,
　385, 389, 393, 425, 426; *5.* 20, 21, 22, 23, 26,
　27, 28, 29, 32, 43, 44, 47, 52, 53, 54, 56, 68,
　70*n,* 158, 159, 176, 271*n.* Letters to, *4.* 37, 38,
　40-41, 216; *6.* 33, 34
Cervantes Saavedra, Miguel de, *2.* 224
Chadwick, Rev. John White, *3.* 285, 286-88,
　291, 300*n,* 352*n*
Chainey, George, *3.* 293*n,* 296*n,* 297*n,* 312,
　448; *5.* 317. Letter to, *3.* 294
Chamberlain, Judge, *4.* 268
Chamberlin, J. E., *4.* 268*n,* 437
Chamberlin, Jessie C. Letter to, *4.* 60
Chambers, Mr., *1.* 176
Chambers, John W., *2.* 133*n,* 369
Chambers, Julius, *4.* 136, 330, 345*n,* 427, 431,
　434, 439; *5.* 118*n,* 195*n,* 332, 337, 341; *6.* 46*n.*
　Letters to, *4.* 136, 155, 181
Chandler, Arthur D., *4.* 86

Channing, Grace Ellery, *4.* 118, 196, 197, 430
Channing, Dr. William F., *1.* 241, 248; *2.* 48,
　52, 56, 60, 63, 65, 66, 145, 211*n,* 230, 239,
　366, 370; *3.* 315, 331, 332, 333, 335, 336; *4.*
　18, 103, 195, 196, 430; *6.* 38. Letters to, *2.* 47;
　4. 106
Channing, Mrs. William F., *2.* 20, 47, 60, 64,
　65, 66, 207, 230
"Chant of National Feuillage, A," *1.* 46
Chapin, William E., *1.* 284, 350*n.* Letter to, *6.*
　5
Chappell, Warren, *5.* 296
Charleston, S.C., Battle of, *1.* 92, 125, 134, 138,
　139
"Charleton (or Charlton), Jay," *see* J. C.
　Goldsmith
Chase, Salmon Portland, *1.* 61, 74, 83, 190*n,*
　196; *2.* 35, 219. Letter from R. W. Emerson
　to, *1.* 64-65
Chasseboeuf, Constantin François, *see* Comte de
　Volney
Chatto & Windus, *1.* 346*n*; *3.* 34, 259*n*; *4.* 43,
　53*n.* Letters to, *4.* 53, 59
Chauncey, Charles W., *1.* 11, 84, 123-24, 126,
　142, 159
Cheever, E. C., *3.* 445
Chevaliers, *3.* 233
Chicago *Evening Journal, 4.* 320*n*
Chicago *Herald, 3.* 281*n*; *4.* 402*n*
Chicago *Inter Queen, 3.* 281*n*
Chicago *Morning News, 4.* 287
Chicago *Tribune, 3.* 45*n,* 46, 176*n,* 181*n,* 430,
　434, 441
Chicago *Weekly News, 2.* 35
Child, Josieh *3.* 136*n,* 137*n,* 141*n,* 193, 248,
　255, 319, 340, 432, 433, 435, 437, 445; *4.* 434;
　5. 304. Letters to, *3.* 132, 140-41, 157-58, 255,
　319; *4.* 235; *5.* 314-15; *6.* 20
"Child-Ghost; A Story of the Lost Loyalist,
　The," *1.* 26*n*
Childhood of Eric Menved, The, 5. 283
"Children of Adam," *1.* 49*n*; *3.* 271*n,* 274, 276,
　286, 287, 336*n*
Childs, George W., *3.* 52*n,* 263, 264, 368*n,* 431,
　433; *4.* 25*n,* 116*n,* 439; *5.* 186*n,* 341. Letters
　to, *3.* 142, 146, 263; *4.* 15
Childs, S. H., *1.* 141*n,* 175*n,* 374
"Child's Reminiscence, A," *1.* 328*n*
Christern, Frederick W., *1.* 257
Christian Intelligencer, The, 3. 281*n*
Christian Kingdom Society, *5.* 348
"Christmas Greeting, A," *4.* 399, 400, 402, 404,
　405, 406, 427; *5.* 24
Christy, George W., *3.* 447
Church, Alfred, J., *3.* 118*n*
Church, F. P., *1.* 285*n,* 341, 342-43, 378; *2.*
　32*n,* 121*n,* 366, 368; *3.* 76. Letters to, *1.* 336,

337-38, 343, 344-45, 346, 354; *2.* 18-19, 21, 22, 32-33, 68, 90-91, 93; *5.* 292, 293; *6.* 9

Church, W. C., *1.* 285*n*, 378; *2.* 22*n*, 365, 367; *3.* 45. Letters to, *1.* 335-36, 337-38, 343, 354; *2.* 18-19, 21, 32-33, 69, 90-91, 93; *5.* 292, 293; *6.* 9

Cincinnati *Commercial*, *1.* 68*n*; *2.* 30*n*; *3.* 176*n*, 181*n*, 434. Letter to, *3.* 24

Cincinnati *Ohio*, *3.* 281*n*

"City Notes in August," *3.* 236*n*, 241*n*

Civilization: Its Causes and Cure; and Other Essays, *4.* 383

Clapp, George, *1.* 339

Clapp, Henry, *1.* 47*n*, 55, 124*n*, 328, 339-40, 341, 364, 371, 372, 378. Letter to, *1.* 55

Clapp, Jr., Henry, *5.* 339; *6.* 68

Clare, Ada, *1.* 124*n*, 339, 349*n*; *2.* 285

Clark, Henry H., *3.* 238*n*, 280. Letter to, *3.* 245

Clark, Nellie F., *1.* 141*n*

Clark, William, *3.* 435

Clarke, Asia Booth, *3.* 376*n*

Clarke, W. B., *3.* 431

Clausen, Carl F., *2.* 143, 150, 163, 175, 176, 185-86, 287, 295

Claxton, Remsen, & Haffelfinger, *3.* 442, 443

Clay, Cassius M., *4.* 430

Clay, Depuis Macellus, *5.* 339

Clemens, Samuel, *1.* 191*n*; *2.* 81*n*, 152*n*, 305*n*; *3.* 405*n*; *4.* 125*n*. Letter to, *4.* 101

Clement, Mr. (editor), *5.* 97*n*

Clement, Willard K., *3.* 436

Clements(?), Billy, *1.* 177*n*

Cleveland, Grover, *3.* 348*n*, 381, 395*n*; *4.* 121, 221

Cleveland *Leader and Herald*, *3.* 398*n*

Clifford, Edward, *3.* 380, 381

Clifford, John Herbert, *4.* 433

Clifton, Mr., *5.* 301

Clito, *4.* 73

Coad, Oral S., *2.* 89*n*

Coan, Titus M., *3.* 445

Coates, Edward, *4.* 204

Cobb, J. T., *3.* 446

Cobb, Mrs. Lucy Livingston, *1.* 278-79

Coburn, Mrs. V. O., *3.* 437. Letters to, *6.* 26, 27

Coffin, Elizabeth M., *5.* 338

Coffman, George, *3.* 432

Cole, George D., *2.* 192*n*, 373

Cole, Mary (Mrs. Frank Baker), *2.* 193

Colein, William, *2.* 280, 284

Coleman, Mr., *3.* 56*n*

Coleman, Rufus A., *1.* 184*n*, 191*n*

Coleridge, Samuel Taylor, *3.* 212; *4.* 330

Colfax, Schuyler, *1.* 211*n*; *2.* 35, 54

Colles, Richard W., *4.* 57*n*, 431. Letters to, *4.* 44-45, 54, 145

Collins, Henry H., *4.* 432

Colophon, *1.* vi

Columbia University, *3.* 297*n*, 304*n*

Columbus, Christopher, *5.* 268*n*

Columbus (Ohio) *Morning Journal*, *1.* 281*n*

Colyer, Dr., *1.* 30*n*

"Come Up from the Fields, Father," *6.* 40*n*

"Commonplace, The," *5.* 24, 27

Comstock, Anthony, *3.* 295, 298*n*, 303, 314, 338, 348*n*; *5.* 316

Concord, Mass., *3.* 244-45, 246, 327

Cone, Helen Gray, *3.* 263*n*

"Confession of Faith, A," *3.* 388, 395

Conley, Eugene, *3.* 433

Conlin, Bernard, *5.* 256*n*

Conover, Simon B., *3.* 353*n*

Conservator, The, *5.* 43*n*, 49, 58, 153, 154, 155, 164, 178*n*

Consuelo, *4.* 107

Contemporary Club, *4.* 67, 147, 150. Letter to, *4.* 150

Contemporary Review, The, *3.* 20*n*; *4.* 34*n*; *5.* 195, 203, 301

"Continuities," *4.* 145*n*

Contraband Camp, *1.* 115

Conway, Eustace. Letter to, *3.* 213

Conway, Moncure D., *1.* 14, 287*n*, 294*n*, 297, 350, 352, 354, 378; *2.* 17, 28, 30, 92, 99*n*, 162*n*, 224*n*, 340, 341*n*, 344, 366, 369; *3.* 20, 22, 25, 38, 44, 46*n*, 47*n*, 60, 213*n*, 437, 441; *4.* 40, 79, 116*n*, 132, 234*n*; *5.* 220, 242; *6.* 25*n*, 41*n*, 45*n*, 46. Letters to, *1.* 332-33, 346-49; *2.* 15-16, 23-24, 96-97, 100; *3.* 31-32, 57; *4.* 76

Cook, Kenningdale, *3.* 440, 442. Letter to, *4.* 19-20

Cook, Marjorie, *4.* 440

Cook, Capt. William, *1.* 376. Letter to, *1.* 255

Cooke, George W., *3.* 287*n*

Cooke, Jay, *2.* 172*n*

Cooper, A. H., *5.* 224

Cooper, Mrs. Hattie E., *1.* 182

Cooper, William, *4.* 201*n*

Cope, Edward Drinker, *4.* 403

Cope's Tobacco Plant, *3.* 141*n*, 157, 158, 159*n*, 435, 436; *5.* 305; *6.* 20

Corbin, Abigail Burroughs, *4.* 139

Corbin, Hiram I., *4.* 139*n*

Corning, Miss, *4.* 246

Corning, Rev. J. Leonard, *4.* 206, 231, 440

Corot, Jean Baptiste Camille, *4.* 393

Corson, Hiram, *4.* 59*n*, 424, 428

Cosmopolitan, The, *4.* 119*n*, 161, 164; *5.* 68. Letter to, *4.* 160

Cosmopolitan Club (Philadelphia), *4.* 161

Costelloe, Benjamin F. W., *3.* 327*n*, 396*n*, 401; *4.* 28*n*, 31, 120, 281, 291; *5.* 26, 47, 225, 227, 229, 230, 231, 233, 255; *6.* 37, 50

Costelloe, Mary Smith, *3.* 321*n,* 326, 329, 345, 355, 365, 367*n,* 393, 395, 396, 400, 451, 452; *4.* 32, 67*n,* 89, 98, 111, 116, 120, 153, 158, 163, 169, 189*n,* 190, 197, 198, 216*n,* 223, 224, 230, 237, 281, 285, 324, 339, 342, 347, 372, 382, 385, 391, 394, 395, 403, 426, 429, 430, 433, 434, 436, 438, 440; *5.* 6, 20, 46, 47, 52, 56, 70, 193, 223, 225, 227, 229, 230, 331, 333, 334, 337; *6.* 37. Letters to, *3.* 358, 360, 370, 372-73, 396-97, 401; *4.* 28, 31, 39, 42, 48, 51-52, 55, 58, 62, 67, 73, 76, 99-100, 104, 106-7, 121-22, 126-27, 129-30, 176, 178, 181, 183, 186, 196, 204, 218, 225-26, 238, 291, 323, 349, 364, 383, 389, 404; *5.* 21-22, 26, 119, 320; *6.* 50
Costelloe, Rachel, *4.* 98, 99, 104, 111, 122, 126*n,* 153, 323; *5.* 52
Cotrel, Thomas, *1.* 98
Cotta, J. G., *2.* 48
Cottell, Elizabeth A., *4.* 439
Coues, Elliott, *5.* 343
Cowan, Frank, *5.* 348
Cox, G. C., *4.* 83*n,* 88, 101, 118-19, 122, 124, 125, 131, 132, 134, 351; *6.* 45*n.* Letters to, *4.* 101, 123, 351
Cox, Miss R. M., *3.* 441
Cox, Samuel S., *3.* 109
Cozzens, Fred T., *5.* 340
Cranford, Capt. Henry Loud, *1.* 197
Crawford, Kenneth, *5.* 344
Cridland, Mrs. Charles, *4.* viii; *5.* ix
Critic, The, 3. 101*n,* 141*n,* 197*n,* 202*n,* 203*n,* 205, 210*n,* 211, 216, 218, 221*n,* 222*n,* 223, 236*n,* 244*n,* 255*n,* 268*n,* 273*n,* 274*n,* 275*n,* 281*n,* 289*n,* 290, 300*n,* 306*n,* 314*n,* 318*n,* 320, 322, 324, 329, 334*n,* 339, 340, 342, 343, 353, 355*n,* 357, 362, 363, 370*n,* 375, 377, 378, 379, 382*n,* 387*n,* 388, 398*n,* 409*n,* 436, 437, 438; *4.* 1, 43, 60, 68*n,* 76, 112, 128, 130, 153, 211*n,* 225, 227, 239, 254, 271, 273, 275, 289*n,* 292, 337, 339, 340, 386, 399, 408, 424, 425, 426, 427; *5.* 46*n,* 60, 64*n,* 68, 70, 71, 74*n,* 78, 94, 115, 122, 130, 145, 146, 149, 153, 235*n,* 244, 257; *6.* 53*n,* 59*n.* Letters to, *3.* 205, 273; *4.* 33, 58, 61, 79, 96, 131; *5.* 46, 67, 152, 319; *6.* 35
Croly, David G., *2.* 204*n,* 371; *3.* 126*n*
Croly, Mrs. Jenny C., *3.* 447
Cross, Rev., *2.* 153
Cruikshank, Robert, *2.* 274*n*
Cummins, Mr., *5.* 291
Cunningham, Helen S., *1.* 218*n,* 375
Cunningham, John S. Letter to, *3.* 265
Cunningham, Oscar, *1.* 176, 181, 184, 217-18, 219, 221, 227, 229, 231
Cupples, Upham & Co., *3.* 451
Curphey, James, *1.* 369, 370, 378
Currie, C. F., *4.* 427; *5.* 123. Letter to, *5.* 67

Curtis, George William, *1.* 329*n;* *3.* 111; *5.* 57
Curtis, Margaret S., *1.* 122*n,* 140*n,* 164, 188*n,* 374. Letters to, *1.* 153-55, 174-75
Curtz, Mr. Letter to, *5.* 46
Custer, George Armstrong, *3.* 53
Cutter, Charles, *1.* 225, 227, 228, 230
Cuttle, Capt. Edward, *5.* 195

Dailey, Charles W., *3.* 451
Dakin, Edward, *3.* 435
Dakyns, H. G., *3.* 60
"Dalliance of the Eagle, The," *3.* 158*n,* 270*n*
Dallin, Ed, *3.* 240*n*
D'Almeida, Charles, *1.* 77-78, 80
Dalmon, Charles William, *4.* 434
Dana, Charles A., *1.* 40*n;* *2.* 332; *3.* 353. Letter to, *3.* 272
Dana, Capt. James J., *1.* 58
Dana, Richard Henry, *1.* 292
Daniel, George, *2.* 274*n*
Daniels, J. W., *3.* 295*n*
Dante Alighieri, *1.* 82; *3.* 336*n;* *5.* 49, 63
Dark Blue, 2. 162; *3.* 60*n*
Dart, Mrs., *4.* 139
Dartmouth College, *2.* 5, 124*n,* 170*n,* 176, 178, 180; *5.* 295*n*
Darwin, Charles, *3.* 357*n*
Davenport, Edward L., *2.* 111
Davidge(?), William, *3.* 445
Davidson, Thomas, *4.* 118*n;* *5.* 33*n*
Davis, Mr. (reporter), *6.* 43
Davis, Andrew Jackson, *1.* 43; *3.* 441
Davis, George K. *2.* 65
Davis, James, *3.* 69, 71
Davis, Jefferson, *1.* 92, 99; *4.* 403, 404
Davis, Joseph P., *1.* 152, 327
Davis, Mrs. Mary O., *3.* 387*n,* 388, 389, 392, 393, 397, 399, 401, 409; *4.* 17, 21, 65, 72, 73, 88, 90, 94, 107, 112, 123, 127, 132, 138, 146, 151, 154, 158, 162, 180, 200, 202, 206, 210, 266*n,* 270, 274. 278, 279, 280, 282, 307, 329, 333, 340, 361, 366, 383, 385, 386, 392, 410; *5.* 24, 27, 30, 34, 38*n,* 43, 52, 67, 81, 82, 83, 84, 87, 94, 95, 105, 107, 108, 120, 125, 132, 133, 137, 140, 147, 152, 155, 165, 168, 173, 183, 190, 193, 195, 196, 206*n,* 212, 225, 229-30, 231, 234, 239, 242, 243, 249, 251, 252, 254, 256, 267, 268, 269, 278, 320. Letter to, *5.* 85-86
Davis, Paulina Wright, *1.* 248; *2.* 60, 65, 281, 315
Davis, Thomas, *1.* 248*n;* *2.* 58, 60, 62, 64, 65, 66
Davis, V. D., *3.* 449
Davis, Warren, *4.* 161; *6.* 48
Davis, William S. Letter to, *1.* 152-53
"Dead Carlyle, The," *see* "Death of Carlyle"

"Dead Emperor, The," 4. 144n, 184n
"Dead Tenor, The," 3. 382n
"Death-Bouquet, A," 5. 19n, 24, 25
"Death Dogs My Steps," 5. 137n
"Death in the School-Room," 1. 26
"Death of Abraham Lincoln, The," 3. 106, 108, 109, 110-11, 112, 113, 117n, 143, 149, 151, 152, 155n, 160, 176, 177, 178, 179n, 217, 219n, 221, 222, 223, 237n, 310n; 4. 19, 22, 24, 25, 26, 27, 28, 35, 75, 78, 79, 80, 81, 83, 84-85, 86, 87, 88; 5. 31-32, 33, 36, 37, 38-39, 40n, 42, 304, 312; 6. 39
"Death of a Fireman," 2. 315n, 316, 318
"Death of Carlyle," 3. 210, 211, 212n, 220n, 290n
"Death of General Grant," 3. 387n, 409n; 5. 318n
"Death of Longfellow," 3. 273, 290n
"Death-Sonnet for Custer, A," see "From Far Dakota's Cañons"
"Death's Valley," 4. 368, 369-70, 376; 5. 340
DeJoe, Williamina H., 5. 339
Delabarre, Edmund B., 4. 387n
Delaware County Institute of Science, 3. 451
De Loach, Dr. R. J. H., 3. viii, 428; 4. viii
"Democracy," 1. 82n, 338, 341, 342, 343, 344, 346, 350, 354; 2. 16, 18-19, 26, 29, 32, 100
Democratic Review, 1. 25n, 26n
Democratic Vistas 2. 1, 5, 19n, 32n, 39, 50, 65n, 81n, 100, 101n, 108, 116n, 118n, 131, 143, 144, 151-52, 154, 161n, 163-64, 174, 184, 269n, 270, 274, 275, 282, 283, 288, 304n, 317; 3. 92, 101, 137n, 142, 162n, 171, 308; 4. 74, 81n, 176n, 179, 182, 183, 235n, 264; 5. 247n, 251; 6. 11, 36-37, 39, 40, 42, 43, 44, 45, 47, 59
Dent, Gen. Frederick T., 2. 184
Denver, Colorado, 3. 165, 168-70
Denver Tribune. Letter to, 3. 182
Deschamps, Chrissie, 2. 255; 3. 59
Detroit Free Press, 3. 181n, 434
Deutsche Presse, 4. 352n
Devoe, William J., 1. 29
Dew-Smith, A. G., 3. 44, 51
Deyo, Chauncey B., 2. 168, 302, 304
Dick & Fitzgerald. Letter to, 4. 152
Dickens, Charles, 2. 94n; 3. 208; 4. 82n, 388, 390; 5. 195n
Dickens, Mrs. Charles, 3. 56n
Dickinson, Mrs. Ellen E., 3. 434
Dickinson, Emily, 2. 139n
Dilke, Lady, 3. 328
Dillard, Mrs. L., 5. 348
Dille, Israel, 2. 268, 272, 276
Dillingham, Charles T., 3. 436, 444
"Dirge for Two Veterans," 3. 153n, 174; 5. 306-7
Dirngee(?), Emma, 5. 348

"Dismantled Ship, The," 4. 144n
Dixon, George E., 4. 435
Dixon, Helen, 5. 205n
Dixon, Thomas, 2. 362, 367, 368, 371, 372, 373; 3. 44n, 430, 432, 440, 441; 5. 305; 6. 20. Letter to, 2. 99-100
Dixon, Wentworth, 5. 205, 244, 245, 342, 348; 6. 57, 58
Dodd, Mead & Co., 5. 39, 334
Doggett, Edward G. Letter to, 3. 195
Dole, William P., 1. 263n
Donaldson, Miss, 3. 25
Donaldson, Blaine, 5. 54. Letter to, 3. 383
Donaldson, Mary E., 5. 54. Letter to, 3. 383
Donaldson, Thomas, 1. vii; 2. v, 307n; 3. 275n, 383, 405n; 4. 24, 28, 101n, 183, 232, 269, 384, 408, 426, 427, 440; 5. 37, 38, 61, 335, 341; 6. 62n. Letters to, 3. 356, 406, 407; 4. 23, 27, 41, 50, 53, 268-69, 348; 5. 53-54, 278
Donizetti, Gaetano, 1. 159, 183
Donnelly, Ignatius, 4. 118n, 130, 168, 171n, 172, 185n, 187, 194, 357, 359, 401; 5. 265n, 266, 332, 341
Doolady, Michael, 1. 344, 350n; 2. 118n, 244n, 275, 294. Letter to, 1. 349-50
Doolittle, Mrs., 1. 177, 184
Doster, Col. W. E., 1. 58n
Doughty, Mrs., 5. 85, 249
Doughty, Maggy, 5. 85, 249
Douglas, Harry J., 2. 224, 363
Douglas Hospital, 5. 287
Douglas, Stephen A., 2. 24n
Dowden, Edward, 1. 5; 2. 1, 4, 127n, 132n, 161, 183n, 216, 328n, 331, 368, 369, 370; 3. 19n, 21n, 28, 29, 34, 35, 36, 48n, 60, 67n, 254n, 315, 318-19, 322n, 341n, 355, 362n, 375, 410, 430, 435, 440, 441, 448; 4. 30n, 32, 34, 44, 54, 372, 433, 439; 5. 43, 49, 305, 334. Letters to, 2. 133-34, 139-40, 153-55, 330-31; 3. 26-27, 58-59, 313; 4. 46, 237; 5. 300-301
Dowden, Mrs. Edward, 3. 27
Dowden, Rev. John, 2. 153; 3. 60
Dowe, Amy Haslam, 3. 90n, 151, 192n, 233; 4. 355; 5. 226
Dowe, Francis E., 3. 90n, 114, 232
Dowe, Mrs. Francis E. (Emma), 3. 114n, 151; 4. 355. Letter to, 3. 90-91
Dowe, Warren, 4. 355
Dowling, Mrs. Katherine J., 5. 334
Doyle, Edward, 2. 3n; 3. 358
Doyle, Francis M., 2. 3n, 148-49
Doyle, James, 2. 3n
Doyle, Michael F., 2. 3n
Doyle, Peter, 1. vii, 5, 6, 11; 2. 3-4, 6, 7, 52, 148, 193-94, 195, 199, 205, 206, 208, 209, 212, 218, 219, 230, 250-51, 272, 276, 304, 315, 322, 361, 363, 366, 373; 3. 3, 4, 6, 26, 187, 358,

373*n*, 432, 433, 434, 435, 443; *4.* 174; *5.* 6, 7, 250*n*. Letters to, *2.* 45-47, 50-52, 55-59, 60-63, 67, 83-85, 86-88, 101-2, 103-13, 114-15, 122-23, 124-25, 126-27, 128-29, 129-30, 131, 165-68, 169, 171, 172, 173, 177-78, 179, 180, 181, 221-23, 224-25, 227-29, 231-33, 235-37, 238-39, 242-43, 244-46, 247-50, 251-55, 256-59, 259-63, 265-66, 267-68, 268-69, 270-71, 274-75, 277-79, 280, 283-84, 285-86, 288-89, 290, 291-92, 293-94, 295-96, 297, 300, 301, 302-3, 305, 306, 307, 308-9, 310, 311-12, 313-14, 316-17, 319-20, 322, 323, 324, 326, 328-30, 332-33, 334-35, 338, 339, 340, 341, 342, 347-49; *3.* 19, 20, 67, 70, 71-72, 87-88, 90, 96, 109, 115, 136, 158-59, 167-69, 184-85, 415. Letter from, *2.* 45*n*

Drake, A. B., *3.* 438, 451

Drake, Theodore A., *1.* 73

Drewry, Louisa, *5.* 335. Letter to, *5.* 58

Drexel & Co., *3.* 35, 43-44

Drinkard, Dr. William B., *2.* 192, 197, 201, 211, 215, 224, 226, 239, 240, 272, 289, 315, 322

Drummond, Mr., *3.* 56*n*

Drum-Taps, 1. 14, 57*n*, 86, 114*n*, 185, 201, 210, 228, 236, 239, 240, 241, 243, 244, 246-47, 257, 258, 263, 269-70, 284, 285, 314, 329*n*, 330*n*, 350*n*; *2.* 18, 40*n*, 273; *3.* 40*n*; *5.* 280, 288, 289; *6.* 4*n*, 9*n*

DuBarry, Edmund L., *2.* 224, 243, 363

Dublin University Magazine, 4. 19*n*

Dublin University Review, 4. 27*n*, 31*n*, 303*n*

Du Chaillu, Paul Belloni, *4.* 390*n*; *5.* 151*n*

Duckett, William, *3.* 406*n*; *4.* 16, 35, 53, 72, 82, 88*n*, 92*n*, 278, 280, 441; *5.* 279*n*

Duffy, Mr., *2.* 54

Dumas, Alexander, *4.* 374*n*

Duncan, Dr. J. M., *2.* 236

Du Pont, Admiral Samuel F., *1.* 92*n*

Dwight, Harry L., *5.* 346

Dwight, Theodore F. Letter to, *5.* 289

Dye, Amos, *2.* 112

Dyer, Oliver, *2.* 89-90

Dyer's Hotel, *2.* 115

"Dying Veteran, The," *4.* 63*n*, 102, 104, 425

Eakins, Thomas, *4.* 132, 134, 135, 143, 147, 154, 157, 160, 163, 176*n*; *5.* 25*n*, 52, 155, 200, 208, 209; *6.* 31*n*, 47*n*, 60*n*

Eaton, Wyatt, *3.* 118, 144, 157; *4.* 329

Echo (London), *4.* 292

Eckler, Peter, *1.* 376. Letters to, *1.* 260; *6.* 4

Edel, Marie L., *4.* 148*n*

"Edgar Poe's Significance," *3.* 289*n*

Edmunds, Sen. George F., *1.* 306*n*, 377; *2.* 224

Edmunds, James M., *2.* 363. Letter to, *2.* 188-89

Edwards, Mr., *3.* 346

Ehrenfeld, C. L., *3.* 445

Eicholz, Hugo, *1.* 277

"Eidólons," *3.* 66*n*

"1861," *1.* 57

"Eighteenth Presidency, The," *1.* 41*n*

Einstein, Edwin, *2.* 373. Letter to, *2.* 343-44

Eisel, Paul J., *4.* viii; *5.* ix

Eldridge, Charles W., *1.* 11, 58*n*, 61*n*, 163, 182, 234, 236, 239, 240, 242, 244, 248, 249, 263*n*, 268, 269, 285, 329; *2.* 3, 49, 54, 64, 103, 116, 124, 127, 128, 194, 198, 208, 222*n*, 229, 230, 233, 236, 239, 240, 248, 250, 251, 253, 254, 260, 265, 268, 272, 274, 276*n*, 285, 296, 308, 311, 313, 315, 317, 321, 335, 344, 363; *3.* 25, 66*n*, 104-5, 178-79, 198, 209, 284, 312, 315, 353, 378, 396*n*, 405*n*, 441, 449, 452; *4.* 45, 68*n*, 71*n*, 86*n*, 106, 110, 129, 353, 357, 367, 375, 406, 407, 425, 430, 439, 440; *5.* 45, 222, 301-2, 342; *6.* 38. Letters to, *1.* 185, 235, 236-37, 242-43; *2.* 64-65, 181-83, 223-24, 226-27, 237, 246, 247, 250-51, 264, 315-16; *3.* 369-70; *4.* 79, 87, 91, 103-4, 117-18, 290-91, 358; *5.* 300, 319

"Election Day, November, 1884," *3.* 379-80

Elgin, Lord, *see* Thomas Bruce

Eliot, George, *4.* 219, 230, 341*n*

Elkton (Maryland) *Cecil Democrat, 4.* 19*n*

Elliott, John, *1.* 100, 104

Elliott, Robert, *3.* 445

Elliott, Samuel, *1.* 366

Ellis, Edwin, *2.* 153

Ellis, F. S., *2.* 162, 368. Letters to, *2.* 405; *3.* 57-58

Ellis, G. Stanley, *5.* 338

Ellis, George, *4.* 224

Ellis & Green, *2.* 161, 162

Ellis, Havelock, *5.* 22*n*, 72*n*, 166, 339

Ellison, Frederick, *1.* 78

Ellsworth, E. A., *6.* 68-69

Elmes, Webster. Letters to, *2.* 180-81, 232

Elster, Kristian, *2.* 295, 305, 309, 338, 364; *3.* 257-58

Elverson, Alice, *3.* 115, 244

Elverson, Jr., Joseph, *3.* 115, 244

Elwell, Miss. Letter to, *3.* 374-75

Elze, Karl, *3.* 335

"Embers of day-fires smouldering," *3.* 201*n*

Emerson, Edward, *3.* 245, 288; *4.* 152*n*, 396

Emerson, Ellen, *4.* 152*n*

Emerson, Ralph Waldo, *1.* 2, 3, 6, 10, 12, 14, 44, 46*n*, 49, 77*n*, 83, 122*n*, 164*n*, 188*n*, 190*n*, 370, 372; *2.* 16, 29, 30, 34*n*, 72, 80, 100, 150, 155, 318, 321*n*, 325, 327, 332*n*; *3.* 40*n*, 49*n*, 50, 76, 138*n*, 172, 174*n*, 179, 218, 239*n*, 244-45, 245-46, 274, 275*n*, 283, 285-88, 294*n*, 300, 326-27, 329, 332; *4.* 4, 21, 69-70, 120, 135,

257*n*, 341*n*, 380*n*, 392; *5.* 162*n*, 205, 222, 235;
6. 6*n*. Letters to, *1.* 61, 68-70; *2.* 71. Letters
from, *1.* 41, 64-66
Emerson, Mrs. Ralph Waldo, *4.* 152*n*
"Emerson's Books (the Shadows of Them)," *3.*
178, 179, 281*n*
Emery, Alfred, *4.* 430
Emmet, J. K., *2.* 108*n*
Emory Hospital, *1.* 78, 81
Encyclopædia Britannica, 3. 335; *4.* 308
"Enfans d'Adam," *1.* 49*n*
Engineering Record, The, 5. 130, 131, 132, 133,
134
England, George, *3.* 201
Engle, Bill, *3.* 290
"English Woman's Estimate of Walt
Whitman, An," *3.* 395
Enos, Dr. DeWitt C., *2.* 68
Epictetus, *3.* 254, 260; *4.* 229; *5.* 136, 205; *6.*
56, 57
Ernani, 1. 306
Erving, William, *3.* 435
Essays from "The Critic," 3. 210*n*, 273*n*, 290
Essays on Poetry and Poets, 6. 32, 33
Essays Speculative & Suggestive, 6. 52
Estes, Dana, *5.* 20*n*, 333
Estes & Lauriat, *2.* 118*n*
"Ethiopia Commenting," *see* "Ethiopia Saluting
the Colors"
"Ethiopia Saluting the Colors," *1.* 338, 341,
342, 354; *2.* 21, 69; *6.* 40*n*
"Europe," *3.* 388*n*
Evangelical Alliance, *2.* 247, 250
Evans, Kate A., *3.* 442
Evans, Rob, *2.* 249, 253
Evarts, William Maxwell, *2.* 30, 37, 38, 39, 40,
41, 42, 43, 71, 79, 117
Evening Tatler, 1. 25*n*
Everrett, John C., *3.* 447
Ewart, R. H. Letter to, *5.* 307
Ewing, Helen, *3.* 69
Examiner, The, 3. 23*n*, 64*n*
Eyre, Ellen, *1.* 372
Eyster, Mrs. Nellie, *2.* 368

F., Dr., *5.* 283
de F. M., *1.* 89*n*
F., W., *3.* 332*n*
Faber, Mrs., *4.* 305*n*
"Fabulous Episode, A," *3.* 370
"Faces," *3.* 270*n*
Fairchild, Col. Charles, *3.* 354-55*n*
Fairchild, Mrs. Charles (Elizabeth), *3.* 354; *4.*
57*n*, 95, 100, 102, 109*n*, 136, 249, 252, 253,
257, 258, 263
Falkenreck, Carl, *5.* 334

Falls, A. J., *2.* 109*n*
"Fancies at Navesink," *3.* 403, 409*n*; *4.* 23, 100
Faris, Mr., *2.* 33
Farmer, Moses G., *1.* 241*n*
Farnam, Charles H., *3.* 437, 438
Farragut, Admiral David Glasgow, *2.* 114
Farwell, Reuben, *1.* 368, 375, 376; *2.* 364, 372;
3. 431. Letter to, *2.* 328
"Father Taylor and Oratory," *3.* 369*n*, 374*n*; *4.*
37, 43
La Favorita, 3. 69*n*
Fawcett, Edgar, *4.* 149
Feinberg, Charles E., *1.* vii, ix-x; *2.* v, vi, *3.* vii,
viii, 428; *4.* vii, viii; *5.* viii, ix
Felt, Francis B., *2.* 363. Letter to, *2.* 214
Felton, Cornelius Conway, *5.* 128
Fenner, Miss, *5.* 332
Ferguson, George, *4.* 354, 426. Letter to, *5.* 202
Ferguson, Sir William, *4.* 303*n*
Fern, Fanny, *2.* 89*n*; *6.* 68
Ferrero, Gen. Edward, *1.* 59, 88, 104, 212, 281*n*
Ferrin, Charles B., *3.* 220, 223
Ferris (attorney), *3.* 403
Field, Walbridge A. Letter to, *2.* 98
Fields, Annie, *4.* 430
Fields, James T., *1.* 57*n*, 77*n*, *2.* 72, 366; *3.*
172*n*; *4.* 388, 390, 396; *6.* 6*n*. Letters to, *2.* 73,
77; *5.* 293
File, Franklin, *5.* 19*n*, 64*n*, 331, 335
"First Dandelion, The," *4.* 144*n*
"First Spring Day on Chestnut Street, The," *3.*
150*n*
Fisher, Judge George P., *2.* 232
Fisher, LeRoy, *1.* 275*n*
Fisher, Mary A., *4.* 440
Fisher, Mary Wager, *see* Mary E. Wager-Fisher
"Five Thousand Poems," *4.* 68*n*, 78*n*
Fletcher, Josiah, *3.* 43*n*
Flood, Jr., John, *2.* 367. Letters to, *2.* 69-70, 74-
75, 118-19
Florence, William Jermyn, *5.* 256
Florio, John, *3.* 298, 301
Flower, B. O., *5.* 119*n*, 338
Flower, Cyril *2.* 368, 369; *3.* 405. Letters to, *2.*
162-63; *5.* 294
Floyd, A. C. Letter to, *2.* 321
Flynn, Richard, *3.* 190, 201; *4.* 368, 369, 371;
5. 104
Foord, John, *4.* 376, 398*n*, 440
Foote, George William, *3.* 55, 60, 431, 443
For Idé og Virkelighed (For Idea and Reality), *2.*
1; *6.* 10
"For Queen Victoria's Birthday," *5.* 46, 47, 53,
54*n*; *6.* 50-51*n*
"For Us Two, Reader Dear," *5.* 119*n*
Ford, Elizabeth, *2.* 372; *3.* 399, 409*n*, 449; *4.*
29, 77, 107, 245, 267, 270, 341, 346, 436; *5.*

50, 111, 207, 223; 6. 27n. Letters to, 3. 370, 400, 402

Ford, Gordon Lester. Letter to, 1. 336-37

Ford, Isabella O., 3. 399, 409n; 4. 23n, 29, 77, 107, 245, 267, 270, 341, 346, 436; 5. 50, 207, 223, 341. Letters to, 3. 400, 402; 6. 27

Ford, Sheridan, 4. 163, 432

Forman, Alfred, 5. 252n

Forman, H. Buxton, 2. 132n, 369; 3. 405, 440; 4. 129, 165n, 219, 434; 5. 58n, 223, 225n, 234, 253, 255, 256, 257, 265, 267, 271n, 331, 332, 335, 336, 341, 344-47; 6. 18. Letters to, 5. 247; 6. 10, 51, 52, 58-60

Forney, Col. J. W., 2. 34n; 3. 150, 163n, 164, 165, 213, 256, 433, 434

Fort(?), Mrs. Pound, 5. 349

Fortnightly Club, 3. 27

Fortnightly Review, The, 1. 14, 287n, 292, 294; 2. 16, 21, 33, 75n, 77; 3. 171; 4. 40n, 119n, 125; 6. 43

Forum, The, 4. 225n; 5. 144

Fosdick, William, 1. 251

Foss, S. W., 3. 370n, 450

Foster, Charles H., 1. 206n, 208

Foster, Emory S., 5. 335

Foster, William, 2. 123

Fountain, Lucy, 2. 131n

Fowler, Col. Edward Brush, 1. 198

Fowler, Frank, 3. 321; 4. 281n, 432

Fowler & Wells, 1. 44

Fox, Mr., 5. 117, 118

Fox, Elijah Douglass, 1. 13, 176, 177, 181, 367, 368, 374. Letter to, 1. 186-88

Fox, George, 4. 191

Fox, Will, 3. 112n

Foy, James, 2. 87, 88

Francesca da Rimini, 3. 363

Francis, Capt. Henry W., 1. 60

Frank Leslic's, 2. 198; 3. 372n

Franklin, Benjamin, 3. 80n

Fraser, George, 3. 441

Fraser, John, 3. 141n, 158n, 432, 436; 6. 20. Letters to, 3. 159; 5. 305-6

Frazee, Capt. A. B., 3. 434

Frazee, Hiram W., 1. 277; 5. 290

Fredericksburgh, Va, 1. 11, 58, 62, 64, 68, 81, 82, 97, 98, 102, 180, 197, 199, 209, 221, 223, 226, 227, 231

Free Love League, 3. 312, 314, 315

Freedman, Florence B., 6. 20n

Freeman, P. T., 3. 442

Freeman, Thomas B., 3. 431, 441, 442

Freiligrath, Ferdinand, 2. 44n, 48, 50, 54-55, 59n, 152; 4. 352n. Letter to, 2. 78

Fremont, John Charles, 1. 167

French, Mr. Letter to, 2. 212-13

French & Richardson, 1. 350

French at Home, The, 6. 61n

Frenz, Horst, 3. viii, 428

Freudenberg, Anne, 1. x; 2. v; 3. vii

Fritsch, Hugo, 1. 3, 11, 86, 142, 366. Letters to, 1. 123-27, 158-60

Fritz, Our German Cousin, 2. 108

Fritzinger, Harry, 4. 210, 366, 400-401

Fritzinger, Walt Whitman, 5. 249n

Fritzinger, Warren, 4. 366, 386, 387, 391, 392, 393, 394, 397, 400-401, 403, 404, 407, 410; 5. 18, 20, 26, 27, 30, 33-34, 38, 43, 46, 48-49, 52, 54, 55, 64, 74, 82, 85, 91, 93, 103, 105, 106, 107, 120, 122, 125, 130, 132, 137, 139, 144, 155, 159, 165, 183, 188, 191, 192, 193, 195, 196, 202, 205, 206, 209, 212, 216, 220, 221, 222, 223, 224n, 225, 228, 230, 231, 234, 235, 241, 242, 243, 247, 249, 251, 252, 254, 256, 259, 267, 268, 269, 279n; 6. 58

"From Far Dakota's Cañons," 3. 53, 54

"From Montauk Point," 4. 144n

"From Pent-up Aching Rivers," 3. 270n

"From Washington," 1. 151, 157, 165, 167

Frost, Robert, 1. 13

Froude, James Anthony, 3. 218n, 316, 326n, 334n; 4. 207, 208, 210

Fry, Lewis, 4. 237

Fryer, Ada, 5. 62, 113, 138, 150, 168, 176

Fryer, Kate, 5. 62, 113, 138-39, 150, 168, 176

Fryer, William, 5. 62, 113, 138-39, 150, 168, 176

Fullerton, William Morlow, 4. 109, 430

Furness, Frank, 3. 150

Furness, Horace Howard, 3. 150, 408n; 4. 15n, 25n; 5. 35, 44. Letters to, 3. 175-76; 6. 23, 24, 50

Furness, William Henry, 5. 35; 6. 24, 50n

Galaxy, 1. 82n, 285, 296-97, 298, 300, 335-36, 337-38, 339, 342, 343, 344, 356n; 2. 15n, 18-19, 24, 26, 30, 32, 34n, 39, 68n, 90n, 93, 94, 121n, 131n, 188, 220n, 295, 326n; 3. 45n, 50, 52, 72, 76n, 416; 4. 234; 5. 279n, 292, 293; 6. 7, 9, 61n

Gale, Miss (actress), 5. 337

Galimberti, Laurence, 4. 439

Gallup, Dr. Donald, 1. x

Gamberale, Luigi, 4. 248n

Gardiner(?), Alexander, 2. 321n

Gardiner, Benjamin, 1. 341

Gardner, Alexander (photographer), 1. 377; 2. 78n

Gardner, Alexander (publisher), 4. 272, 293, 295n, 321n, 350n, 359n, 439

Garfield, James A., 1. 193; 3. 232, 239, 246n, 262n

Garibaldi, Giuseppe, 1. 341n

Garland, Hamlin, 4. 158n, 167, 218, 228, 236, 239, 249, 252, 253, 257n, 258, 268, 271n, 289, 343, 361-62, 429, 432, 434, 435, 436, 438, 439, 440, 441; 5. 21n, 204, 334. Letters to, 4. 226, 234, 268

Garren, Harry. Letter to, 6. 61

Garrigues, Gertrude, 3. 167n

Garrison, Charles G., 5. 343

Garrison, E. V., 3. 450

Garrison, Judge J. F., 4. 348

Garrison, Wendell Phillips, 1. 339n

Garrison, William Lloyd, 1. 160n, 339

"Gathering the Corn," 3. 137, 140

Gayler, Charles, 2. 108n

Gellett, Edwin C., 4. 436

Gems from Walt Whitman, 4. 382

Gentleman's Magazine, The, 2. 153n; 3. 21, 27

Gere, Thomas A., 3. 314n

Gerstenberg, A., 4. 62n

Gettysburg, Battle of, 1. 114, 121, 139, 174

Gibbons, Charles, 2. 371

Gibbons, Thomas, 3. 434

Gibbs, Sheriff T. B., 3. 265

Gibson Brothers, 1. 270n

Gilchrist, Alexander, 2. 1, 134-36; 3. 169n, 208n, 272n

Gilchrist, Anne, 1. vii, 6, 273n; 2. 1-2, 4, 91, 98n, 100, 131, 161, 168, 323n, 344, 368, 369, 370, 371, 372, 373; 3. 1-2, 5, 25n, 29n, 33, 44, 51, 56, 60, 74, 78, 83, 86, 88, 89, 91, 92-93, 97, 98, 99, 100, 101, 103, 105n, 112n, 113, 116, 118, 129, 131, 135, 138n, 141, 145, 147, 148, 154, 156, 158, 162, 170, 174, 179, 180, 244, 253, 262, 265, 272, 283, 288n, 301, 322n, 339, 349, 364, 395, 396, 397, 400, 401, 408-9, 412-13, 431, 432, 440, 441, 443, 444, 445, 446, 447, 448, 449, 450, 451, 452; 4. 16, 18, 21, 45n, 91, 92n, 287, 370; 5. 2, 6, 81, 147, 220, 310, 311, 313, 320; 6. 16n, 41n. Letters to, 2. 140, 145, 164-65, 170, 234-35, 336, 341; 3. 30-31, 62, 66, 75, 78, 79, 80-81, 82-83, 84-85, 90, 95, 96-97, 98, 101-2, 106, 107-8, 117, 119, 124-25, 128, 130, 138-39, 140, 142, 150-51, 161-62, 169-70, 172-73, 180, 187, 192-94, 203, 219-20, 253-54, 298-99, 302-3, 309-10, 328-29, 340, 388-89, 392-93, 411. Letters from, 2. 134-38, 141-43

Gilchrist, Beatrice, 3. 56n, 84, 86, 87, 88, 91, 93, 97, 98, 99, 106, 108, 113, 126, 128, 129, 135, 136, 145n, 156-57, 162, 174, 178, 179, 187, 193, 203, 240, 245n, 246, 253-54, 262, 432, 443, 444; 4. 16; 5. 312. Letters to, 3. 97-98, 104-5, 135, 148

Gilchrist, Grace, 3. 56n, 84, 86, 87, 88, 91, 93, 97, 106, 108, 126, 141, 147, 151, 154, 162, 187, 254, 262, 303, 329, 339, 365n, 389, 393; 4. 16

Gilchrist, Herbert 2. 165n; 3. 2, 56n, 84, 85, 86, 87, 88, 90, 93, 95, 96, 97, 98, 99, 100, 101n, 102, 105n, 106, 108, 116, 117, 119, 125, 126, 130, 135, 138-39, 140, 141, 142, 143, 151, 154, 156, 159n, 162, 179, 187, 193, 203, 208, 240n, 251, 254, 265, 288n, 290, 301, 303, 309n, 329, 340, 381, 389, 393, 409, 411, 413, 444, 445, 446, 447, 448, 449, 451, 452, 453; 4. 16, 18, 21, 30, 34, 46, 47, 51, 54n, 64, 72, 82, 85-86, 92, 94, 95, 97, 98, 99, 100, 102, 103, 105, 107, 108, 110, 111, 116, 117, 119, 120, 121, 122, 123, 124, 126, 128, 130, 132-33, 138, 167, 169, 186, 190, 191, 199, 201, 205, 207, 208, 211, 212, 218, 226, 236, 244, 254, 282, 312, 326, 341, 342, 343, 346, 350, 359, 361, 363, 364, 365, 366, 367, 370, 371, 393, 403, 407, 425, 427, 428, 429, 430, 431, 432, 435; 5. 2, 6, 47, 51, 55, 63, 77, 81, 95, 117, 151, 152, 154, 155, 190, 200, 208, 237n, 256, 310, 312, 315, 319n; 6. 41, 43, 45, 51. Letters to, 3. 64-65, 74, 91, 92-93, 104, 110, 111-12, 112-13, 118, 130-31, 144, 147-48, 151, 152-53, 156-57, 171, 177-78, 189, 261-62, 272, 339, 364, 398-99, 404-6, 408-9, 411, 412-13; 4. 44, 49, 57, 78-79, 127-28, 156, 162-63, 189; 5. 175

Gilchrist, Percy, 2. 164n, 235, 336, 341n; 148, 160n, 193

Gilder, Helena de Kay, 3. 445

Gilder, Jeannette L., 3. 141, 144, 145n, 204, 375, 430, 432, 436, 438, 440; 4. 1, 58n, 118, 224n, 434; 5. 44n, 79n, 256, 257, 337, 338. Letters to, 3. 202, 205-6, 210, 222, 236, 268, 289-90, 318, 320-21, 322, 324, 355-56, 362, 370, 377; 4. 68, 88; 5. 145; 6. 19

Gilder, Joseph B., 3. 141n, 210, 300n, 352n, 375; 4. 1, 86, 87, 154, 224n, 267, 288, 427, 430, 434, 435, 436, 437; 5. 67n, 152n, 257, 335, 336, 337, 338, 339; 6. 59, 67, 69. Letters to, 3. 268, 289-90, 320-21, 322, 324, 342, 355-56, 362, 377, 378, 387; 4. 45, 68, 76; 5. 145

Gilder, Richard Watson, 3. 108n, 110-11, 118n, 141n, 170, 198, 274n, 374, 375, 410, 444, 449, 450; 4. 1, 25n, 26, 82n, 173n, 347n, 426, 427; 5. 28, 29, 54, 331. Letters to, 3. 120, 195-96, 200, 391; 4. 55, 85

Gilder, Rosamund, 3. viii, 195n, 428

Giles, Richard F., 6. 65

Gillette, Daniel G. Letters to, 2. 246, 255-56

Gillette, Dr. F. B., 1. 379

Gilmore, General, 5. 289

Gimbel, Col. Richard, 1. ix

Girard, Stephen, 4. 348

Gladstone, William, 4. 55n

Gleed, Charles S., 3. 435

Glicksberg, Charles I., 1. viii

Godey, Walter, 2. 232, 237, 239, 240, 243n, 246, 251, 254, 264, 272, 296, 306n, 363, 371

Godkin, Edwin L., *1*. 334

Goethe, Johann Wolfgang von, *4*. 129, 259, 260, 391*n*

Gohdes, Clarence, *1*. viii; *2*. v

Goldsmith, J. C. ("Jay Charlton"), *4*. 40

Goldy, Amy Whitman, *3*. 404*n*

Goldy, Ethel B., *3*. vii

Goldy, Ruth Stafford, *see* Ruth Stafford

Goldy, William, *3*. 381*n*, 405

Good Gray Poet, The, 1. 12, 14, 263*n*, 268*n*, 281*n*, 303*n*, 323*n*, 329*n*, 339, 354; *2*. 31*n*, 55; *3*. 103, 314*n*, 316, 317, 320, 325, 328*n*, 331, 332, 333, 334*n*, 336

Good-bye My Fancy, 3. 136*n*; *4*. 242*n*; *5*. 30, 54, 56, 59, 60, 68, 69, 70, 77, 80, 82, 83, 89, 91, 96, 112, 116, 125, 126, 143, 144, 158, 163, 166, 167, 168, 169, 170, 171, 173, 174, 175-76, 177, 180, 181, 182, 184, 185, 186, 188, 189, 190, 191, 192, 193, 195, 196, 200, 201, 202, 203, 204, 207, 215, 216, 244, 246, 247, 251, 255-56, 260; *6*. 56, 59, 60

Gordan, Dr. John, *1*. x; *2*. v; *3*. vii

Gordon, Adam Lindsay, *5*. 62

Gosse, Edmund, *2*. 341*n*, 371; *3*. 189*n*, 385, 451; *4*. 224*n*, 362, 387*n*, 392; *5*. 34*n*, 144, 195. Letters to, *3*. 48, 384

Gould, Elizabeth Porter, *4*. 257, 302, 382, 441; *5*. 224, 341, 348. Letters to, *4*. 96; *5*. 93

Gould, Theodore, *1*. 144

Gower, Lord Ronald, *4*. 62*n*

"Grand Is the Seen," *5*. 137*n*

Grand Union Hotel (New York), *3*. 249

"Grant," *see* "Death of General Grant"

Grant, Jenny, *2*. 344

Grant, Ulysses S., *1*. 116, 202, 204, 205, 206, 211, 213, 214, 215, 216, 217, 219, 220, 223, 226, 228, 231, 232, 233, 237, 239, 243, 252, 253, 261-62; *2*. 15, 35, 54, 58, 70, 72*n*, 79, 81, 88*n*, 116*n*, 147, 173*n*, 183, 184; *3*. 154*n*, 378, 401; *4*. 57*n*, 316. Letters to, *2*. 280-81, 306; *5*. 297-98

Grashalme (German translation of *Leaves of Grass), 4*. 129, 207-8, 212, 220, 265, 269, 270, 272, 286, 287, 293, 295, 296, 297, 298, 319, 330, 401, 406-7; *5*. 349

Gray, Freda, *3*. vii, 223*n*

Gray, James, *1*. 344, 350*n*

Gray, John F. S., *1*. 10-11, 123-24, 125, 126, 127, 142, 158, 159, 241, 343, 373, 375. Letter to, *1*. 80-85

Grayson, Edward B., *1*. 307, 309

Grayson, Mrs. Edward B., *1*. 278, 302, 304, 306, 307, 309, 312

Grayson, William, *1*. 307

"Great Are the Myths," *3*. 272*n*

"Great Army of the Sick: The Military Hospitals in Washington, The," *1*. 75*n*, 256

Greek Poets, 4. 224, 267, 268, 271

Greeley, Horace, *2*. 183, 186; *3*. 63*n*

Green, Rev., *4*. 372

Green, J. M., *3*. 441

Green, S. W., *2*. 186*n*, 275*n*, 369; *3*. 441. Letter to, *3*. 43

Greene, C. H., *5*. 342

Greene, Stephen, *3*. viii, 428

Greene, Mrs. Ward, *4*. viii

Greene, Fort, *1*. 137, 148, 260

Greenway, Dr. Cornelius, *3*. viii, 428

Greg, Thomas Tylston, *4*. 436

Gregg, Miss, *1*. 177, 184. Letter to, *1*. 143

Grey, Samuel H., *4*. 440

Gridley, C. Oscar, *3*. 405. Letters to, *6*. 34

Grier, Edward, *1*. x; *2*. v; *3*. vii, 145*n*

Grier, Dr. Matthew J., *2*. 200*n*, 239*n*, 240, 288, 289, 302*n*

Griffith, Mrs. F. D., *3*. vii

Grimm, Herman, *3*. 300

Grosart, Alexander B., *3*. 58

Gross, S. E., *6*. 35

Grover, Edwin O., *5*. ix

Grundy, Fanny M., *4*. 440

Guernsey, Frederic R., *3*. 237, 283*n*, 289, 447; *4*. 223*n*

Guerrabella, Genevra, *1*. 96

Guiteau, Charles J., *3*. 262

Gunther, Mr. Letter to, *4*. 25

Gurd, Matilda, *3*. 249; *5*. 27

Gurd, William, *4*. 232, 256, 398; *5*. 27*n*, 29, 31*n*, 70

Gurney(?), Benjamin, *3*. 443; *6*. 14*n*

Gurowski, Count Adam, *1*. 124*n*, 236, 263*n*, 275

Gustafson, Harry W., *3*. 450

Gutekunst, F., *3*. 228, 243*n*, 434; *4*. 364; *6*. 24*n*

Gwynne, Carey, *1*. 108, 249

Habberton, John, *4*. 206, 212

Haeckel, Ernst Heinrich, *3*. 357*n*

Haggerty (or Hagerty), Thomas, *1*. 340

Haight, Grace B., *2*. 149, 156, 369

"Halcyon Days," *4*. 144*n*

Hale, Edward Everett, *1*. 25*n*; *2*. 178*n*

Hale, John Parker. Letter to, *1*. 39-40

Hale, Jr., Nathan. Letter to, *1*. 25-26

Hale, Phillip, *2*. 369, 373. Letter to, *3*. 53

Hales, Samuel, *4*. 425

Haley, Mrs. C. S., *4*. 434

Half-Hours with the Best American Authors, 4. 38

Halifax (Nova Scotia) *Chronicle, 3*. 434

Hall, George, *4*. 438

Hall, Thomas J., *3*. 434

Halleck, Fitz-Greene, *3*. 154*n*

Halleck, Gen. Henry Wager, *4.* 56-57
Hallett, Henry L., *3.* 314
Hallett, Samuel, *1.* 167
"Halls of Gold and Lilac," *2.* 204*n*, 258, 259, 262
Halpern, Mrs. Barbara, *3.* viii, 428; *4.* viii
Halstead, Marst, *3.* 24*n*
Hames & Co., *3.* 436
Hamilton, William, *3.* 434
Hamlet, 3. 332*n*
Hamlet's Note-book, 4. 24, 26, 29, 187
Ham Smith, W. J., *3.* 140*n*
Hanley, Charles W., *5.* 340
Hanley, T. E., *1.* ix
Hansen, Falbe, *2.* 283*n*
Hanson (actor), *4.* 373*n*
Hanson, Harry, *6.* 74
Hapgood, Maj. Lyman S., *1.* 11, 60, 62, 79, 86, 109, 116, 119, 121, 130, 133, 134, 137, 143, 149, 150, 157, 160, 163, 170, 174, 185, 186, 187, 189, 191, 199, 204, 218, 224, 226, 230, 233, 235, 237, 239
Hardie, John, *3.* 433
Harding, Rebecca, *1.* 77*n*
Hardy, Lady, *3.* 60
Hardy, Katherine, *5.* 337
Hardy, William, *3.* 231
Hare, Rebecca Jane, *3.* 368*n*
Harewood Hospital, *5.* 287, 290
Harkness, Dr. Jack, *4.* 199
Harlan, James, *1.* 14, 235*n*, 262*n*, 275*n*, 376; *2.* 26, 80*n*, 151, 160
Harlan (or Harland), Thomas, *1.* 321
Harleigh Cemetery, *4.* 5-6, 403, 407, 408; *5.* 43, 47, 52, 66, 89, 95, 98, 105, 129, 196, 197, 202-3, 206, 207, 220, 228, 231, 232, 239, 240, 265, 267, 268, 269
Harned, Anna, *4.* 130, 134, 264
Harned, Frank, *4.* 182, 231, 371
Harned, Herbert Spencer, *4.* 242, 243, 245, 259, 261, 264, 278, 324, 399
Harned, Thomas B., *1.* vii; *4.* 88*n*, 129, 134, 150, 156, 159, 161, 165*n*, 166*n*, 178, 179, 180, 187, 192, 207, 214, 220, 231, 232, 242, 245, 254, 259, 261, 270, 278, 283, 302, 306, 307, 308, 314, 317, 320, 324, 333, 336, 341, 342, 343, 350, 352, 358, 371, 372, 374, 377, 388, 391, 394, 399, 403, 409, 427; *5.* 29, 31, 59, 72, 74, 85, 86, 89, 105, 108, 116, 117, 141*n*, 161, 178, 191, 227, 265, 267, 274; *6.* 47*n*. Letters to, *4.* 130, 133, 165, 182-83, 264, 335, 349; *5.* 278
Harned, Mrs. Thomas B., *4.* 129, 134, 160, 169, 170, 174, 176, 242, 243, 259, 261, 264, 278, 280, 306, 314, 317, 320, 341; *5.* 31, 85, 86, 89, 220-21
Harned, Jr., Thomas B., *4.* 134, 264, 320

Harney, Rev. G. L., *4.* 197*n*
Harper & Brothers, *4.* 427, 440
Harper's Bazaar, 4. 86*n*; *5.* 49*n*
Harper's Fifth Reader, 4. 378
Harper's New Monthly Magazine, 2. 269, 272, 277, 278, 282, 287, 295; *3.* 111*n*, 204, 239*n*, 357, 360, 364, 376, 391*n*, 402*n*, 435, 436, 438, 439; *4.* 48*n*, 51, 119*n*, 122, 148*n*, 226*n*, 256, 271, 275, 276, 369-70, 376, 388, 425; *5.* 57, 68. Letters to, *1.* 46-47; *4.* 368
Harper's Weekly, 1. 326, 329*n*, 372; *2.* 198, 206, 211; *3.* 110*n*, 387*n*, 452; *4.* 86, 347*n*, 376, 380, 385, 399, 400, 404, 427; *5.* 318
Harrington, 1. 108; *4.* 386
Harrington, Elinor J., *3.* vii, 90*n*, 151*n*
Harris, Charles H., *1.* 177, 248*n*, 375
Harris, Ira, *3.* 155*n*
Harris, Mrs. J. S., *5.* 340
Harris, Joseph, *1.* 238, 332, 375
Harris, William Torrey, *3.* 171. Letters to, *3.* 166-67, 187-88
Harrison, Benjamin, *4.* 196, 229, 232, 233, 328, 395; *5.* 21, 84, 101*n*, 193, 199, 225
Harrison, Clifford, *5.* 340
Harrison, Gabriel, *3.* 451
Harrison, Mrs. H. M., *5.* 205*n*
Harrison, L. Birge, *3.* 450
Harrison, Preston, *5.* 348
Hart, Michael C., *2.* 125
Harte, Bret, *1.* 346*n*; *2.* 81*n*, 94*n*, 368
Hartigan, James, *5.* 62, 113, 138, 150, 168, 176
Hartmann, C. Sadakichi, *4.* 108, 110, 136, 192, 208, 213*n*, 224*n*, 322, 325, 331, 340, 368, 433; *5.* 49*n*, 61, 68. Letter to, *4.* 61
Hartranft, Rufus C., *5.* 334
Harvard Monthly, 4. 143
Harvard Signet Society, *4.* 143*n*
Haskell, E. B., *3.* 283*n*
Haskell, Erastus, *1.* 3, 6-7, 119, 127-30, 131, 146; *5.* 283-85
Haskell, S. B., *1.* 131, 173, 373; *5.* 284. Letters to, *1.* 119, 127-30, 146
Haskell, Jr., Mrs. Samuel, *1.* 309
Haslett(?), Thomas, *2.* 88
Hasset (or Hassett), Thomas, *2.* 47, 57
Hastings, Warren, *4.* 18
Hatch, Mrs. Anna, *5.* 346
Hatch, Dr. B. F., *1.* 43*n*
Hatch, Mrs. Cora L. V., *see* Cora L. V. Tappan
Haweis, Rev. H. R. *3.* 100
Hawkins, Walter, *5.* 250*n*
Hawkinson, C. J., *2.* 239, 243
Hawley, Dr. William A., *4.* 426; *5.* 331; *6.* 68
Hawthorne, Miss, *5.* 151*n*
Hawthorne, Julian, *5.* 151*n*
Hawthorne, Nathaniel, *1.* 26*n*, 339*n*; *3.* 219*n*, 244*n*; *4.* 388, 390, 396

Haxtun, Capt. Milton, *3.* 240*n*

Hay, John, *3.* 53*n, 408n,* 441; *4.* 55*n,* 75, 83*n,* 425, 430; *5.* 348

Haynes, Donald R., *3.* vii

Heard, George, *3.* 445

Hearne, James, *3.* 436, 446

Hearst, William Randolph, *5.* 338

Hedge, Frederic Henry, *1.* 80*n*; *4.* 239

Heenan, John, *1.* 55*n*

Heffernan, Miriam, *1.* x

Hegel, Georg Wilhelm Friedrich, *2.* 151, 154; *3.* 167*n,* 171; *4.* 381

Hegeman, Thomas, *1.* 36

Heine, Heinrich, *2.* 289*n*; *4.* 55

Heinemann, William, *5.* 253*n,* 257, 267; *6.* 60

Helmick, Frederick, *5.* 342

Hemenway, O. O. Letter to, *4.* 378

Hempstead & Son, O. G., *4.* 170*n,* 432. Letter to, *4.* 168

Hemsley, W. J., *4.* 432

Henderson, S. R., *5.* 136

Hendrickson, Mr., *1.* 135, 151

von Herkomer, Sir Hubert, *3.* 60

Heron, Matilda Agnes, *1.* 83

Herrick, Anson, *1.* 230

Hershey, O. F., *4.* 436

Hewins, Henry C., *1.* 289-90

Hewins, Joseph S., *1.* 289-91

Heyde, Charles L., *1.* 8-9, 50, 97*n,* 102, 135, 138, 216-17, 267*n,* 277, 299, 303, 306, 307, 321, 365, 372, 377, 378; *2.* 3, 79, 80*n,* 98*n,* 146, 197, 204, 361, 368; *3.* 100*n,* 384*n,* 438, 442, 450, 451, 452; *4.* 381*n,* 390*n,* 427, 430, 434, 435, 437, 439, 440, 441; *5.* 7, 88, 134, 173, 194*n,* 200, 214*n,* 223*n,* 232*n,* 238*n,* 248*n,* 249*n,* 331, 333-45, 347, 348

Heyde, Hannah Whitman, *1.* 8-9, 31, 33, 36, 50, 54, 58, 68*n,* 71, 72, 78, 85, 87, 95, 97, 101, 102, 106, 109, 111, 116, 118, 131, 135, 138, 140, 146, 165, 172, 189, 192, 194, 204, 208, 209, 213, 215, 216-17, 220, 224, 226, 227, 229, 232, 233, 250, 257, 273, 276, 278, 280, 288, 297, 298, 299, 300, 303, 305, 306, 310, 314, 319, 320, 324, 364, 365, 366, 367, 368, 369, 370, 372, 376; *2.* 3, 14, 38, 39, 42, 73-74, 79, 80*n,* 86, 124*n,* 145, 157, 182, 183, 191*n,* 194, 196, 197, 199, 200, 201, 203*n,* 204, 213, 220, 315, 360, 361, 362, 363, 366, 370; *3.* 24, 69, 100*n,* 166, 180*n,* 359*n,* 384*n,* 432, 433, 434, 435, 436, 437, 438, 439, 444, 447, 449, 451; *4.* 51, 179, 282, 355, 380, 391, 424, 425, 426, 427, 438; *5.* vii, 7-8, 88, 122, 123, 124, 127, 142, 152, 178, 200, 222, 231, 239, 331, 332, 334, 345, 347, 348. Letters to, *5.* 67, 134-35, 148, 157-58, 160, 163, 172-73, 175, 179, 185, 186, 191, 193-94, 210, 214-15, 223, 226, 232, 238, 240, 242, 247-48, 249-50, 255, 257, 259-

60, 264, 267-68, 270, 273-77

Heyn, Joseph G., *5.* 349

Heywood, Ezra H., *3.* 312, 314, 320, 335, 338, 448; *4.* 157

Hickman, Robert ("Beau"), *2.* 238, 243

Hicks, Elias, *1.* 111; *4.* 79, 141, 151, 163, 164, 165, 182, 184, 189, 191, 194, 198, 199, 201, 205, 206, 210, 213, 224; *5.* 69, 92

Hider, Lizzie H. (later Mrs. Wesley Stafford), *3.* 112*n,* 131, 194, 210

Hieniken(?), Theodore, *3.* 194, 223, 262; *5.* 314

Hieniken (?), William, *5.* 314

Higginson, Thomas Wentworth, *3.* 283; *4.* 86*n*; *5.* 49*n*

Hildreth, Charles L., *5.* 349

Hill, Miss, *1.* 181

Hillard, Katharine, *2.* 160*n,* 224, 241; *3.* 25, 26, 32, 114, 117, 119, 125, 128, 146*n,* 432. Letters to, *5.* 302-4

Hilliard, F. A., *5.* 342

Hinds, Katy, *1.* 301; *2.* 65

Hine, Charles, *1.* 371; *2.* 130, 131, 366; *3.* 368*n,* 382*n,* 383*n,* 384*n,* 440. Letter to, *2.* 33

Hine, Mrs. Charles, *2.* 368; *3.* 438

Hinton, Miss Leslie, *3.* 314*n*

Hinton, Col. Richard J., *2.* 30, 33*n,* 45, 50, 157*n,* 189*n,* 248, 250, 256, 296, 369; *4.* 263, 322*n,* 434, 439; *5.* 296; *6.* 68. Letters to, *2.* 246; *5.* 289-90, 295

Hirsh, Mr., *3.* 57*n*

Hiskey, Tilghman, *3.* 433. Letters to, *3.* 182-83, 185

History of King Arthur, see Romance of King Arthur, The

Hoadley, Florence A., *3.* viii, 61*n,* 428

Hoag, F. A., *3.* 192, 203, 234

Hoar, Ebenezer Rockwood, *2.* 80, 117

Hoare, C. W. Letter to, *6.* 11

Hodgkinson, Samuel, *5.* 241, 253

Holbrook, Edward D., *1.* 329*n*; *5.* 291

Holcomb, Helen J., *5.* 346

Holdsworth, J. E., *5.* 332, 347

Holland, E. E. P., *5.* 340

Holland, Josiah Gilbert, *1.* 343; *3.* 198*n.* Letter to, *3.* 66

Hollingswood, James B., *1.* 291*n*

Hollis, Carroll, *5.* 289*n,* 295*n*

Holloway, Emory, *1.* viii, x; *2.* v, vi, 18*n*; *3.* vii, 380*n*

Hollyer, Samuel, *4.* 197, 426, 436. Letters to, *6.* 47

Holmes, Henry A., *4.* 438

Holmes, John A., *1.* 64, 111

Holmes, Mrs. Mary Jane, *3.* 278

Holmes, Oliver Wendell, *1.* 346*n*; *2.* 102*n*; *3.* 246, 247, 337, 405*n*; *5.* 78, 82, 83

"Home Again," *3*. 188*n*

Home News, The (London), *6*. 51*n*

Homer, *1*. 5, 263; *3*. 118, 120*n*, 152*n*, 219, 394; *4*. 325*n*; *5*. 32*n*, 259*n*

Hood, Dr. T. B., *4*. 302, 311

Hooker, Gen. Joseph, *1*. 92, 94, 98*n*, 99, 101, 106, 114*n*

Hopkins, Albert, *5*. 348

Hopkins, Johns, *4*. 348

Horne, Herbert P., *4*. 127, 434

Horne, R. H., *6*. 10

Horner, Helen A., *2*. 367

Horner, Mary, *3*. 204*n*

Horton, George, *5*. 344

Hoskins, *see* Samuel Hodgkinson

"Hospital Visits," *see* "Our Wounded and Sick Soldiers–Visits among the Hospitals"

Hotten, John Camden, *1*. 332*n*, 346*n*, 348, 349, 353; *2*. 13, 15, 16, 20, 31, 133*n*, 152, 365. Letters to, *2*. 16-17, 21-22, 28-29

Houghton, Lord, *see* Richard Monckton Milnes

Houghton, Mifflin & Co., *3*. 228, 453; *4*. 25*n*; *5*. 132, 140, 144, 145*n*, 146, 189, 222, 258; *6*. 32. Letter to, *4*. 148

House, Edward Howard, *1*. 47, 48, 328

Hovey, Franklin H., *3*. 215

Howard, Albert Waldo, *5*. 334

Howard, Dr. Alma, *3*. viii, 428

Howard, Carrie(?), *1*. 248*n*

Howard, Garaphelia, *1*. 248*n*; *2*. 272, 276, 304. Letter to, *5*. 287

Howard, Jr., Joseph, *1*. 190

Howard, Sallie (?), *1*. 239, 247

Howe, Col. Frank E., *3*. 240*n*

Howe, Julia Ward, *2*. 173*n*

Howe, M. A. De Wolfe, *1*. 57*n*

Howe, W. T. H., *1*. viii

Howell, Benjamin D., *1*. 95, 150*n*

Howell, C. A., *3*. 60

Howell, Henry D., *1*. 95

Howells, Beulah, *2*. 123

Howells, Joseph Charles, *1*. 183, 240, 247

Howells, Mrs. Joseph Charles, *1*. 184, 239, 244; *2*. 123

Howells, William Dean, *1*. 281*n*, 339; *3*. 67*n*; *4*. 125*n*, 148*n*, 228, 256, 271, 275, 276, 277, 341; *5*. 195*n*

"How I Get Around at Sixty, and Take Notes," *3*. 202, 204, 205, 216, 222, 223, 255*n*, 268*n*

"How I Made a Book," *4*. 36, 37, 39; *6*. 33

"How Leaves of Grass Was Made," *3*. 409*n*; *4*. 36*n*, 37

Hudson, Mrs. Sarah A., *1*. 366

Hueckberny, C. A. J., *3*. 435, 445

Hugg, Judge, *4*. 88*n*

Hughes, Harry D. Letter to, *4*. 67

Hughes, Oscar F., *1*. 78

Hugo, Victor, *1*. 257; *2*. 153*n*, 331; *3*. 82, 118, 391, 394; *5*. 319

"Human Voice, The," *5*. 24, 27

Humphrey, James, *1*. 310-11

Humphreys, George, *5*. 232, 251, 348

Hungerford, Edward, *1*. 44*n*

Hunter, Benjamin, *3*. 127

Hunter, John Ward, *1*. 310-11

Huntington, Joshua, *2*. 276*n*

Huntington, William S., *2*. 172. Letter to, *6*. 7

Huntington, Mrs. William S., *2*. 276, 304; *3*. 25

Huntington & Sons, *1*. 284-85, 340, 350*n*

Hurd(?), Charles E., *4*. 338*n*; *5*. 58*n*

Hurlbert, William Henry, *3*. 314

Hurt, Henry, *2*. 51, 56, 105, 113, 366. Letter to, *2*. 52-53

Hutcheson, David, *3*. 445

Hutchins, Ethel L., *3*. vii, 24*n*

Hutchinson, Thomas, *5*. 338

Hutchinson, William ("John Sands"), *3*. 289

Hutton, Rev. F. R. C., *5*. 83*n*, 91

Hyatt, Thaddeus, *5*. 346, 348

Hyer, Joe, *6*. 58

"If I Should Need to Name, O Western World," *3*. 379

Illustrated American, The, *5*. 39, 77, 331, 346

Illustrated London News, *5*. 76, 127*n*, 170, 201

Image, Selwyn, *4*. 271*n*

"Indian Bureau Reminiscence, An," *3*. 358, 359, 360, 364

Ingemann, Bernhard Severin, *5*. 282

Ingersoll, Col. Robert G., *3*. 204, 207, 295*n*, 297, 444; *4*. 142*n*, 164, 172*n*, 221, 341; *5*. 51, 53, 54, 55, 80, 84, 87, 89, 90, 91, 92, 94, 95, 97, 99-100, 101, 102, 103-4, 107, 108, 109, 112, 114, 115, 118, 119, 120, 122*n*, 125, 126, 127, 129-30, 133, 138, 151, 155, 157, 158, 176, 177-78, 180, 183, 225, 263, 275-76, 332, 335, 337, 347, 348; *6*. 51*n*, 53, 54. Letters to, *3*. 175; *5*. 104, 272-73

Ingersoll, Mrs. Robert G., *5*. 121, 273

Ingpen, Roger E., *5*. 337

Ingram, John H., *3*. 193, 435, 445. Letter to, *6*. 15

Ingram, William, *2*. 231-32; *4*. 154, 200, 210, 228, 333, 337, 371, 407, 433, 434; *5*. 52, 73-74, 108, 133, 272, 337. Letters to, *4*. 120, 158, 209-10, 370-71; *5*. 319

Innes, George, *4*. 368*n*, 376

Innes, Randolph, *3*. 436

"Interpolation Sounds," *4*. 198*n*

Ireland, Alexander, *3*. 57. Letter to, *3*. 49

Ireland LeRoy, *4*. 369*n*

Irving, Henry, *3*. 28*n,* 356, 383; *4.* 41*n,* 348,
384*n; 5.* 349; *6.* 41
Irwin, Mrs. Letter to, *1.* 258-60
Irwin, Frank H., *1.* 258-60
Irwin, P., *1.* 29*n*
"I Sing the Body Electric," *3.* 270*n,* 271*n*
"Is Walt Whitman's Poetry Poetical?" *2.* 278*n*
Ives, Lewis T., *3.* 402. Letter to, *3.* 239-40
Ives, Percy, *4.* 429, 431; *5.* 258*n.* Letters to, *3.*
239-40, 402-3

Jackson, Eliphalet W., *1.* 120, 133
Jackson, Gen. Stonewall, *1.* 196*n*
Jackson, William F., *5.* 337
Jaffe, Harold, *4.* vii
James, Henry, *2.* 139*n; 4.* 30*n*
James, Sr., Henry, *3.* 246, 247
James, Joseph ("Sonny"), *2.* 119
James, William, *2.* 57*n; 4.* 143*n*
Jansen, J. M., *1.* 118*n*
Janson, Kristofer. Letter to, *3.* 334
Jardine, D., *3.* 38, 45, 430, 441; *6.* 13
Jefferson, Joseph, *5.* 256
Jefferson, Thomas, *2.* 189, 335
Jellison, W. A., *1.* 375
Jenkins, Howard M., *3.* 437
Jenks, John S. Letters to, *6.* 5
Jennings, J. E.(?), *1.* 177
Jesus, *5.* 140*n*
Johann, John A., *3.* 146
Johns Hopkins College, *5.* 159, 178
Johns Hopkins Hospital, *4.* 327, 332; *5.* 20*n,*
198*n*
Johnson, Andrew, *1.* 261, 265, 267, 275, 277,
279, 280, 307, 315*n,* 316; *2.* 20, 23*n,* 25*n,* 26*n,*
31*n,* 34-35, 70*n,* 80*n,* 173*n; 5.* 286, 288
Johnson, Arnold B., *1.* 235, 239; *2.* 286; *5.* 300
Johnson, Charles(?), *3.* 136
Johnson, John Newton, *2.* 325, 364, 371, 372,
373; *3.* 430, 431, 432, 435, 438, 440, 441, 442,
443, 452; *4.* 94, 103, 107, 158*n,* 159, 428
Johnson, Lionel, *3.* 453
Johnson, Mrs. Nancy M., *2.* 268, 271-72, 304,
311; *3.* 25, 33, 440
Johnson, Robert Underwood, *3.* 450; *4.* 214; *5.*
95. Letters to, *3.* 167, 373-74; *4.* 133
Johnson, Dr. Samuel, *1.* 2; *4.* 165, 170
Johnson, Thomas, *4.* 362*n,* 363, 393
Johnson, Walt Whitman, *4.* 95
Johnson, William H., *4.* 381*n*
Johnston, Albert, *3.* 3, 7, 80, 98, 122-25, 138,
156, 159, 247, 248, 252, 348, 360, 382, 388,
433, 434; *4.* 74, 86, 124, 254; *5.* 193; *6.* 38.
Letters to, *3.* 186, 271-72, 374
Johnston, Alma Calder (Mrs. John H.), *3.* 120,

121, 156, 249, 252, 271, 311*n,* 348, 360, 374,
382, 396, 398, 432; *4.* 86, 119, 124, 215, 219,
254, 409*n; 5.* 89, 102, 144, 338; *6.* 38. Letters
to, *3.* 246-47, 248, 388, 417; *4.* 73, 200-201,
299-300; *5.* 18
Johnston, Amelia (Mrs. John H.), *3.* 68, 72,
81*n,* 121*n,* 160; *4.* 254*n; 5.* 304. Letter to, *3.*
80
Johnston, Bertha, *3.* 271; *5.* 52, 144, 335, 339.
Letter to, *5.* 144
Johnston, E. S. (or G. T.), *1.* 35
Johnston, Grace, *3.* 271; *5.* 160
Johnston, Harold ("Harry"), *3.* 81*n,* 98, 120,
121, 127, 160, 271
Johnston, Ida, *2.* 323*n; 3.* 88-89, 433. Letter to,
3. 85
Johnston, Dr. John, *1.* vii; *4.* 3, 96, 345, 346,
428, 430, 432, 441; *5.* 1, 3-4, 7, 63, 65, 66, 70,
71, 72, 74, 76, 77, 79, 82, 83, 84, 90-91, 92,
97, 121, 137, 142, 149, 184, 188, 190, 198,
200, 203, 205, 206*n,* 215, 218, 219, 221, 222,
223, 227, 228, 233, 234, 245, 252, 254, 255,
266, 274, 332, 334, 336-48; *6.* 57. Letters to,
4. 95; *5.* 82, 84, 88, 110, 118-19, 122, 124,
126-27, 134, 135, 145-46, 148-49, 157, 162-63,
165-68, 170-71, 174, 178-80, 182, 184-85, 188-
89, 192, 194-97, 205-6, 208, 210-11, 213-14,
216, 217-20, 224-25, 227, 229-32, 234-41, 243-
45, 248, 250-54, 256, 258, 261-63, 267, 269,
271, 275-76; *6.* 57-58
Johnston, John H. (jeweler), *3.* 3, 4, 7, 71,
79*n,* 81*n,* 83*n,* 109, 110, 112, 120, 122, 123,
124, 147, 150, 151, 156, 158, 159*n,* 186*n,* 236,
245, 246, 247, 248, 249, 271*n,* 276*n,* 348*n,*
374, 432, 433, 434, 435, 437, 445, 447, 449,
450, 453; *4.* 82*n,* 84, 143, 160*n,* 200-201, 222*n,*
254, 261, 263, 308, 343, 382, 430, 431; *5.* 52*n,*
86*n,* 90, 92, 129, 132, 144, 193*n,* 234, 246,
263, 305, 314, 336, 345, 346; *6.* 66. Letters to,
3. 40, 67-68, 70, 72, 80, 98-99, 138, 183, 252,
311, 348, 360, 368, 382-83, 384, 388, 396, 398;
4. 74, 84, 86, 118-19, 124, 165-66, 299-300; *5.*
18, 89, 91; *6.* 30-31, 37-38, 42, 45-46
Johnston, Col. John R., *2.* 256; *3.* 39*n,* 85, 89,
119, 177, 354*n; 6.* 68. Letter to, *2.* 322
Johnston, Jr., John R. ("Jack"), *2.* 323*n; 3.* 3,
85, 92*n,* 433, 434. Letter to, *3.* 88-89
Johnston, Katherine, *3.* 127, 271; *4.* 427, 436.
Letter to, *4.* 254
Johnston, May, *3.* 80, 98, 121, 156, 271, 374,
388; *5.* 339, 345
Johnston & Co., T. & J., *3.* 434
Johnstone, Rev. T. B., *5.* 124, 145
Johnstown (Pa.) Flood, *4.* 345, 346, 347
Jones, Adrian, *2.* 169, 171
Jones, Henry Festing. Letters to, *3.* 116, 119-20,

128
Jones, John Paul, 4. 326
Jones, Nathaniel G., 3. 433
Jones, W. A. B., 3. 441
Jordan, Bim M., 5. 349
Jordan, Mary A., 5. 340
Journal of Speculative Philosophy, The, 3. 166n,
  167n, 171, 188n
Judge, W. Q., 4. 57n
Judson, Edward Z. C., 1. 52n
Julius Caesar, 3. 108n
"Junius," 3. 284

Kalbfleisch, Martin, 1. 193, 209, 230
Kansas Magazine, The, 2. 157, 159, 163; 5. 295;
  6. 9n
Kant, Immanuel, 4. 239
Karpstyin(?), Louis, 3. 446
Katz, John Z., 4. viii
deKay, Charles, 3. 149, 448
"Keep Off The Grass," 5. 317
Kegan Paul, Trench & Co., 3. 255n
Kelley, Mrs. Letter to, 5. 278
Kelley, Louis S., 4. 440
Kelling, Prof. Harold D., 4. viii; 5. 319n
Kellogg, Clara Louisa, 1. 183
Kelly, Frederick, 2. 54
Kelly, James Edward, 3. 329
Kelly, Judge Milton, 1. 329n, 378; 5. 291
Kelly, William H., 3. 444
Kenaga, D. H., 4. 438
Kenilworth, 2. 88
Kennedy, Victor, 5. 62n
Kennedy, William Sloane, 1. vii, 281n, 295n; 3.
  197n, 218, 341-42, 369n, 375, 414, 446, 447,
  450, 451, 452, 453; 4. 1, 15, 31, 34, 41, 43n,
  53, 56n, 77, 87, 91, 102, 110, 117, 128, 134,
  139, 140, 141, 142, 150, 157n, 160, 162, 166,
  167, 204, 208, 228, 243, 253, 254, 256, 258,
  261, 263, 270, 273, 276, 277, 278, 281, 284,
  287, 290, 306, 313, 321, 322, 341, 355, 359,
  365, 367, 372, 377, 380, 382, 384, 387, 390,
  391-92, 394, 395, 403, 427, 428, 429, 430, 431,
  432, 433, 434, 435, 436, 437, 438, 439, 440,
  441; 5. 2-3, 5, 6, 7, 19, 24, 38, 49, 53, 59, 60,
  65, 66, 70, 72, 75, 84, 115, 127, 147n, 149,
  153, 155, 160, 163, 166n, 171, 176n, 190, 198,
  200, 203, 213, 263, 332-45, 349; 6. 47, 51,
  53n. Letters to, 3. 260, 281, 317, 337-38, 339,
  340-41, 374, 385, 391, 393-94, 400-401, 402,
  410; 4. 25, 27, 28, 33-34, 35, 36, 39, 40, 41-42,
  43-44, 47, 50, 52, 57-58, 60, 65-66, 68-72, 74-
  75, 78, 80-81, 83-89, 91-95, 97-100, 103, 105-9,
  112, 114, 118-19, 122, 125-28, 131-32, 135-37,
  140, 144-47, 149-50, 152, 157-59, 163-65, 168-

69, 173, 179, 184, 193, 203, 212, 218, 220,
  223-24, 226-27, 241-42, 248-49, 252, 258, 263,
  272-73, 276, 279, 285-86, 289, 294-96, 303,
  305-6, 308, 317-19, 321, 325-26, 331, 333-35,
  337, 340, 344, 350, 354, 361, 372-74, 378, 380-
  82, 384-85, 395, 406; 5. 22-23, 26, 32, 37, 41,
  44, 50, 54-55, 58, 64, 68, 69, 71, 74, 76-80, 86-
  88, 94, 97, 102, 108, 110, 114, 116, 121, 136,
  139-40, 150, 153-54, 159, 162, 164, 166, 170,
  177, 196-97, 202, 204, 216, 223-24, 228, 236-
  37, 246; 6. 55-56
Kensington Museum, 4. 121, 126
Kent, Charles, 2. 31n; 3. 52
Kenyon, Margrave, 5. 340
Kephart, Andrew J., 1. 315, 316, 319, 322-23
Kepler, Johannes, 5. 195
Kerr, Andrew, 2. 55n; 5. 289. Letters to, 1.
  270, 283-84, 286
Kerr, Mrs. Anna M., 4. 431
Kerswell, R. W., 4. 64
Kesson, J., 5. 282n
Keyser, Charles S., 1. 371
Kidd, Mrs. Donald E., 2. vi
Kilgore, Damon, 3. 199n. Letters to, 3. 61, 75-
  76
Kilpatrick, Gen. Hugh Judson, 1. 166, 210n
Kimball, Sumner I., 5. 184
King & Co., Charles S., 3. 438
King, Moses, 5. 346
King, Preston, 1. 73
Kingsley, Charles S., 1. 11, 84n, 127, 143, 158,
  366, 373
Kinnear, Dr., 4. 115n
Kipling, Rudyard, 6. 59n
Kirk, John Foster, 3. 150
Kirk, Sophia, 4. 436
Kirkwood, James P., 1. 105, 216, 327; 3. 386.
  Letter to, 1. 213-15
Kitton, Fred G., 4. 430
Klein, Jacob. Letters to, 4. 207, 211
Klinkicht, M., 4. 402n
Knapp, Albert G., 1. 212n; 3. 440, 449
Kneedler, H. S., 3. 447
Knerr, Calvin B., 5. 342
Knight, Joseph, 2. 341n
Knortz, Karl, 3. 261n, 349, 363, 375, 410, 449;
  4. 32n, 36, 129, 208, 212, 220, 270, 287, 293,
  295, 331, 352n, 401n, 436, 438; 5. 349; 6. 30n,
  69. Letters to, 3. 288-89, 316, 317, 343, 351,
  362, 389-90, 404; 4. 31, 77, 90-91, 101, 209,
  265, 289, 319, 330
Knower, Benjamin, 1. 11, 85, 127, 143, 158
Knowles, James, 3. 402n, 410, 439, 450; 4. 90n,
  385n, 425, 427, 430; 5. 334. Letter to, 5. 25-26
Knox, J. Armory, 5. 346
Knox, John Jay. Letters to, 1. 310, 356

Kossabone, Jenny, *5*. 80
Kroll, Ernest, *5*. ix

Labar, Richard E., *3*. 240*n*, 256*n*, 436; *4*. 400; *5*. 335
Lader, Lawrence, *1*. 117*n*, 146*n*
Lady Audley's Secret, *1*. 297
"Lafayette in Brooklyn," *4*. 48*n*, 425
Lamb, Mary, *2*. 1; *3*. 340*n*
Lane, Alf. L., *1*. 120, 133, 375
Lane, Elmer B., *4*. 432
Lane, Moses, *1*. 58*n*, 67, 71, 73, 80, 96, 98, 101, 105, 117, 143, 226, 233, 251, 275, 327, 356*n*, 365, 366, 372, 373; *2*. 27*n*. Letters to, *1*. 98-99, 201-2
Lang, Cecil, *5*. 318*n*
Langfield, William R., *5*. 211*n*
Langley, Miss E., *4*. 305*n*, 323*n*, 436, 437
Lanier, Sidney, *3*. 443; *4*. 87*n*
Lanman, Charles, *3*. 327
Larned, Francis M., *4*. 286*n*
"Last of the Sacred Army, The, *1*. 26*n*
Latchford, Henry, *4*. 439
Lathrop, George Parsons, *2*. 190*n*; *3*. 216*n*, 218, 436, 443, 452
Lawney, Eleanor M., *3*. 450
Lawrence, Richard Hoe. Letter to, 6. 24
Lawrence, Kansas, *3*. 164, 165
Lay, Alfred, *3*. 366*n*, 367, 368*n*, 371, 387*n*, 389, 393
Lay, Mrs. Alfred, *3*. 371, 372, 387*n*, 389, 393
Lay, Harry, *3*. 373*n*
Lay, Tasker, *3*. 366-67
Lazarus, Emma, *4*. 270
Lazarus, Josephine, *4*. 173*n*
Leap (conductor), *5*. 129
Lear, King, *5*. 203, 204
Leary's Book Store, *3*. 306
Leaves of Grass, *1*. 246-47, 300, 303, 330, 335, 340, 343, 346-49, 351, 354; *2*. 1, 48, 50, 142, 151, 154, 158, 160; *3*. 146*n*, 149*n*, 150, 193, 211, 238-39, 247, 259, 269, 307, 326, 329, 336, 338, 344, 369, 395, 405, 410; *4*. 33, 34, 50, 69-70, 117, 150, 153-54, 164, 215, 219, 227*n*, 230, 247, 299, 347, 362, 379, 384, 390, 391, 396, 408; *5*. 32*n*, 35, 42, 61, 63, 65, 72-73, 78*n*, 79, 81, 92, 94, 112, 115, 138, 150-51, 157*n*, 158, 203, 204, 246*n*; 6. 10
  First Edition, *1*. 41, 43, 298, 336-37; *2*. 21, 94*n*, 99-100, 140; *3*. 92, 242*n*, 287, 308, 370*n*; *4*. 32*n*, 257*n*; *5*. 63*n*, 227*n*, 286; 6. 8, 30, 47*n*, 62
  Second Edition, *1*. 40*n*, 44; *3*. 92, 373; 6. 30
  Third Edition, *1*. 10, 44, 45, 46*n*, 49, 50-51, 52-53, 85-86, 95, 236*n*; *2*. 30*n*, 32*n*; *3*. 92, 104*n*, 186, 196-98, 199-200, 226, 237*n*, 299; 6. 30
  Fourth Edition, *1*. 244, 282, 284-285, 286, 288, 292, 295, 297, 300*n*, 302, 314, 329*n*, 335*n*, 344, 349, 350*n*, 354; *2*. 18, 22, 33, 39, 46, 48, 55, 58, 59, 76, 78, 81, 273, 274, 275, 294; *3*. 92; *5*. 287-88, 289; 6. 4, 5, 8, 30
  Fifth Edition, *1*. 350; *2*. 29, 81*n*, 100, 103, 105, 108, 111, 112, 113, 116*n*, 118*n*, 131, 133, 143, 144, 150, 163, 166, 167, 168, 169, 174, 175, 244, 263; *3*. 42, 92; *4*. 386; *5*. 294, 298; 6. 10, 11, 30
  Sixth Edition, *2*. 7, 172*n*, 259*n*, 283*n*, 323*n*, 330, 332, 335, 343, 344, 345; *3*. 21, 26, 27, 29, 31, 32, 33, 34, 35, 37, 38, 39, 40, 41, 43, 44, 45, 47, 48, 49, 51, 52, 53, 55, 56, 57, 58-59, 62, 64, 65, 67, 68, 72, 73, 88, 92, 96, 99, 101, 103, 104, 116, 120, 128, 129, 130, 132, 133, 137-38, 141, 142, 157, 159*n*, 174, 180*n*, 190, 191, 192, 193, 195, 201, 206, 209, 211, 218, 227, 252, 256, 275*n*, 282, 288, 307, 322, 372; *4*. 25*n*, 53, 54, 62, 75, 106, 137, 152, 204, 207, 211; *5*. 280*n*, 301, 303, 307; 6. 13, 14, 15, 16, 23, 24, 26, 27, 30, 61*n*
  Seventh Edition, *3*. 139*n*, 224, 225, 226-27, 227-31, 232, 233, 234-35, 236, 238-39, 240, 241-42, 243, 244, 245, 246, 247, 248, 249, 250, 252, 253, 254, 255, 256, 257, 258, 259, 260, 262, 267, 268, 269, 270-71, 272, 273, 274, 275, 276, 278, 279, 280, 282-84, 291, 292, 294, 295, 296, 297-98, 299, 300, 301, 302, 303, 304, 305, 306*n*, 309, 310*n*, 311*n*, 312, 314, 315*n*, 317, 323, 329, 335*n*, 348, 350, 370*n*, 371, 375, 376, 382, 385, 399, 401, 414; *4*. 19-20, 29*n*, 38, 41*n*, 45, 59, 71, 86, 108*n*, 145, 147, 172, 312, 321*n*; *5*. 313, 314-15, 316-17, 321; 6. 25, 27, 30
  Eighth Edition (*Complete Poems & Prose*), *3*. 389; *4*. 181, 200, 201, 202, 203, 204, 209, 211, 213, 217, 218, 221, 222, 224, 225, 226, 231, 232, 233, 234, 235, 236, 237, 238, 239-40, 241, 242, 243, 244, 245, 247, 248, 249, 250, 252, 254, 255, 256, 258, 259, 261, 262, 263, 264, 265, 266, 267, 269, 271, 272, 274, 275, 276, 281, 282, 283, 284, 285, 287, 289, 290, 291, 294, 295, 298, 299, 300, 301, 302, 304, 309, 310, 312, 318, 319, 323, 336, 342, 347, 353, 357, 359, 362, 387, 399, 405; *5*. 23, 33*n*, 38, 42, 44, 47, 52, 58, 65, 66, 70, 74*n*, 76, 77, 78, 81, 94, 99, 100-1, 103, 106, 107, 110, 111, 113-14, 115, 116, 117, 129, 130, 136, 137, 138, 139, 140, 143, 146, 150, 158, 167, 171, 176, 180, 182, 183, 185, 186-87, 197-98, 230*n*, 238, 247, 255, 264, 266, 321; 6. 52-53, 59
  Eighth Edition (with *Sands at Seventy* and *A Backward Glance*), *4*. 293, 309, 311, 312, 313, 317, 318, 320, 323, 324, 325, 326, 327, 328, 330, 331, 333, 336, 338, 339, 343, 345, 347,

352, 361, 362, 363, 368, 378, 382, 387, 388, 392; 5. 18, 22, 52, 58, 69, 70, 79, 83, 85, 88, 90, 97, 99, 101, 102*n*, 124, 135, 205*n*
  Ninth Edition, 5. 223, 239, 243, 245, 247, 251, 255, 266, 268, 269, 270, 271, 272, 275, 276*n*; 6. 59, 60
Leaves of Grass, Scotch Edition, 3. 328*n*, 344
"Leaves of Grass and Modern Science," 5. 43, 49
Leaves of Grass Imprints, 1. 53; 3. 316
"L. of G.'s Purport," 5. 119*n*, 185*n*
Leavitt & Co., George A., 3. 196-97, 200, 433
Lebknecker, Arthur E., 3. 252, 437
LeConey, Chalkley, 5. 27
Lee, John, 2. 85, 87, 88
Lee, John Fitzgerald, 3. 258, 261, 316*n*, 447. Letter to, 3. 259-60
Lee, Robert E., 1. 99, 106, 110, 112-13, 114, 134, 139, 169, 176, 180, 212, 214, 215, 219, 220, 226, 228; 5. 71
Lee, Shepard, Dillingham, 2. 214, 273
Leech, John, 2. 274*n*
LeGendre, Charles W., 1. 88, 104, 212, 222-23
Legg, Charles E., 4. 373, 375
Leggett, Mrs. Elisa S., 3. 239*n*, 434, 436, 445, 448; 5. 347. Letter to, 5. 248
Leisure Moments, 4. 67
Leland, Charles G., 1. 54*n*
Leland, Henry, 1. 54*n*
Leman, Dr., 1. 71
Leon & Brothers, 3. 439
Lerris, O. K., 5. 107, 125
Lesley, Prof. J. Peter, 3. 25; 5.302
Lesley, Mrs. J. Peter, 3. 26, 32
Lesley, Maggie, 3. 25
deLesseps, Vicomte Ferdinand Marie, 4. 248
Lessing, Gotthold Ephraim, 3. 255*n*
"Letter from Washington," 1. 141, 148, 157, 159, 163, 165
Lewes, George Henry, 4. 129
Lewin, Walter, 4. 103*n*, 431
Leycester, Rafe, 5. 305
Leypoldt, F. Letter to, 3. 92
Lezinsky, David L., 5. 48, 53*n*, 158, 331. Letters to, 5. 106-7, 125
Liberty (Boston), 3. 348*n*; 4. 353, 363, 372, 374, 375
Liberty and Literature, 5. 100, 102, 103, 107, 108, 114, 115, 118, 119, 125, 126, 138, 151, 155, 157; 6. 53*n*
Librarian of Congress, 5. 332. Letters to, 2. 345; 3. 373
Liebenan, Andrew J., 1. 375
"Life," 4. 145*n*
"Life and Death," 4. 145*n*
Life of Samuel Johnson, 4. 239
Light, 5. 305

Lincoln, Abraham, 1. 2, 78, 82-83, 108, 113, 163-64, 171, 174, 212, 213, 215, 220, 254, 292*n*, 315*n*, 321*n*, 334; 2. 26*n*, 35, 41, 115*n*, 232*n*, 317*n*; 3. 53*n*, 65*n*, 106, 108, 109, 110-11, 114*n*, 117*n*, 149, 151, 155, 163*n*, 212*n*, 222, 402*n*; 4. 21, 89, 148*n*, 352; 5. 39, 84, 288*n*, 321*n*
Lincoln, George B., 1. 273
Lincoln, W. I., 5. 347
Lindell, Capt. Respegius Edward, 3. 182-83, 185, 433, 436, 445
Lindsey, Ed., 3. 168*n*
Linensparger, Isaac, 1. 181, 375
Linkenheil, Lizzie, 3. 94
Linton, William J., 2. 256, 364, 372; 3. 117, 452; 4. 222, 315*n*, 434. Letters to, 2. 171-72, 186, 323-24, 326, 333-34, 340-41; 3. 116-17; 4. 210; 6. 16
Lion, Oscar, 1. ix; 2. vi, 291*n*
Lippincott, J. B., 3. 435; 4. 156*n*
Lippincott's Monthly Magazine, 3. 150, 263*n*; 4. 43, 55, 91*n*, 99, 100, 127, 153*n*, 157, 161, 385*n*, 426; 5. 41*n*, 42, 56, 59*n*, 70*n*, 113, 118, 120, 121, 122, 127, 133, 137, 140, 146, 147, 149, 150, 151, 153, 154, 156, 158, 159, 164, 165, 167, 168, 169, 170, 171, 176, 210*n*, 214, 215, 216, 217-18, 220, 221, 224, 229, 230, 239, 261; 6. 57-58
Liptay, Paul, 2. 315
Literary News (New York), 4. 331
Literary World, The, 3. 178, 179, 210*n*, 213*n*, 258*n*, 275*n*, 281*n*, 434, 436; 4. 249; 5. 244, 343. Letter to, 3. 212
Littell's Living Age, 2. 29, 188; 3. 21*n*
Littledale, Harold, 3. 60
Littlefield, John Harrison. Letter to, 2. 72
Lloyd, J. William, 5. 346
Lloyd, Rev. William, 4. 149
Loag, Samuel, 3. 68
Lobb, Henry, 3. 56*n*
Locker-Lampson, Frederick, 3. 134, 444, 445, 446. Letters to, 3. 174-75, 179-80, 188
Lockwood, Ingersoll, 4. 426, 432
Loftus, J. P. Letter to, 4. 137
Logue, Mr., 4. 154
London, The, 3. 135
London, Canada, 3. 181-82, 183-85, 186, 201
London (Canada) *Advertiser,* 3. 180*n*, 181*n*, 184*n*, 188*n*, 435; 4. 151, 153
London (Canada) *Free Press,* 3. 180*n*
London *Chronicle,* 1. 335
London *Daily News,* 2. 218*n*; 3. 30, 31*n*, 36, 38*n*, 39*n*, 44, 47, 98, 399*n*
London *Examiner,* 3. 52, 56, 65, 431
London *Illustrated News,* 4. 402
London *Morning Star,* 2. 28
London *Piccadilly,* 4. 401*n*, 403

London Review of Politics, Society, Literature, Art, and Science, 2. 29
London *Star,* 6. 51*n*
London *Sun,* 3. 53*n*
London *Telegram,* 4. 385, 386
London *Times,* 3. 46, 63*n*, 82, 132, 136, 430
London *Universal Review,* 5. 32, 35, 39, 79, 80
Long, Alexander, *1.* 211
Longaker, Dr. Daniel, *5.* 177, 178, 179, 180, 181, 183, 184, 185, 186, 187, 191, 192, 194, 195, 196, 197, 198, 202, 210, 213, 214, 217, 225, 226, 231, 244, 252, 259, 263, 269, 271, 276*n,* 347. Letters to, *5.* 191-92, 199, 209
Longfellow, Henry Wadsworth, *1.* 77*n,* 339*n*; *2.* 30*n,* 78*n,* 171*n,* 317*n*; *3.* 52, 167*n,* 214*n,* 246, 247, 273, 281*n,* 370*n,* 446; 4. 49; *5.* 206. Letter to, *3.* 212-13
Longinus, *3.* 332*n*
Long Islander, The, 1. 9, 38*n*; 3. 235*n,* 241*n*
Loomis, Prof. Elias, *3.* 294
Loskey(?), Thomas, *4.* 425
Lotos Club, *5.* 171*n*
Louis the Fourteenth and the Court of France, 4. 216, 219, 224
Louisville (Ky.) *Courier Journal,* 3. 181*n,* 434
Louisville (Ky.) *Daily Journal,* 3. 212*n*
Lovell, J. G., *5.* 253*n,* 257, 267
Lovering, Henry B., 4. 56, 65-66, 425
Loving, Jerome M., 6. 73
Low, George L., *1.* 203*n*
Low, Thomas B., *1.* 203*n*
Lowe, Miss, *1.* 160
Lowell, Anna, *1.* 332
Lowell, James Russell, *1.* 48, 280*n,* 346*n*; *2.* 72*n*; *3.* 333; *4.* 83*n,* 148*n,* 249, 289*n*; *5.* 214, 235. Letters to, *1.* 47-48, 57
Lowery, John, *1.* 64
Lozynsky, Artem, 6. 21*n*
Lucas, John. Letters to, *3.* 102; 6. 17
Luckey, Leon P., 2. 280*n,* 371
Lucretius, *3.* 339*n*
Lucrezia Borgia, 1. 178*n,* 183
Ludwig, George W., *3.* 450
Lung, Rev. Augustus H., *5.* 310
Lüttgens, C. H., *5.* 59*n*
Lutz, Robert, *3.* 452
Lychenheim, Mr., *4.* 358*n*
Lyman, Judge Samuel Fowler, *3.* 26
Lynch, Arthur, *5.* 268-69, 345
Lynn (Mass.) *Saturday Union,* 3. 370*n*
Lytton, Edward Bulwer-, *see* Bulwer-Lytton, Edward
Lyvere, Clarissa, 6. 3

M, E. P., *3.* 253*n*
McAlister, Dr. Alexander, *4.* 267; *5.* 277

McAlpine, William Jarvis, *3.* 386
McCandlish, George, *4.* viii
McCartee, George B., *2.* 233
McCarthy, Justin, *3.* 64*n*
McCarthy, Jr., Justin H., *2.* 341*n*; *3.* 52*n,* 65, 441; 4. 251*n,* 435
McClellan, Gen. George Brinton, *1.* 99, 242
McClintock, Gilbert S., *2.* vi; *4.* viii
McClure, J. E., *1.* 27*n*
McClure, S. S., 4. 108, 399*n,* 404, 405, 406, 425, 441. Letters to, 4. 102, 104, 114, 119, 402
McClure's Magazine, 4. 399*n*
MacColl, Norman, *3.* 51-52
McCowell, Thomas, *1.* 60, 223
McCown & Co., A. R., *3.* 88*n,* 106
McCulloch, Hugh, *1.* 279*n*
McDermott, Mr., *5.* 32
McDonald, Frank, *1.* 191
McDowell, William O., *5.* 344
McFarland, William H., *1.* 374
McGill College, *5.* 250*n,* 251
McIlhaney, A. K., *4.* 440
McIlvain, Charles, *5.* 337, 349
McKay, David *3.* 197*n,* 310*n,* 313-14, 324, 325, 329, 330, 335, 337, 338, 344, 350*n,* 371*n,* 399, 401, 409*n,* 410*n,* 414; *4.* 124, 172, 219, 220, 221, 228, 229, 235, 236, 242, 251, 266, 272, 277, 281, 291, 293, 302, 306, 309, 311, 312, 313, 336, 343, 345, 347, 354, 365, 381, 383, 384, 387, 394; *5.* 42, 65, 76, 100-101, 126*n,* 127, 137, 183, 185, 186*n,* 188, 230, 252, 255, 266, 275, 337, 341, 343; 6. 29*n,* 40. Letters to, *3.* 375; *4.* 170, 221, 225, 255, 257, 405, 410; *5.* 42, 103, 110-11, 140, 186-87; 6. 56-57
McKee, Thomas J., *4.* 161, 426, 432
McKenzie, Norman, *3.* 182*n,* 435, 445
McKenzie, William P., *4.* 440
McKinney, Francis, *2.* 54
McKinsey, Folger, *3.* 450; *4.* 19*n*
McKnight, Mrs. Sarah R., *2.* 41
McLaughlan, Charles, *2.* 54
McLeod, A. L., *5.* 62*n*
McMahon, John, *3.* 154*n*
McMurray, L. A. Letter to, *5.* 57
McNallie, Ridgway, *3.* vii, 380*n*
McQuire, James C. Letter to, *2.* 175
McReady, Lt. Fred, *1.* 100, 167, 212, 222, 223, 226, 227, 229, 373
McWatters, George S., *1.* 379
Mabbott, Thomas Olive, *2.* 266*n*; *3.* ix, 429
McCaulay, G. C., *3.* 319, 322*n,* 405, 410, 448
Macaulay, Thomas Babington, *4.* 18
Macdonald, Katie, *3.* 435, 445
Macdonald, T. F., *3.* 450
Machefer, Ted, *5.* 138, 150, 168, 176
Mackenzie, W. Colin, *3.* 435, 445
Magazine of Art, The, 4. 148*n*

Magazine of Poetry, The, 4. 280, 289, 294
Maginley, H. R., 5. 334
Maginnis, Craig, 3. 449
Mahay, John, 1. 91, 120, 134
Main(?), Mrs., 5. 349
Main, H. P., 6. 62n
Major, George M., 4. 424
Malet, Sir Edward, 4. 62n; 5. 244
Manchester Guardian, 5. 203, 271n
Mann, Miss, 3. 244, 251
Mann, Horace, 3. 245n
Mann, J. C., 2. 363, 371. Letter to, 2. 290
Mann, Thomas, 3. 245n
"Mannahatta," 4. 144n
Manning, Cardinal Henry Edward, 4. 221
"Man-of-War-Bird," *see* "To the Man-of-War Bird"
Mansfield, E. D., 3. 159n
Mapes, Mrs. Mary E., 4. 336; 5. 86, 331
Maretzek, Max, 1. 86n, 159n, 183
Marino, A. J., 3. ix, 429
Mario, Giuseppe, 2. 191
Marks, Mr., 3. 56n
Marsh, Edward Sprague, 5. 335. Letter to, 3. 322
Marston, Cecily, 3. 60
Marston, George, 3. 279, 283, 348n
Marston, Philip Bourke, 3. 61n, 65. Letter to, 3. 58
Marston, Sr., Mrs. Roy L., 6. 65
Martin, Mrs., 1. 332
Martin, John D., 1. 73
Marvin, Frederic R., 2. 372
Marvin, Joseph B., 2. 99n, 317, 338, 341, 344, 364, 371; 3. 20, 26, 52, 89, 135n, 150, 170n, 198, 209, 352, 431, 432, 433; 4. 75, 357, 430; 5. 302; 6. 38. Letter to, 5. 298-99
Mason, Col. E. C., 2. 214n
Mason, Julius W., 1. 249, 251, 275, 308, 368, 369, 376; 2. 215
Matther, T. W., 4. 426, 434
Matthew, G. J., 5. 339
Matthews, Mrs., 3. 55
Matthews, Brander. Letter to, 3. 304
Matzkin, Ruth, 2. v
Mawson, Edward, 3. 452
Maxim, Mrs. Mattie, 3. 438, 450
Maxwell, Gerald, 4. 429
Maybee, Elizabeth, 2. 215n
Mayer, Townsend, 3. 56n
Mayfield, John S., 3. ix, 428; 4. viii
Maywood, H. J., 5. 340
Mazzini, Giuseppe, 2. 100n
Mazzoleni, Francesco, 1. 183, 185n, 307n
Mead, James H., 2. 214n
Mead, Sarah (Sally), 2. 202, 210, 211, 215, 264; 3. 114, 443

Meade, Gen. George Gordon, 1. 92n, 114, 125, 134, 136, 151, 163, 166, 170, 180, 214, 221, 232, 262
Mearns, David C., 1. x; 2. v
Medea, 1. 83
Medori, Giuseppini, 1. 86, 178, 183, 185n
Meier, E. D., 5. 338
Meigs, Gen. Montgomery C., 1. 74
Melville, Herman, 3. 365n
"Memorandum at a Venture, A" 3. 274, 276, 279, 285, 298n
"Memoranda During the War," 1. 70n, 171-72; 2. 266n, 329n; 3. 24n, 27, 33n, 34n, 35n, 36n, 40, 41, 44, 48, 51, 52, 55, 56n, 92, 144n, 173n, 176n, 221n, 275n; 6. 14n
Mencken, H. L., 1. 263n
Menken, Adah Isaacs, 1. 55n
Mercer, Edmund, 5. 337
Meredith, Owen, 3. 228
Merrick, Richard T., 1. 334n
Merrill, W. R., 4. 97
Metcalf, Lorretus S., 3. 205
Metcalf, Dr. W. G., 3. 185n
Metropolitan Museum of Art, 4. 20n; 5. 193
Meyer, Annie Nathan, 5. 339
Meyerbeer, Giacomo, 2. 169
Michel(?), S. F., 3. 441
Michelangelo Buonarroti, 1. 82
Milburn, Dr. J. Parker, 2. 106, 108n, 113, 128-29, 171, 222, 245, 251, 256, 258, 260, 266, 280, 283, 286
Milburn, W. C. ("Wash"), 2. 108, 113, 168, 171, 223, 231, 254, 256, 280, 284, 313
Miller, Cyrus C., 5. 348
Miller, Edwin H. (?), 1. 177, 181
Miller, F. DeWolfe, 1. 260n, 261n, 263n, 270n; 2. v, 120n; 3. vii, 63n, 149n, 170n; 6. 4n, 75, 76
Miller, Joaquin, 2. 138n, 155, 161, 181, 182, 278n, 334, 344n, 364, 369, 371, 372; 3. 20, 38, 40, 45, 52, 68, 72, 105n, 146n, 246, 247, 440, 443; 5. 349; 6. 13
Miller, John, 2. 54
Miller, John Dewitt, 5. 337, 339
Miller, John P., 3. 432
Miller, Rosalind S., 5. vii
Miller, "Professor" William, 3. 154n
Millet, Frank D., 4. 255
Millet, Jean François, 3. 339n; 4. 166, 234, 329
Millis, William H., 1. 12, 367, 375, 376; 2. 363, 364, 365, 371, 372, 373; 3. 436
Mills, Elwood, 5. 30
Mills, William, 3. 444
Milnes, Richard Monckton (Lord Houghton), 2. 344, 373; 3. 20, 44. Letter to, 3. 395
Milton, John, 1. 1; 5. 32n
Minchin, Mrs. M. B., 3. 450; 5. 346

Minto, William, *3*. 52*n*

Minton, Maurice M., *5*. 39*n*, 334

Mr. Donnelly's Reviewers, *4*. 294*n*, 357, 359

Mitchell, Dr. J. K., *4*. 187, 188, 189, 192; *5*. 52, 122-23, 130, 136*n*, 147

Mitchell, Dr. S. Weir, *3*. 111*n*, 114, 115*n*, 116*n*; *4*. 25*n*, 187*n*, 441; *5*. 50*n*, 122. Letter to, *5*. 44

Mitchell, Dr. W. E., *5*. 349

Mix, Mrs. Mary, *1*. 278, 279, 280, 307, 309, 311, 312; *2*. 27

Modern School, The, *1*. viii

Modern Thought, *3*. 305

Moffitt, Mrs. Eva E., *3*. 238, 240, 249*n*

Molière (Jean Baptiste Poquelin), *3*. 321

Moll, Mrs. June, *4*. vii

Moller, Jacob, *3*. 447

Molloy, Fitzgerald, *3*. 305*n*

"Monitor," *1*. 64

Monk, George W., *1*. 112

Monk, William D., *1*. 112*n*

Monroe, James, *1*. 301

Montaigne, Michel Eyquem de, *3*. 298, 301, 308; *4*. 357*n*

Montgomerie, Annie, *see* Anne M. Traubel

Montgomery, George Edgar, *3*. 344

Montgomery, Walter, *2*. 111*n*

Montgomery, William V., *3*. 222*n*

Montreal *Witness*, *3*. 434

Moody, William Vaughan, *3*. 354*n*

Moore, Henry W., *3*. 94

Moore, Ralph, *5*. 62*n*, 98, 105, 203, 207, 225, 267, 274

Moore, Ralph E., *5*. 345

Moore, Thomas, *3*. 157

Moran, Edward, *3*. 157

Moran, Peter, *3*. 157

Moran, Thomas, *3*. 157

Morehouse, Mr., *4*. 317

Morgan & Co., J. S., *3*. 401*n*

Morgan, John D. F., *3*. vii

Morgan, R. Rooke, *5*. 349

Morgan, Rachel, *3*. 112*n*; *5*. 313

Morgan, Will, *3*. 112*n*, 131

Morley, John, *2*. 16, 77, 361, 367. Letter to, *2*. 75

Mormon, Mrs., *2*. 149

Morrell, L., *5*. 336, 344

Morrell(?), R. J. Letter to, *3*. 143

Morris, Charles. *4*. 429. Letter to, *4*. 38

Morris, Harrison S., *4*. 409*n*, 441; *5*. 80, 106, 109, 174*n*, 178, 207, 259, 343. Letter to, *5*. 254

Morris, George R., *5*. 334

Morris, William, *2*. 138*n*

Morrison, B. G., *3*. 440

Morrow, Rev. James, *3*. 297*n*

Morse, George R., *5*. 334

Morse, Josie, *2*. 373

Morse, Sidney H., *2*. 99*n*; *3*. 135*n*, 432, 444; *4*. 92, 93, 95, 97*n*, 99, 103, 105, 107, 108, 110, 111, 112, 119, 120, 121, 124, 126*n*, 127, 132, 133, 134, 135, 136, 137, 139, 140, 150, 151, 156, 158, 159, 160, 163, 189, 207, 213*n*, 215, 220, 307, 354, 393, 426, 431, 432, 433, 435; *5*. 236*n*, 255*n*, 274*n*, 333, 335; *6*. 43, 45*n*, 47. Letters to, *4*. 154, 213

Morton, Levi Parsons, *4*. 196

Moulton, C. W., *4*. 435

Moulton, Ellen Louise Chandler, *4*. 165, 166, 167, 268; *5*. 349. Letters to, *3*. 65, 209

Moxon's Popular Poems, *5*. 296

Moyne, Ernest J., *4*. 19*n*

Muchmore, W. M. Letter to, *1*. 38-39

Muir, Percy, *3*. viii, 429

Mulford, Lt. Col. John Elmer, *1*. 369

Mullan, Capt. John, *1*. 87, 90, 207*n*

Mullen, Edward F. (?), *1*. 85, 127

Muller, Mr., *5*. 315

Mullery, Jesse, *1*. 247, 368, 369, 376, 377

Mullery, William, *1*. 376

Munday, Luther, *5*. 347

Munson, Judge Lyman E., *2*. 25

Munyon, Mr., *5*. 28

Munyon's Illustrated World, *4*. 136*n*, 141*n*, 426; *5*. 23, 120, 170*n*, 331

Murdock, Baalam, *2*. 113

Murger, Henri, *5*. 222*n*

Murphy, Andrew E., *3*. 390

Murphy, Jenny, *2*. 108

Murray's Magazine, *4*. 431; *5*. 229

Murrell, Capt. Hamilton, *4*. 325

Musgrove, W. A., *4*. 182*n*, 190, 227*n*, 229, 230, 231, 333

"My Book and I," *4*. 36*n*, 43, 55, 58, 63*n*, 66, 424

"My Canary Bird," *4*. 144*n*

"My Long Island Antecedents," *3*. 262

"My Picture Gallery," *3*. 223*n*

"My 71st Year," *4*. 347*n*, 370, 385, 427

"My Task," *5*. 119*n*

"Mystic Trumpeter, The," *2*. 157, 159, 163, 164; *3*. 272*n*; *4*. 67*n*; *5*. 294*n*; *6*. 9

Napoleon Bonaparte, *1*. 214; *2*. 288

Napoleon, Louis, *1*. 76; *2*. 110

Nash, Mr. and Mrs. Michael, *2*. 105, 108, 113, 168, 232, 254, 260, 261, 262, 267, 280, 313, 317, 326, 332, 335, 342; *3*. 70, 71, 72, 96, 415; *5*. 299

Nast, Thomas, *2*. 45*n*

Nathan, Benjamin, *2*. 104

Nation, The, *1*. 339; *2*. 276, 278; *3*. 21*n*, 285*n*,

341*n*, 349, 352; 4. 17, 43, 139, 141
National Magazine, 2. 337*n*
National Review, The, 5. 183, 184
"Native Moments," 3. 270*n*
"Nay, Tell Me Not To-day the Publish'd Shame," 2. 204
Neale, Mrs. Doris, 2. vi; 3. vii; 4. viii
Neat, Thomas, 1. 173, 375
Needham, Mrs., 3. 105
Neilson, Kenneth P., 5. 307*n*
Nelson, Andrew or N. (?), 1. 310
Nencioni, Enrico, 4. 159*n*; 5. 61
Nettleship, John Trivett, 2. 153; 3. 55, 60, 65, 431
Nevins, Allan, 1. 167*n*
New Bowery Theatre, 1. 81
New Eclectic Magazine, The, 2. 44*n*, 78*n*
New England Magazine, The, 4. 379, 381; 5. 69, 77, 81, 83, 121, 122, 137, 147*n*, 194, 197, 198, 200, 201; 6. 56
New Orleans *Daily Crescent*, 1. 9, 27*n*, 28*n*, 29, 30*n*, 32, 34*n*, 35
"New Orleans in 1848," 4. 64
New Orleans *Picayune*, 1. 30*n*; 4. 429. Letter to, 4. 64
New Quarterly Magazine, 3. 141
New Review, 5. 243
New Voice, The, 2. 30*n*
New York *American Queen*, 3. 305
New York *Atlas*, 1. 35, 231*n*
New York *Christian Intelligencer*, 1. 43
New York *Citizen*, 1. 356; 2. 40
New York *Clipper*, 2. 45, 53
New York *Commercial Advertiser*, 2. 139, 177; 4. 24*n*
New York *Daily Graphic*, 2. 123*n*, 204, 206, 209, 210, 212, 220, 243*n*, 258, 259, 260, 261, 262, 272, 283, 294, 303*n*, 318; 3. 126*n*. Letters to, 2. 318; 3. 390
New York *Dispatch*, 1. 35
New York *Evening Mail*, 2. 110*n*, 116*n*
New York *Evening Mirror*, 1. 35
New York *Evening Post*, 1. 320; 2. 132*n*, 138, 220*n*, 303*n*; 3. 115*n*, 121*n*, 340*n*, 349, 352
New York *Evening Sun*, 4. 83*n*, 89
New York *Globe*, 1. 35
New York *Herald*, 1. 35, 58*n*, 75*n*, 80*n*, 81*n*, 115*n*, 170*n*, 176*n*, 211*n*, 308, 316*n*; 2. 56, 226, 238*n*, 285; 3. 38*n*, 45*n*, 141*n*, 204, 205, 218, 430; 4. 1, 5, 127*n*, 136*n*, 143-44, 146, 149, 151, 153, 155, 156, 157, 158, 159, 160, 161, 162, 164, 167, 170, 180, 198, 199, 200, 205, 212, 224, 257-58, 322, 325, 330, 331, 347*n*; 5. 49*n*, 68*n*, 172*n*; 6. 13*n*. Letters to, 3. 46; 4. 136, 206; 6. 46
New York *Home Journal*, 2. 130; 3. 281*n*
New York International News Company, 5. 35

New York *Leader*, 1. 339*n*
New York *Ledger*, 1. 53
New York *Mail and Express*, 3. 386*n*; 4. 437
New York *Morning Journal*, 5. 66, 67, 335
New York *Saturday Press*, 1. 54*n*, 55, 236*n*, 328*n*, 338*n*, 339*n*
New York *Sontagsblatt*, 2. 78*n*
New York *Staats-Zeitung Sontagsblatt*, 3. 289*n*
New York *Star*, 3. 409*n*
New York *Sun*, 1. 35, 75*n*, 337*n*; 2. 132*n*, 167*n*, 332*n*, 343*n*; 3. 120, 124*n*, 149*n*, 253*n*, 272*n*, 296*n*, 352-53, 437; 5. 19*n*, 160, 282
New York *Times*, 1. 35, 58*n*, 64*n*, 70*n*, 75, 81*n*, 82*n*, 99*n*, 105, 108*n*, 110*n*, 112*n*, 136, 138, 141, 148, 157, 159, 163, 165, 176*n*, 190*n*, 199*n*, 219*n*, 220*n*, 221*n*, 223*n*, 227*n*, 228*n*, 232*n*, 245*n*, 248*n*, 251, 252, 254*n*, 256, 269*n*, 271*n*, 300, 301, 303, 324, 341*n*, 2. 15, 30, 35*n*, 49*n*, 52*n*, 54, 58*n*, 59*n*, 78*n*, 104*n*, 112*n*, 114*n*, 122*n*, 138*n*, 166*n*, 178*n*, 179*n*, 210*n*, 256*n*, 257*n*; 3. 110*n*, 149*n*, 248*n*, 304*n*, 320, 341*n*, 344, 352, 399*n*, 437; 4. 83*n*, 100, 149*n*
New York *Tribune*, 1. 35, 40*n*, 44*n*, 47*n*, 53*n*, 81*n*, 98*n*, 109, 122*n*, 167*n*, 270*n*, 308, 320*n*, 328*n*, 338*n*; 2. 30*n*, 103, 132*n*, 160, 189*n*, 239*n*, 245*n*, 247, 250, 282, 283, 287, 294, 317, 321, 337*n*, 344*n*; 3. 23*n*, 25, 36*n*, 38*n*, 39, 52*n*, 53*n*, 95*n*, 110*n*, 112, 118*n*, 121*n*, 124*n*, 126*n*, 127, 128, 129, 136*n*, 140*n*, 152*n*, 153, 154, 155, 157*n*, 163, 178*n*, 180, 181*n*, 199, 214, 215*n*, 236*n*, 241*n*, 250, 257*n*, 275*n*, 276*n*, 281, 282, 284, 285, 286*n*, 291, 292*n*, 299*n*, 300*n*, 303, 304*n*, 315, 320, 327*n*, 341*n*, 342, 376*n*, 382, 402*n*, 434, 436, 437; 4. 124, 130, 131*n*, 134, 235*n*, 246, 248*n*, 259, 280, 291, 295, 314, 327; 5. 82*n*, 244, 275, 320*n*; 6. 10-11*n*. Letters to, 3. 180, 235; 5. 314
New York *Sunday Courier*. Letter to, 1. 47
New York *Sunday Mercury*, 1. 55*n*
New York *Weekly Graphic*, 1. 70*n*; 2. 267, 268, 271, 277, 278, 280, 285; 5. 298
New York *Weekly Tribune*, 5. 292
New York *World*, 1. 167*n*, 339*n*; 2. 59, 126*n*, 130, 132*n*, 204*n*; 3. 110, 297*n*, 304*n*, 314, 437; 4. 1, 118, 322, 328*n*, 330, 345*n*, 346, 348, 426, 427; 5. 5, 118, 119, 195*n*
Newbould, John A.(?), 1. 183
Newcastle-on-Tyne *Chronicle*, 4. 425
Newman, John H., 2. 152*n*
Newport, David, 4. 151*n*
Newton, Mr., 3. 56*n*
Newton, A. Edward, 5. 338
Niblo's Theatre, 2. 111
Nicholson, Miss, 3. 431
Nicholson, D., 3. 153*n*, 444
Nicholson, Thomas, 3. 182*n*, 234*n*, 433, 437, 447. Letters to, 3. 189-90, 200-201, 218-19,

231-32, 248, 349-50

Nicolay, John G., *4.* 55*n*

Nielson, Rasmus, *2.* 283*n*

Niemeyer(?), T. W. Letter to, *6.* 24

Nietzsche, Friedrich, *1.* 1; *2.* 5; *3.* 1

Nilsson, Christine, *2.* 169

Nineteenth Century, The, *3.* 319, 376*n*, 403; *4.* 23, 91, 234, 277, 385*n*, 394; *5.* 30, 53, 54, 68

Nineteenth Century Club, *4.* 142*n*

Ninth Army Corps, *1.* 86, 100, 107, 108, 130, 135, 139, 186, 232, 308, 311

Noble, L. F. Deh. Letters to, *3.* 282, 288

Noel, Roden, *2.* 162, 369; *3.* 56*n*, 60; *4.* 137*n*, 424, 428; *5.* 223. Letters to, *6.* 32, 33

Norma, *1.* 86

Norman, Henry, *4.* 62, 430; *6.* 20. Letter to, *4.* 63

Norris, Dr., *3.* 406*n*

North American Review, The, *1.* 122*n*; *3.* 132*n*, 188*n*, 204, 205, 209, 236*n*, 262*n*, 274, 276, 279, 285, 318*n*, 344, 362*n*, 376*n*, 402*n*, 435, 437, 438; *4.* 36, 39*n*, 43, 48*n*, 55, 221, 275; *5.* 18, 84, 100, 101, 107, 108, 109, 111, 114, 115, 116, 120, 132, 133, 150, 153, 154, 158, 169, 173, 339; *6.* 33, 53. Letters to, *3.* 277; *4.* 61; *5.* 99, 100, 112; *6.* 27

"North Star to a South, A," *see* "A Christmas Greeting"

Northrup, Daniel L., *1.* 98. Letter to, *1.* 101-2

Norton, Charles Eliot, *2.* 54*n*; *3.* 56*n*; *4.* 125*n*

Notes on Walt Whitman, As Poet and Person, *1.* 281*n*, 329*n*, 335*n*, 340, 341, 351, 354, *2.* 33*n*, 55, 80*n*, 81, 97*n*, 127*n*, 131, 274, 275, 317; *3.* 81, 103, 144, 316, 317, 355*n*; *5.* 89*n*, 99, 247*n*, 304; *6.* 14*n*, 59

Nouvelle Revue, La, *4.* 231*n*, 272, 273, 276, 277, 278, 286

Nourse, A. B., *3.* 453

November Boughs, *1.* 208*n*, 209*n*, 210*n*, 219*n*, 225*n*, 266*n*; *3.* 318*n*; *4.* 22, 46, 53, 55, 56, 77, 100, 117, 123, 151, 159, 160, 162, 173, 176, 177, 178, 179, 180, 183, 187, 188, 189, 190, 191, 192, 193, 194, 195, 196, 197, 198, 199, 200, 201, 202, 203, 204, 205, 206*n*, 208, 209, 211, 212, 213, 214, 217, 218-19, 220, 221, 222, 224*n*, 226, 228, 229, 232, 235, 236, 237, 238, 241, 244, 245, 246*n*, 258, 265, 266, 270*n*, 271, 272, 275, 276, 277, 278, 281, 282, 283, 287, 289, 291, 293, 304, 305, 320*n*, 323*n*, 348, 367*n*; *5.* 80, 113, 176, 184, 196, 202; *6.* 56, 60

"November Boughs," *4.* 99, 100, 105, 127, 425

Noyes, Mrs. Ada, *see* Ada Clare

Noyes, Crosby Stuart, *2.* 56, 224, 227; *3.* 88, 170, 280*n*, 437

Nuova Anatologia, *4.* 159*n*

O*ates, Charles G. Letter to, *3.* 58

Observer, The, (London), *6.* 51*n*

"O Captain! My Captain!" *3.* 129, 304; *4.* 148, 427, 430, 440; *5.* 5, 34*n*, 45*n*, 57*n*; *6.* 40*n*, 50*n*

O'Connor, Ellen M., *1.* 10, 59*n*, 63, 83, 108, 130-31, 141, 157, 163, 174, 185, 218, 234, 235, 236, 237, 239, 241, 243, 248, 249, 275*n*, 281, 283, 285, 294, 299, 301, 305, 308, 314, 315, 317, 319, 328, 330, 335, 339, 355, 367, 374, 375, 376, 377; *2.* 7, 15, 26, 32, 35, 36, 39, 41, 43, 49, 55, 64, 65, 80, 83, 85, 92, 99, 103, 116, 127, 128, 145, 162, 182, 184, 193, 195, 196, 198, 204, 205, 206, 207, 208, 224, 226, 254, 260, 264, 281, 284, 286, 292, 296, 308, 315, 316, 335, 338; *3.* 330, 331, 395; *4.* 2, 136, 151, 162, 164, 173, 174, 177, 195, 223, 229, 233, 246, 251, 253, 260, 272, 273, 277, 279, 283, 284, 285, 286, 287, 288, 290, 291, 292, 294, 295, 296, 297, 298, 299, 300, 302, 304, 306, 307, 308, 310, 313, 314, 315, 316-17, 321, 322, 323, 324, 325, 326, 329, 332, 334, 336, 338-39, 340, 346, 351, 353, 354, 356, 357, 363, 364, 365, 367, 368, 370, 372, 373, 376, 377, 378, 382, 384, 389, 394, 397, 398, 399, 401, 402, 407, 431, 432, 436-41; *5.* 22, 90*n*, 91, 92, 94, 95, 100, 108, 127, 132, 140, 144, 146, 184, 190, 220, 228, 229, 238, 239, 240, 263, 266, 333-36, 338-42, 344, 346; *6.* 68. Letters to, *1.* 182-84, 240-41, 243-44, 256-57, 267-68, 269-70, 315-16, 341-42; *2.* 20-21, 48-49, 63-64, 122, 123-24, 229-30, 239-40, 268, 271-72, 275-77, 279, 281, 284-85, 289, 292, 293, 296-97, 298, 302, 303-4, 311, 314-15, 321-22, 342-43; *3.* 19, 24-25, 25-26, 32-33, 54, 65; *4.* 112, 115, 151, 155, 250, 252, 260-61, 277, 288, 300-301, 334, 337, 353, 362-63, 367, 374, 375, 377, 395-96, 401, 406-7; *5.* 44, 45, 90, 93, 96, 145, 189, 264

O'Connor, Henry, *3.* 190

O'Connor, Jean, *1.* 63, 83, 108, 239, 240, 243, 248, 269, 335, 342; *2.* 15, 20, 49, 64, 83, 85, 86, 103, 122, 123, 128, 162, 182, 226, 230, 281; *3.* 330, 331, 341*n*

O'Connor, William D., *1.* 3, 4, 6, 11, 12, 14, 59*n*, 63, 77*n*, 83, 108, 130-31, 141, 157, 163, 174, 182, 185, 191*n*, 218, 235, 237, 240, 242-43, 244, 256*n*, 263*n*, 268, 269, 274*n*, 283, 286, 294, 299, 300, 301, 303, 305, 308, 311, 314, 315, 317, 319, 324, 325, 326, 332, 335, 340, 342, 346*n*, 354, 375, 376, 377, 378; *2.* 3, 15, 26, 32, 35, 36, 39, 41, 43, 48, 51, 55, 58, 64, 66, 76, 78, 80, 83, 91, 109, 122, 123, 124, 145, 158, 162, 181, 184*n*, 192*n*, 214*n*, 227, 230, 236, 286; *3.* 2, 38*n*, 39*n*, 65*n*, 103, 111*n*, 153*n*, 164*n*, 170*n*, 183*n*, 294*n*, 301, 309, 316, 317, 361*n*, 367*n*, 393, 396*n*, 404, 405*n*, 410, 414,447, 448, 449, 450, 451, 452; *4.* 5, 26, 27, 37*n*, 43, 44, 52, 53, 59, 60, 68-69, 71, 73, 74, 75, 77, 78, 79, 81, 87, 94, 95, 97*n*, 100, 106, 108, 109, 110, 114, 115, 118, 125, 126-27, 128,

132, 135, 136, 139, 140, 142, 143, 147, 149,
151, 153, 156, 157, 158, 160, 163, 164*n*, 167,
169*n*, 174, 186, 187, 194, 203, 204, 215, 217,
219, 220, 222, 223, 224, 227, 229, 239, 241,
243, 247, 249, 250, 252, 253, 258, 260-61, 263,
271, 273, 275, 277, 279, 280, 281, 283, 284,
285, 286, 288, 289, 305, 306, 308, 309, 311,
312, 315, 317, 319, 320, 321, 322, 326, 330,
331, 333, 334, 335, 336, 337, 338, 339, 340,
353, 358, 359, 363, 372, 374, 375, 378, 386*n*,
397, 399, 401, 406*n*, 407*n*, 424, 426, 428, 429,
431-35; *5.* 3, 6, 7, 45*n*, 65, 70, 90, 91, 92, 93,
94, 95, 96, 100, 101, 107, 122, 132*n*, 140, 146,
147, 183, 188, 189, 220, 222, 228, 239, 258,
288, 302, 316, 319; *6.* 38. Letters to, *1.* 234,
235-36, 238-39, 241-42, 246-49, 256-58, 272,
284-85, 287-88, 327-30, 338-40, 342-43, 347-49,
351, 355-56; *2.* 13, 48-49, 54-55, 59-60, 85-86,
89-90, 92, 98-99, 102-3, 115-16, 127-28, 130; *3.*
275-77, 279, 282-84, 285-88, 291-92, 293-94,
294-95, 295-98, 300-301, 303-4, 305, 307-8,
311, 312, 313-16, 318-19, 319-20, 321, 325-28,
330, 331-34, 335-37, 338-39, 341-42, 343-44,
346-47, 349, 350, 351-54, 357, 358, 362-63,
377-78, 387, 394-95; *4.* 15, 17-19, 23-24, 26,
29, 43, 45, 54-55, 129, 134, 141, 143-44, 162,
164, 166, 169-73, 175, 177, 184, 188-89, 193,
195-97, 213-14, 217-18, 220, 222-23, 228, 233-
34, 236, 241-42, 246, 272, 274-75, 278, 284-87,
290-304, 306-8, 310-11, 313-24, 326-29, 332-33
Odel, Moses Fowler, *1.* 58, 193, 209
Odets, Clifford, *1.* ix
O'Donovan, William Rudolf, *3.* 118; *5.* 186,
190, 192, 193, 200, 207, 209, 222, 225, 226,
231
O'Dowd, Bernard, *4.* 3; *5.* 3, 7, 65, 127, 158*n*,
331, 332, 334-38, 344. Letters to, *5.* 62, 98-99,
112-13, 138-39, 142-43, 150-51, 167-68, 176,
201, 260
O'Dowd, Eric, *5.* 151, 168, 176
O'Dowd, Eve Fryer, *5.* 62, 113, 138, 150, 168,
176
O'Dowd, Mrs. Neil, *5.* ix
"Of That Blithe Throat of Thine," *3.* 386*n*
O'Grady, Standish James, *2.* 153; *3.* 21, 27,
446; *5.* 104*n*, 213*n*, 348
O'Kane, Thomas, *2.* 263, 273, 275, 345*n*, 363;
5. 297. Letters to, *2.* 244, 294
Oldach, Frederick, *4.* 225, 245, 266, 277, 311;
5. 185, 187. Letters to, *4.* 225, 239-40, 242,
290, 338; *5.* 76, 113-14
"Old Actors, Singers, Shows, &c., in New
York," *5.* 179, 183
"Old Age Echoes," *4.* 385*n*, 394, 427; *5.* 25,
30, 41, 42, 120*n*, 146*n*
"Old Age's Lambent Peaks," *4.* 161, 204, 205,
251, 426
"Old Age's Ship & Crafty Death's," *4.* 261,

262, 267, 393, 426; *5.* 20, 21, 22, 23, 25, 26
"Old Brooklyn Days," *5.* 66, 67
Old Capitol Prison, *1.* 77, 106
"Old Chants," *5.* 118, 137, 183*n*
"Old Man's Rejoinder, An" *5.* 67, 68, 70, 71,
72, 74, 78; *6.* 53*n*
"Old Poets," *5.* 18, 81, 99, 100, 101, 102, 107,
108, 109, 110, 112, 113, 114-15, 119
"Old Salt Kossabone," *4.* 144*n*
Oliver, John, *4.* 439
Olmstead, Harold, *3.* vii, 191*n*
Once A Week, 5. 201*n*, 202*n*. Letter to, *5.* 156
O'Neill, Charles, *5.* 288*n*
"On, on the Same, Ye Jocund Twain!" *5.* 46*n*,
47, 53, 54, 56, 118-19*n*, 201*n*
Onderdonk, Jr., H., *6.* 68
"Orange Buds by Mail from Florida,"
4. 145*n*
"Orbic Literature," *2.* 30, 31, 33
Orbis Litterarum, 1. viii
O'Reardon, W. J., *4.* 439
O'Reilly, John Boyle, *3.* 224, 258, 354, 436,
439, 446, 451; *4.* 57*n*, 100, 102; *5.* 71*n*
"Osceola," *5.* 23*n*
Osgood & Co., James R., *1.* vii; *2.* 321*n*; *3.* 1,
196*n*, 230-31, 236, 237, 238, 239, 241, 247,
249, 253*n*, 257, 260, 274, 275, 276-77, 279,
280, 283, 287, 292, 294, 301*n*, 306*n*, 315, 436,
437, 446, 447; *4.* 235*n*; *5.* 313, 315, 316-17.
Letters to, *3.* 224, 225-27, 227-29, 232, 234-35,
238, 241-43, 255-56, 267-68, 268-70, 270-71,
273, 281
Osler, Thomas, *2.* 248, 252, 253
Osler, Dr. William, *3.* 406*n*; *4.* 51*n*, 147*n*, 174,
175, 177, 179, 187*n*, 207, 212, 215, 221, 224,
227, 229, 232, 240, 241, 242, 243, 245, 246,
260, 328, 329; *5.* 21*n*, 159, 198*n*
"O Star of France," *2.* 110*n*, 121; *5.* 293
Otis, Albert B. Letter to, *2.* 190
Ottinger, G. M., *3.* 151*n*
Otto, William Tod, *1.* 246, 248, 368, 376
"Our Eminent Visitors (Past, Present, and
Future)," *3.* 355-56, 357, 363
"Our Wounded and Sick Soldiers—Visits
among the Hospitals," *1.* 75*n*, 256
"Out from Behind this Mask," *2.* 172*n*
"Out of May's Shows Selected," *4.* 145*n*
"Out of the Cradle Endlessly Rocking," *1.*
328*n*; *2.* 16*n*, 233*n*; *3.* 319*n*, 343; *4.* 5, 67*n*
"Out of the Rolling Ocean the Crowd," *1.*
236*n*
Outing, 3. 355*n*, 391-92, 394, 396
"Over and Through the Burial Chant," *see*
"Interpolation Sounds"
Overland, 5. 162
Overland Monthly, The, 2. 97*n*; *5.* 285*n*. Letter
to, *2.* 94
Owen, Charles Norton, *4.* viii

Pacific Railroad, *2*. 96
Paget, Wal, *4*. 148*n*
Paine, Thomas, *2*. 231*n*; *3*. 61, 75; *5*. 242
Pall Mall Budget, The, 3. 101*n*
Pall Mall Gazette, 4. 52*n*, 55, 62, 63, 85*n*, 102*n*,
  127*n*, 128, 148*n*, 216*n*, 230, 292, 293, 295; *5*.
  40*n*, 46*n*, 244, 280, 341; *6*. 20*n*, 40, 41, 42,
  43*n*, 51*n*
"Pallid Wreath, The," *5*. 145, 146, 148, 149,
  152*n*, 153
Palmer, Courtland, *4*. 141. Letter to, *4*. 142
Palmer, Prof. G. H., *3*. 451
Palmer, Nettie, *5*. 62*n*
Palmer, Nicholas D., *1*. 376
Pardee, Timothy Blair, *3*. 183; *4*. 119*n*, 143,
  144, 146, 178, 229, 239, 360; *5*. 47*n*, 308
Pardoe, Julia, *4*. 216, 219, 224
Parepa-Rose, Euphrosyne, *1*. 324
Parker, Aurelia, *1*. 292, 369
Parker, Lt. Col. E. S., *1*. 253*n*
Parker, Erastus Otis, *1*. 289-91, 302, 307-8, 319,
  370
Parnell, Charles Steward, *5*. 119*n*, 132
Parton, James, *1*. 44*n*; *2*. 89-90
Parton, Mrs. James, *6*. 68
"Passage to India," *2*. 5, 77*n*, 94, 96, 100, 101*n*,
  108, 116*n*, 144, 274; *3*. 92, 129; *4*. 343; *6*. 11
Patent Office Hospital, *1*. 70, 82
Path, The, 4. 57*n*
Pathfinder, 1. 236*n*
"Patroling Barnegat," *3*. 204, 219*n*
Patten, Robert L., *3*. vii
Patterson, Theodore. Letters to, *3*. 416-17
Patti, Carlotta, *2*. 191
Paul, Saint, *5*. 75
"Paumanok," *4*. 144*n*
Payne, William W., *4*. 320*n*, 438; *5*. 335
Payton, George, *see* George Peyton
Peabody, George, *2*. 91
Peak, William, *3*. 131
Pearsall, G. F. E. Letter to, *3*. 49-50
Pease, Mrs. Augusta W., *5*. 258*n*
Pease, Ben, *3*. 112*n*, 432
Pease, Edward R. Letters to, *3*. 347-48, 370
Peck, Mrs. D. C., *3*. 437
Peck, John L., *3*. 434
Peddrick, W. C. ("Wash"), *2*. 280
Peirson, Clayton Wesley, *4*. 269*n*
Pennsylvania Academy of the Fine Arts, *5*.
  155*n*
Pepys, Samuel, *4*. 124, 129; *5*. 195*n*
Percy, Florence (Elizabeth Chase Allen), *1*.
  303; *2*. 34*n*
"Perfect Human Voice, The," *see* "The Human
  Voice"
Perkins Mr., *1*. 11, 127, 142, 158
Perkins, Jr., Mrs. Joseph R., *1*. ix; *2*. vi

Perkins, Julia A. J., *5*. 336
Perot, Mrs. Elliston L., *3*. 114
Perrigo, George W., *1*. 378
Perry, Bliss, *1*. viii; *2*. 330*n*
Perry, Jeannette B., *5*. 336
Perry, Nora, *2*. 64, 66
"Personalism," *2*. 15*n*, 18-20, 21, 22, 23, 26, 29,
  31, 32, 34
Petersen, Clemens, *2*. 173, 282, 287, 295, 310;
  3. 257
Peterson, Arthur, *3*. 139, 171, 254
Peterson, Henry, *3*. 386*n*
Petrola, Salvador, *2*. 247
Peyton, George, *2*. 132, 368
Pfaff, Charles, *5*. 44*n*
Pfaff's Restaurant, *1*. 10, 11, 74*n*, 75*n*, 84*n*, 124;
  2. 344
Philadelphia *American, 5*. 42*n*
Philadelphia *City Item, 1*. 54*n*; *2*. 257
Philadelphia *Daily News, 3*. 384*n*; *4*. 113, 115
Philadelphia *Evening Bulletin, 3*. 281*n*; *4*. 230
Philadelphia *Evening Telegraph, 3*. 408*n*
Philadelphia *Inquirer, 5*. 50*n*, 183
Philadelphia *Ledger, 2*. 226
Philadelphia *Press, 3*. 150*n*, 170*n*, 175*n*, 177*n*,
  181*n*, 184*n*, 203*n*, 263*n*, 275*n*, 280*n*, 293, 296-
  97, 304*n*, 340*n*, 375, 378*n*, 379*n*, 387*n*, 397,
  402*n*, 434, 436, 437, 438; *4*. 24, 25*n*, 28, 36*n*,
  62*n*, 64, 67*n*, 96-97, 115, 135, 221, 224, 280,
  291, 295, 314, 327, 389, 390*n*, 425; *5*. 19*n*,
  23*n*, 24, 64*n*, 101*n*, 105, 108*n*, 130, 155*n*,
  201*n*, 222*n*, 259*n*, 260*n*, 316; *6*. 43*n*, 54*n*.
  Letters to, *3*. 275; *4*. 35; *5*. 108
Philadelphia *Public Ledger, 3*. 52*n*, 54*n*, 142*n*,
  146*n*, 233, 240, 241*n*, 254, 256, 262, 263*n*,
  434; *4*. 15*n*, 149*n*; *5*. 46*n*, 186*n*, 222*n*
Philadelphia *Record, 4*. 325; *5*. 38*n*, 265*n*
Philadelphia *Times, 3*. 76*n*, 146*n*, 161, 281*n*,
  371; *4*. 232; *5*. 108, 344
Philips, Melville, *4*. 224*n*, 390*n*; *5*. 23*n*, 200*n*,
  331, 342. Letters to, *5*. 27-28, 201
Phillips, Mr., *3*. 75
Phillips, Mrs. Francis Frederic, *1*. ix; *2*. vi
Phillips, Wendell, *1*. 160*n*
Philp, James B. (or Franklin), *1*. 333; *2*. 218
Philp & Solomon, *1*. 333*n*; *2*. 361. Letter to, *5*.
  292
Photographic Times, 5. 347
Piatt, John J., *1*. 281
Pictorial World, The, 2. 372
Piercy, Mrs. Henry R., *1*. 97
Pierrepont, Edwards, *1*. 334*n*
Pilgrim's Progress, 2. 90
Pillsbury, Parker, *3*. 438, 450
Pintard, Phoebe, *2*. 210
Piper & Co., William H., *2*. 113*n*, 244*n*, 263,
  273, 277*n*. Letter to, *2*. 144

Pittman, Mrs. J. L., *5.* 347

Plato, *5.* 149*n*, 205; 6. 57

Platt, Isaac Hull. Letter to, *3.* 190

Pleasanton, Gen. Alfred, *1.* 149

Pleasants, Matthew F., *1.* 284, 292*n*; *2.* 43*n*, 106, 117; *5.* 289

Poch, Carmen, *1.* 307*n*

Poe, Edgar Allan, *1.* 26*n*; *2.* 64*n*, 121*n*, 342*n*; *3.* 179, 193

Poems by Walt Whitman (Rossetti's edition), *1.* 294*n*, 346-49, 350-51, 352-54; *2.* 1, 13, 15, 16-17, 20, 21-22, 29*n*, 133, 218*n*; *4.* 53*n*; *5.* 296

Poems of American Patriotism, 3. 304*n*

Poems of Walt Whitman, [*Selected.*] *The, 4.* 22*n*, 53*n;* 6. 32*n,* 39

Poet as Craftsman, The, 4. 32*n*

Poet-Lore, 4. 271, 367; *5.* 64, 86, 94-95, 115*n*

"Poetry of America, 1776-1876," *3.* 116, 117

Poetry of the Future, The, 3. 204, 205, 209, 275*n*

"Poetry of the Period, The," *3.* 73

"Poetry To-day in America," *3.* 132*n*, 204, 205, 209; 6. 53

Poets of America, 3. 192*n*

"Poet's Recreation, A," *3.* 36*n*, 110*n*, 118*n*, 122-26, 127, 128, 129

"Poet's 68th Year, A," *4.* 96, 425

"Poet's Western Trip, A," *3.* 170*n*

Poets' Tribute to Garfield, The, 3. 232*n*

Pond, Major James B., *4.* 91, 430; *5.* 260. Letters to, 4. 84, 86

Pooley, Lt. Samuel M., *1.* 60, 252-53, 255

Poore, Benjamin Perley. Letter to, *3.* 22

Pope, Alexander, *3.* 332*n*

Pope, Charles, *3.* 434

Popoff, Dr. P., *3.* 342*n*

Porter, Rev. Elbert Stothoff, *1.* 43

Porter, Jane, *2.* 259*n*

Porter, Linn B., *3.* 295*n*

Porter & Coates, *3.* 198

Posnett, Hutcheson Macaulay, *4.* 42*n*

Post, Charles W., *3.* 434

Post Hospital, *1.* 280, 331

Postmaster, Camden, N.J. Letter to, *5.* 306

Potter, Edward T., *4.* 34*n*, 429. Letters to, 4. 138, 185

Potter, Gen. Robert B., *1.* 88*n,* 104

Pound, Ezra, *5.* 119*n*

Powell, Frederick York, *3.* 326, 451; *4.* 436

Powell, Rosamund E., *4.* 65*n,* 156

"Prairie Sunset, A," *4.* 144*n*

"Prairies in Poetry, The," *3.* 277*n*

Pratt, Alfred, *1.* 263-64, 311, 376, 378; *2.* 367. Letters to, *1.*264-66, 286-87, 333-34, 345-46; *2.* 82, 93

Pratt, Mrs. Charles Stuart, *3.* 432

Pratt, N. M. & John B., *2.* 367. Letters to, *1.* 263-64; *2.* 93

"Prayer of Columbus," *2.* 5, 259, 262*n*, 264, 269, 272, 277, 278, 282, 287, 295, 305, 310

Prentice, George D., *3.* 212

Prentiss, T. M. *5.* 342

Preston, Paul, *2.* 53*n*

Price, Abby A., *1.* viii, 10, 42, 135, 141, 148, 151, 173, 184, 240, 248, 285, 300, 306, 319, 328, 340, 366, 378; *2.* 20, 48, 49, 64, 85, 98, 99, 103, 197-98, 202, 224*n*, 315, 360, 363; *3.* 221; *4.* 65*n*; 6. 48*n*. Letters to, *1.* 49-50, 161-64, 253-54, 282-83, 291-92, 301-2, 318-19, 321-22, 335; *2.* 25-27, 44, 66, 80-81, 83, 120, 200, 241-42, 264, 266-67, 281-82; *3.* 62

Price, Arthur, *1.* 161, 282, 292, 319, 335; *2.* 120, 149, 156, 225*n*; *3.* 234*n*, 304; 6. 48. Letter to, 4. 65

Price, Edmund, *1.* 42, 292, 301; *2.* 26; *3.* 222, 304

Price, Emily (Emma), *1.* 50, 135, 141, 148, 161, 173, 253, 282, 292, 297, 301, 308, 319, 322; *2.* 20, 26, 43, 66, 80, 83, 103, 200; *3.* 222, 304; 6. 48

Price, Helen E., *1.* 10, 42, 50, 162, 253, 282, 292, 300, 301, 319, 322; *2.* 26, 43, 66, 80, 83, 123, 191*n*, 200, 201*n*, 209*n*, 220*n*, 225*n*, 242; *3.* 234*n*, 436; *4.* 65; *5.* 339. Letters to, *2.* 266-67; *3.* 62, 221-22, 252, 304-5; *4.* 161-62; 6. 48

Probasco, Louis, *1.* 67, 87, 101, 131, 216

Probasco, Samuel, *1.* 66*n*, 365, 367

Progress (Philadelphia), *3.* 23*n*, 150*n*, 178, 275*n*, 313*n*, 355*n*

Prometheus, 4. 268

"Proud Music of the Storm," *2.* 71*n*, 73, 77, 81*n*; *5.* 293*n*; 6. 6

Proudfit, Daniel L., *3.* 432, 449

Providence Hospital, *5.* 287

Providence (R.I.) *Journal, 4.* 109*n*

Publisher's Weekly, 4. 221*n*

Putnam, Rev. A. P., *3.* 441

Putnam, Avery D., *2.* 122*n*

Putnam, George Palmer. Letter to, *2.* 75

Putnam's Monthly Magazine, 1. viii, 343; *2.* 37, 75*n*

Putnam's Sons, G. P., *3.* 433, 444

Pyne, Mr., *1.* 150

Quartermaster Hospital, *1.* 276

Queen Elizabeth, 1. 300

"Queries to My Seventieth Year," *4.* 145*n*

Quigley, Mr., *4.* 164

Rabelais, François, *3.* 340*n*

Rackliffe (or Racliffe), William, *1.* 194, 302

Radical, The, 1. 273; *2.* 99, 168; *3.* 340*n;* 4. 92*n*

Radical Review, The, 2. 317*n*, 338*n*

Rae, E. H., *1.* 78

Ramsdell, Hiram J., *1.* 329, 370, 378; 5. 294. Letter to, 5. 291

Rand & Avery, *1.* 52; 3. 237, 238, 239, 244, 246, 247, 248, 296, 312. Letter to, 3. 280

Randall, John K., *3.* 377*n*

Ransom, Frank H., *3.* 436

Rathbone, Mr., *4.* 255

Rathbone, P. H., *4.* 255*n*

Rauch, Fred W., *3.* 433, 445

Rawlins, Gen. John Aaron, *2.* 88

Ray, Judge Charles A., *3.* 297

Ray, Mrs. Eleanor, *1.* x

Raymenton, Dr. W. H., *6.* 69

Raymond, Mr., *1.* 11, 142

Raymond(?), Charles A., *3.* 443

Raymond, Henry J., *1.* 299*n*, 300*n*, 303, 324, 341; 3. 320

Raymond, Lewis, *see* Lewis Wraymond

Reade, Charles, *2.* 124

"Real Summer Openings," *3.* 152*n*, 153, 157*n*

Ream, Vinnie. Letter to, 6. 8

Reamer, Alexander K., *3.* 452

Rean, F. W., *4.* 441; 5. 338

"Red Jacket (from Aloft)," *3.* 378, 379, 380

Redden, Val. Stuart, *5.* 346

Reddie, Cecil, *5.* 342

Redfield, James S., *2.* 101*n*, 131*n*, 186*n*, 214, 273*n*, 364, 372. Letter to, 2. 118

Redgate, Stephen, *1.* 112, 366

Redpath, James, *1.* 188*n*, 365, 372, 373, 374; 2. 30*n*; 3. 403, 439, 452, 453; 4. 21, 48*n*, 55, 425, 429, 431; 5. 164; 6. 68. Letters to, *1.* 121-23, 164, 171-72; 3. 403, 412; 4. 36, 37, 39; 6. 33

Reed, John H., *4.* vii

Reed, Milford C., *1.* 373; 4. 346, 347, 427, 439

Reeder, W. M. *5.* 346

Rees Welsh & Co., *3.* 294, 295, 296, 298*n*, 300*n*, 301, 303, 306*n*, 310*n*, 313-14, 447, 448; 5. 316. Letters to, 3. 291, 292

Reeves & Turner, *5.* 252*n*

Reich, Jacques, *5.* 24, 333

Reich, Lorenz, *3.* 439, 453

Reid, Ogden, *3.* 152*n*

Reid, Whitelaw, *2.* 364, 371; 3. 110, 283, 292*n*, 315*n*, 433, 434, 441, 443. Letters to, 2. 317; 3. 23, 53, 129, 137, 140, 152, 153-54, 181, 281

Reidel (Reisdell?), William, *3.* 434

Rein, Mrs. *2.* 49, 281

Reinhalter & Co., J. E., *5.* 95, 105, 203*n*, 225, 264*n*, 337, 341, 345

Reisdell, William, *3.* 176. Letter to, *3.* 176

Reisser Restaurant, *5.* 87, 91, 130

Reminiscences of Abraham Lincoln, 4. 21, 32

Reminiscences of Walt Whitman, 4. 33*n*

Repplier, Agnes, *5.* 259

Resnick, Nathan, *1.* 340*n*

"Resurgemus," *3.* 388*n*

"Return of the Heroes, The," *1.* 336, 337, 356; 4. 405; 5. 176*n*, 292

"Revenge and Requital: A Tale of a Murderer Escaped," *1.* 26*n*

Review of Reviews, The, 4. 1; 5. 20, 29, 32, 145, 146*n*, 157, 170, 182, 219, 229, 238

La Revue Independante, 4. 248, 249

Reynell, Charles W., *3.* 34, 44, 51

Reynolds, Clare, *5.* 182*n*, 332, 341

Reynolds, Mrs. Henry, *2.* 366

Reynolds, Walter Whitman, *2.* 361, 362, 367, 368, 369

Rhinds, Mrs., *1.* 340

Rhodes, Albert. Letter to, 5. 279; 6. 61

Rhodes, John H., *1.* 98

Rhys, Ernest, *3.* 410, 452, 453; 4. 32, 68-69, 72, 74, 78, 81, 94, 99, 107, 114, 120, 126, 127-28, 130, 132, 133, 134, 135, 136, 137, 139, 140-41, 144, 145, 146, 147, 149, 150, 151, 152, 153, 156, 160, 163, 168, 172, 189, 190, 192, 207, 254, 270, 293, 366, 394, 407, 425-41; 5. 46, 158, 164, 223, 242, 331, 334, 336; 6. 18*n*, 51*n*, 53*n*. Letters to, 3. 407; 4. 22, 52, 66-67, 98, 117, 192-93, 211, 254, 358-59, 367; 5. 22; 6. 32, 36-37, 38, 39, 40, 41, 42-43, 44-45, 47, 49, 50-51, 53

Rice, Charles Allen Thorndike, *3.* 205, 209, 402*n*, 412, 435, 436, 446, 452; 4. 22, 32, 36*n*, 48*n*, 275, 436. Letter to, 3. 403

Rich, Theodore, *1.* 372

Richardson, Jack, *3.* 435, 436, 445

Richardson, Kate, *1.* 376

Richardson, Louis G., *5.* 349

Richeton, Leon, *3.* 436, 446

Richmond (Va.) *Sentinel,* 1. 248*n*

"Riddle Song, A," *3.* 178, 179*n*, 180

Rideing, William H., *5.* 99*n*, 113*n*, 133*n*, 332, 336, 338

Riegel, Calving P., *1.* 115*n*

Riker, Silvanus S., *2.* 106

Riley, Emma, *3.* 450

Riley, Thomas, *2.* 54

Riley, William Harrison, *3.* 149-50, 305*n*, 444; 4. 432; 5. 77*n*. Letter to, 3. 148-49

Ripley, Philip, *3.* 431

Ristori, Adelaide, *1.* 300, 306

Ritter, Mrs. Fanny Raymond, *3.* 153*n*, 174, 349, 431. Letter to, 5. 306-7

Ritter, Frédéric Louis, *3.* 153*n*, 174; 5. 306-7

Rives, Franklin, *2.* 257, 259

"Roaming in Thought," *3.* 139

"Robert Burns," *3.* 318, 320; 4. 55

"Robert Burns As Poet and Person," *3.* 318*n*; 4. 39*n*, 43, 55, 425

Robert le Diable, 2. 169

Roberto Devereux, 1. 159; *2.* 169

Roberts, Charles H., *5.* 346

Roberts, Howard, *3.* 175

Roberts, Milton S., *1. 375*

Roberts, Morley C., *4.* 429

Roberts, R. D., *4.* 29; *5.* 50, 207

Roberts Bros., *2.* 156*n*, 244, 321. Letter to, *2.* 139

Robertson, Mr., *2.* 28*n*

Robertson, John, *5.* 179*n*

Robinson, Mr., *3.* 56*n*

Robinson, Harriet W., *3.* 206*n*

Robinson, John(?) B., *3.* 451

Robinson, Nugent, *4.* 430; *5.* 201

Robinson, Tracy, *5.* 338

Robinson, William, *5.* 349

Roche, Regina Marie, *2.* 245*n*

Rochester (N. Y.) *Evening Express, 2.* 30, 33*n*, 44*n*

Roe, J. E., *5.* 263*n*

Rogers(?), Amos, *3.* 306

Rogers, Mrs. Elizabeth W., *3.* 278, 306; *4.* 163; *5.* 317

Rogers(?), Jane, *3.* 278, 306; *5.* 317

Rogers, John M., *2.* 362, 364, 368, 369, 372; *3.* 430; 431, 440, 443

Rolleston, T. W. H., *3.* 59*n*, 259*n*, 320, 322*n*, 349, 362*n*, 388, 404, 410, 433, 435, 436, 437, 438, 444, 445, 446, 447, 448, 449, 450, 451, 452; *4.* 27*n*, 31, 207, 209, 212, 220, 237, 265, 270, 272, 287, 288, 289, 295, 319, 330, 352*n*, 401*n*, 403*n*, 404, 427, 433, 436, 437, 440; *5.* 33*n*, 104*n*, 122*n*, 213, 306*n*, 348; *6.* 30*n*. Letters to, *3.* 254, 260-61, 318, 363, 369, 375, 377; *5.* 320-21

Romance of King Arthur, The, 4. 66-67; *6.* 32

Rome, Andrew, *1.* 337; *5.* 63, 251, 252, 253, 335. Letter to, *2.* 94

Rome, Thomas, *5.* 63, 251. Letter to, *2.* 94

Romeo and Juliet, 3. 249*n*

Romsey, Mr., *4.* 39

Roosevelt, Theodore, *3.* 53*n*, 408*n*

Rose, Mrs. E. L., *5.* 115

Rose, Dr. George S., *1.* 94

Rose, James Anderson, *3.* 96*n*

Rose, Margaret, *3.* vii, 304*n*

Rosenberg, Carl, *2.* 286

Rosencrans, Gen. William Starke, *1.* 68, 151, 156, 158

Rossetti, Dante Gabriel, *2.* 138*n*; *3.* 58*n*, 60, 62*n*, 179*n*; *4.* 32

Rossetti, Willim Michael, *1.* 4, 5, 14, 294*n*, 332*n*, 335*n*, 346-47, 348-49, 378, 379; *2.* 1, 2, 4, 13, 16, 20, 30*n*, 31*n*, 44*n*, 55*n*, 87*n*, 98*n*, 99*n*, 130, 133*n*, 134*n*, 136-37, 140*n*, 152*n*, 153*n*, 154*n*, 164-65, 168, 332, 337*n*, 340*n*, 344*n*, 363, 364, 366, 367, 368, 369, 372, 373;

3. 22*n*, 31, 32, 48*n*, 63*n*, 64*n*, 72, 74, 128, 148, 174, 203, 301, 355*n*, 399, 404, 407*n*, 409, 410, 411, 414, 430, 431, 434, 437, 439, 440, 441, 442, 451, 452, 453; *4.* 18, 29*n*, 32, 44, 49, 52*n*, 115*n*, 163, 352, 428, 429; *5.* 33*n*, 127, 220*n*, 301, 305; *6.* 13, 15*n*, 25*n*, 66. Letters to, *1.* 350-51, 352-54; *2.* 91-92, 131-32, 159-62, 327-28; *3.* 20-21, 23, 28-30, 33-36, 37-38, 42, 43-45, 51-52, 55-56, 59-60, 129, 130, 409; *4.* 30; *5.* 296, 302

Rossi, Ernesto, *3.* 249*n*

Rothman, Fannie, *2.* v, 72*n*

Round Table, The, 1. 270*n*, 320; *3.* 327

Rousseau, Jean-Jacques, *3.* 308

Routledge, Edmund, *1.* 355; *2.* 17. Letters to, *2.* 13-14, 24

Routledge & Sons, George, *1.* 379; *2.* 13. Letters to, *1.* 355; *2.* 17-18, 19

Rowland, John A., *1.* 311; *2.* 109, 111

Rowlandson, H. (T. W. H. Rolleston), *4.* 27*n*

Rowley, Charles, *4.* 80

Roy, Prof. G. Ross, *3.* ix, 429

Royal Academy, *4.* 120, 121

Royce, Josiah, *5.* 128*n*

Rubens, Peter Paul, *4.* 157*n*

Ruff, Josephine, *4.* 80*n*

Ruggles, Dr. Edward, *1.* 90, 143*n*, 165*n*, 190*n*, 251, 253*n*, 312, 316, 319-20

Rush, Jr., George, *4.* 200*n*, 228*n*, 371; *5.* 334

Ruskin, John, *2.* 99*n*; *3.* 63*n*, 149, 150, 174, 305, 307, 348*n*; *4.* 33, 34, 122; *5.* 77, 163*n*

Russell, Jr., Benjamin, *1.* 370, 378

Russell, Bertrand, *3.* 407*n*

Russell, Charles H., *1.* 11, 83, 84, 124, 126, 142, 159; *2.* 108*n*

Russell, Earl (John Francis Stanley), *3.* 406*n*

Russell, Dr. LeBaron, *1.* 121*n*, 155, 161, 164, 175, 254-55, 256, 374. Letters to, *1.* 188, 199-200

Russell (?), Thomas, *2.* 368

Russell, W. Clarke, *1.* 354*n*

Rutherford, Mark, *see* William Hale White

Ryan, Gen. Washington, *2.* 257

Ryder, Miss, *5.* 75

Ryder, Jr., Anson, *1.* 369, 370, 377, 378; *3.* 436; *5.* 75. Letters to, *1.* 258, 276-77; *2.* 76; *5.* 285-86, 290-91

Ryerson, Fred S., *4.* 438

Ryman, F. S., *4.* 432

S., L. S., *3.* 438

S., W. A., *4.* 221*n*

"Sail Out for Good, Eidólon Yacht!" *5.* 59, 118*n*, 137*n*, 140

Sailer, Charles C., *2.* 167

Saint Botolph Club, *4.* 140*n*

St. Clair, Charlotte, *1*. 377
Saint-Gaudens, Augustus, *4*. 83*n*, 87
St. John (New Brunswick) *Press*, *3*. 435
St. Louis *Post-Dispatch*, *3*. 167*n*
St. Louis *Republican*, *3*. 164*n*
Ste. Marie, Henry, *1*. 320
Saintsbury, George, *2*. 314*n*, 318*n*; *4*. 30*n*; *5*. 299*n*
Salaman, Mr., *3*. 56*n*
Salesman, *1*. 37*n*
"Salut au Monde," *3*. 369*n*
Sammis, Dr. O. K., *1*. 88, 371. Letter to, *2*. 23
Sampson, Low, Marston, Low & Searle, *2*. 118*n*, 273*n*, 370; *6*. 10. Letter to, *6*. 12
Sanborn, Franklin B., *3*. 39-40, 244-45, 280*n*, 288, 436, 437, 445; *4*. 70, 140*n*, 152*n*, 220*n*, 249, 252, 253, 256, 258, 270, 305, 396, 436; *5*. 80, 161. Letters to, *3*. 185, 316
Sanborn, Kate, *3*. 321*n*
Sand, George, *2*. 265*n*; *4*. 107
Sands, John, *see* William Hutchinson
San Francisco *Bulletin*, *4*. 270, 271
San Francisco *Examiner*, *5*. 338
Sappho, *4*. 304*n*
Sarony's, *3*. 126, 135*n*, 140*n*, 432, 443; *4*. 402*n*; *5*. 39; *6*. 47
Sarrazin, Bernard, *4*. viii, 330*n*; *5*. ix
Sarrazin, Gabriel, *2*. 367; *4*. 98*n*, 230*n*, 272*n*, 273, 276, 279, 281, 283, 284-85, 286, 287, 289, 293, 295, 298, 330, 331, 332, 339, 352, 372, 379, 384, 394, 401, 409*n*, 436, 437; *5*. 32, 33*n*, 35, 39, 81, 83, 104, 1-22*n*, 127, 150-51, 181, 200*n*, 213, 228, 335, 338, 343. Letter to, *4*. 330-31; *5*. 80, 141, 220
Sartoris, Mr., *3*. 161
Saturday Evening Post, *1*. 11
Saturday Night (Philadelphia), *3*. 115*n*
Saturday Review of Politics, Literature, Science, and Art, *2*. 28*n*; *4*. 304, 305, 306
Saunders (or Sanders), Frederick, *1*. 221-22
Saunders, John, *2*. 319
Sawyer, Thomas P., *1*. 331, 366, 373, 375. Letters to, *1*. 90-94, 106-7, 139, 185-86
Saxton, Maj. Samuel Willard, *2*. 120
Sayle, Wellesley, *4*. 435
Schabelitz, J., *4*. 220, 270; *6*. 30*n*
Schiller, Friedrich von, *3*. 21*n*
Schilling, Agnes, *5*. 130*n*
Schliemann, Heinrich, *5*. 259
Schmidt, Rudolf, *1*. viii; *2*. 1, 4, 147*n*, 297*n*, 369, 370, 371, 372; *3*. 316, 317, 322*n*, 362*n*, 430, 437, 441, 447, 448; *4*. 439; *6*. 10. Letters to, *2*. 143-44, 150-53, 163-64, 172-73, 175-77, 185-86, 269-70, 282-83, 286-88, 295, 304-5, 309-10, 337-38; *3*. 21, 54-55, 188, 257-58, 310-11; *4*. 408
Schneider, Louis, *2*. 247

Schneider, Mrs. William F., *3*. vii, 322*n*
Schoff, Stephen Alonzo, *1*. 52
Scholl, Emil, *3*. 436
Schuchhardt, C., *5*. 259*n*
Schuyler, Montgomery, *3*. 110, 452
de Schweinitz, Dr. G. E., *5*. 243-44
Scott, C. L., *1*. 12, 373
Scott, John A., *3*. 206*n*. Letter to, *6*. 23
Scott, Sir Walter, *2*. 88, 335; *3*. 179*n*; *4*. 86*n*, 383; *5*. 282*n*
Scott, Walter (publisher), *3*. 407*n*, 409*n*; *4*. 22, 52, 74, 98, 103*n*, 117, 176, 192, 358, 367; *5*. 166; *6*. 36-37, 44-45
Scott, William B., *2*. 99*n*, 340*n*; *3*. 44, 51
Scott & Williams, *1*. 378
Scott-Moncrieff, Elizabeth J., *3*. 42, 440
Scottish Art Review, The, *4*. 244*n*, 270*n*, 277, 358
Scottish Review, The, *3*. 355
Scovel, Harry Sidney, *3*. 435, 445
Scovel, James Matlack, *2*. 337*n*; *3*. 39*n*, 105, 119*n*, 177*n*, 191, 196*n*, 199, 215, 353*n*, 387, 432, 433, 434, 443, 444, 445, 446, 451, 452; *4*. 15, 16, 29, 88*n*, 429, 431, 435; *5*. 75, 333, 334, 336, 340, 349. Letters to, *3*. 63-64, 389; *5*. 306
Scribner, Armstrong & Co. Letter to, *5*. 303
Scribner's, *1*. 257. Letter to, *3*. 81
Scribner's Monthly, *1*. 343*n*; *2*. 233; *3*. 66*n*, 76*n*, 110*n*, 120, 141, 144*n*, 163*n*, 171, 179, 193, 195, 198*n*, 200, 214*n*, 218*n*, 251*n*, 282, 316, 317, 408*n*; *4*. 15; *5*. 49, 137, 140, 153, 155, 162, 332
Scull, Walter Delaplaine, *4*. 388, 440
"Sea Captains, Young and Old" ("Song of All Seas, All Ships"), *2*. 204*n*, 212
Sears, George E., *5*. 333, 344
Sears, J. C., *5*. 335
Sears, Mrs. J. C., *5*. 53*n*
Secular Review, *6*. 28*n*
Secularist, *3*. 44, 52, 431
Seeger, Dr. Ferdinand, *3*. 38, 45, 440, 441; *6*. 13
Seigfried, Mr., *3*. 192
Sellinghast, C. B. Letter to, *2*. 22
Selwyn, George (WW's pseudonym), *3*. 387*n*
Semmes, Capt. Raphael, *1*. 87
Sempers, Charles T., *4*. 143*n*, 432
Sequard, Dr., *4*. 401
Seward, William H., *1*. 10, 61, 73-74, 78, 83, 171, 254. Letter to, *1*. 41-42. Letter from R. W. Emerson to, *1*. 65-66
Sewell, Gen. William J., *3*. 431, 434, 450
Seybold, Ernest Denton, *5*. 349
Seymour, Gov. Horatio, *1*. 145*n*; *2*. 36
Shakespeare, William, *1*. 257; *2*. 111; *3*. 219, 307, 340*n*, 351*n*, 394; *4*. 43, 70, 118, 127, 187*n*, 213*n*, 295, 396; *5*. 86, 178, 183, 265*n*, 266

"Shakspere-Bacon's Cipher," 4. 119, 243n, 425; 5. 25
"Shakspere for America," 5. 64n, 86, 94-95, 101, 115n
Shambaugh, Mr., 5. 289
Shannon, Jr., Dr. Edgar F., 2. 184n
Sharkland, Robert, 3. 227
Sharp(?), 3. 299n
Sharp, Ben K., 3. 6, 194
Sharp, William, 5. 183, 184, 347
Sharpe, Elizabeth J., 4. 429
Shaw, Albert D., 3. 436
Shaw, George Bernard, 1. 1; 4. 127n
Shedd, Henry, 2. 103, 109, 113
Sheer, George, 3. 94
Sheldon & Co., 1. 336n; 2. 32n, 366. Letter to, 2. 34
Shelley, Percy Bysshe, 2. 153n; 4. 165n, 330
Shepard, Col. Elliott F., 1. 262, 368, 376; 3. 110
Shephard, Charles E., 3. 437
Shephard, Esther, 4. 106n
Sheppard, C. W., 3. 60, 430, 431
Sheridan, Gen. Philip Henry, 4. 198, 200
Sheridan, Richard Brinsley, 4. 18
Sherman, Caroline K., 4. 402n, 440
Sherman, Senator John, 6. 11n
Sherman, Gen. William Tecumseh, 1. 261, 264; 4. 316
Sherman & Co., 3. 296, 298n, 330n
Shiells, Robert, 4. 124
Shillaber, Benjamin Penhallow, 1. 191, 255, 256, 374
"Ship Ahoy!" 5. 153, 154
Shivers, Dr. C. H., 4. 16
Shoemaker & Co., J. M., 4. 267n
Shoemaker, W. L., 4. 429
Sholes, C. H. Letter to, 3. 181
Sholes, Hiram, 1. 91, 93, 378. Letter to, 1. 331-32
Shore, Eli, 5. 341
Shorrock, Thomas, 5. 96n, 244, 245
Sidney, Sir Philip, 4. 354n
Sierra Grande Mining Company, 3. 346n; 6. 69
Sigel, Gen. Franz, 1. 226
"Sight in Camp in the Daybreak Gray and Dim, A," 3. 272n
Sill, James L., 4. 438
Sillard, Robert M., 5. 336, 346
Silver, Louis H., 3. ix, 429
Silver, Rollo G., 1. viii, ix, 261n; 2. v, vi, 40n, 266n, 342n; 3. vii, ix, 152n, 347n, 429; 4. viii, 19n; 5. ix, 211n
"Silver and Salmon-Tint," 2. 204n, 260n, 262n
Simmons, Horace C., 4. 436
Simonson, Joseph M., 2. 34
Simpson, Abraham, 1. 261n, 270n, 370, 377,

378; 2. 365 6. 4. Letter to, 1. 330-31
Simpson, Theresa C., 3. 42, 51, 440
Sims, Palin H., 3. 452
Sims, Capt. Samuel H., 1. 63n, 104, 167, 212, 222, 241n; 5. 285
Sinclair, Gregg M., 3. ix, 429
Sing(?), Julius, 2. 367
"Singer in the Prison, The," 1. 324n
"Singing Thrush, The," (later "Wandering at Noon"), 2. 204n, 206
Skinner, Charles M. Letter to, 3. 385-86
Skinner, William C., 3. 451
"Slang in America," 3. 403n, 409n
"Sleepers, The," 3. 270n
Sleeptalker, The, 5. 282-83
Slenker, Elmina D., 5. 349
Sloane, Charles F., 4. 432
Small, Alvah H., 1. 373
Smalley, G. W., 2. 30n
Smith (Brooklyn builder?), 2. 237
Smith (Brooklyn merchant), 1. 35
Smith, A. L., 5. 69
Smith Aaron, 1. 249, 370, 375, 376
Smith, Alexander, 4. 399
Smith, Alys, 3. 326, 329, 345, 355, 360, 365, 367n, 370, 372, 373, 395, 401, 407n; 4. 17, 28, 39, 42, 48, 52, 80, 92, 98, 99, 104, 107, 111, 120, 122, 126, 130, 163, 170, 181, 186, 281, 323n, 324, 349, 385, 388, 389, 393, 399, 403, 404, 440; 5. 20, 21, 23, 27, 47, 52, 53, 56, 70, 223, 225n, 230, 320, 333, 335. Letter to, 4. 324
Smith, Annie Taiman, 3. 442
Smith, Bethuel, 1. 367, 368, 373, 374, 375, 376; 2. 364, 372. Letters to, 1. 149-50; 2. 318-19
Smith, Christopher, 1. 375, 376
Smith, Mrs. Donald F., 5. 299n
Smith, E. J., 5. 347
Smith, Edgar M., 3. 234n, 236n
Smith, George, 2. 103, 113
Smith, Mrs. Hannah W., 3. 321n, 326, 329, 366n, 371n; 4. 168, 323, 324, 437; 5. 225n
Smith, Huntington, 4. 437
Smith, J. L., 6. 69
Smith, J. W., 5. 102n
Smith, Lizzie H., 1. 375
Smith, Lloyd, 3. 321n; 4. 89
Smith, L. Logan. Letter to, 4. 137
Smith, Logan Pearsall, 3. 321n, 326, 329, 345, 355, 365, 370, 373, 401; 4. 31, 48, 52, 58, 76, 92, 120, 126, 129, 165, 169, 194, 212, 251, 363, 364, 373, 434, 435, 436; 5. 6, 20, 21, 52, 53, 56, 70, 74, 76, 115, 223, 225n, 230, 269, 332, 336, 337, 338, 341, 344, 346; 6. 50. Letters to, 4. 104-5, 116; 5. 69-70
Smith, Marian, 1. 375, 376; 2. 371, 372
Smith, Mary Whitall, see Mary Smith Costelloe

Smith, N. F., 5. 342

Smith, Pliny B., 3. 450

Smith, Robert Pearsall, 3. 320n, 323, 326, 327, 329, 345, 346, 347, 348, 354-55, 356n, 358, 360, 381n, 401, 451; 4. 17n, 31, 55, 58, 80, 82, 87, 88, 89, 98, 99, 100, 107, 121, 126, 127, 128, 130, 140, 151, 163, 168, 178, 181, 186, 218, 230, 254, 267, 281, 321, 323, 324, 370, 372, 376, 382, 390, 392, 393, 404, 427, 432, 438, 439, 440; 5. 6, 20, 21, 36, 52, 55, 65, 70, 81, 111, 127, 193, 223, 225, 227, 229, 230, 236n, 336, 337; 6. 45n, 50, 51, 69. Letters to, 3. 365-67, 380-81; 4. 81, 92, 111, 120-21, 126, 169-70, 190; 5. 45-46, 53, 56

Smith, Susan Garnet, 1. 372

Smith, Dr. Thomas C., 1. 277

Smith, William, 5. 341

Smith, William Farrar, 1. 219

Smith, William Hawley, 5. 332. Letter to, 5. 136

Smith, Mrs. William Hawley, 4. 430

Smith & Brooks, Ham, 3. 141

Smith & McDougal, 2. 101n

Smith & Starr, 4. 428

Smithson, Mrs. Edward, 3. 211n

Smithsonian Institute, 1. 41-42, 84, 115

Snowdon, Louisa, 4. 431

"Sobbing of the Bells, The," 1. 193n; 3. 232n

Socrates, 3. 152n; 4. 74n; 5. 31

"Socrates in Camden with a Look Around," 3. 404n

Solomon, Adolphus S., 1. 333n

Solomon, King, 4. 304n

"Some Diary Notes at Random," 3. 360n, 409n

"Some Personal and Old-Age Jottings," 5. 137, 140

"Some Personal and Old-Age Memoranda," 5. 121n, 137, 140, 147, 149, 151, 154, 158, 159, 164, 167, 171

"Some War Memoranda. Jotted Down at the Time," 4. 48n, 51, 61, 425

Somerby, Charles P., 2. 244n, 274n, 345n, 364, 372, 373; 3. 441. Letter to, 3. 42

Somers, Mrs., 5. 30

"Song for Occupations, A," 5. ix

"Song of All Seas, All Ships," see "Sea Captains, Young and Old"

"Song of Myself," 3. 270n, 272n; 5. 39n, 162n

"Song of the Exposition," see "After All, Not to Create Only"

"Song of the Redwood-Tree," 2. 255, 258, 262n, 264, 269, 272, 282, 287, 295, 305, 309; 4. 38n, 429

"Song of the Universal," 2. 291n, 303, 305, 306n, 308, 309

La Sonnambula, 1. 183; 5. 257

Sonnenchein & Co., 3. 385; 4. 99; 5. 79

"Soon Shall the Winter's Foil Be Here," 4. 5, 144n, 151n

Soralejea, Byramjie, 5. 348

Sorrell, Charles, 2. 45, 51, 57

Sorrell, James, 2. 45, 51, 57

Soule, Silas S., 1. 365, 372

"Sounds of the Winter," 5. 41n, 120n

Southwick, F. Townsend, 5. 117n, 338, 342

Southwick, Mrs., 1. 177

"Spain," 2. 204n, 209

Sparkes, Charles W., 4. 439

Spaulding, A. H., 4. 431

Spaulding, Mrs. Ada H., 4. 155n, 303, 312, 437; 5. 43, 331, 333, 344, 347

Specimen Days, 1. 64n, 171n, 250n, 332n; 3. 2, 75n, 118n, 121n, 122n, 124n, 141n, 269, 291, 292, 294, 296, 298, 299, 300, 301, 302, 303, 304, 306, 309, 310, 311, 312, 313n, 314, 316, 317, 318, 319, 320n, 323, 329, 335n, 344, 348, 350, 370n, 371, 375, 382, 385, 399, 401, 414; 4. 19, 23n, 29n, 66-67, 70n, 74, 117, 145, 171, 172, 200, 242, 255n, 312; 5. 63n, 316, 317; 6. 27, 28, 36, 52, 53, 60. Scotch edition, 3. 323, 329, 344

Specimen Days in America, 4. 63n, 80n, 99, 103, 105, 122, 125; 6. 36-37, 38, 39, 40, 41, 43, 44

Specimens of Early English Metrical Romances, 4. 224

Spectator, The, 5. 21

Speed, James, 2. 26, 44, 117. Letter to, 5. 288-89

Speed, John Gilmer, 3. 434

Spieler, Mr., 3. 69n

Spielmann, M. H., 4. 431, 433; 5. 340. Letters to, 4. 147-48

Spinola, Francis B., 1. 53

"Spirit That Form'd This Scene," 3. 236n

Spofford, Ainsworth R., 3. 292n, 448; 6. 69. Letters to, 3. 247, 299; 6. 14

Spofford, C. A., 4. 430

Spofford, Harriet Prescott, 3. 335

"Spontaneous Me," 3. 270n, 271n

Sporting Life, 2. 45

Spragge, G. W., 3. vii, 189n

Sprague, Amasa & William, 2. 66, 67

Sprague, Mrs. Frank J. 1. viii; 3. 66n

Springfield (Mass.) Republican, 1. 342n; 2.132n, 303n, 321, 335n, 337n, 338n; 3. 20n, 21n, 29n, 39n, 40n, 277n, 281n, 283, 297n, 306n, 375, 387n, 389n; 4. 102n, 228, 270, 271, 425; 5. 161, 316. Letters to, 3. 253, 304

Stafford, Benjamin Franklin, 3. 131, 234

Stafford, "Burt," 3. 361

Stafford, Prof. Cora E., 4. viii

Stafford, Deborah (later Mrs. Browning), 3. 41, 111, 115n, 119, 126, 130-31, 139, 145, 161, 189, 194, 203, 208, 210, 238, 251, 261, 278,

365, 405*n,* 406*n,* 431, 432, 435, 445; *4.* 78, 79, 185, 191, 206, 238, 282, 326, 361

Stafford, Dora, *4.* 17*n,* 90, 201, 209, 236; *5.* 32

Stafford, Edmund D., *3.* 361, 363*n*

Stafford, Edward L., *3.* 363

Stafford, Edwin, *3.* 77*n,* 111, 131, 145, 177, 189, 204, 206, 221, 222, 238, 251, 256, 261, 262, 265, 272, 278, 290, 324, 346, 381, 405, 432, 437; *4.* 16, 21, 22*n,* 51, 64, 72, 80, 82, 98, 138, 146, 163, 185, 191, 194, 260, 282, 317, 326, 361; *5.* 17, 33, 55, 116, 123, 126, 152, 200, 239, 309. Letters to, *3.* 41; *5.* 315

Stafford, Mrs. Elizabeth, *3.* 131

Stafford, Elmer E., *3.* 91*n,* 324, 431, 435, 442, 443, 445

Stafford, Mrs. Eva (Harry's wife), *3.* 371*n,* 406*n;* *4.* 17*n,* 89, 111, 185, 201, 209, 236; *5.* 30, 32, 33, 51, 53, 119, 200, 211, 239, 269, 338. Letters to, *3.* 381, 392; *5.* 51

Stafford, George, *3.* 2, 3, 6, 37, 41, 75*n,* 77, 78*n,* 82, 83*n,* 84, 85, 86, 89*n,* 91, 93*n,* 94, 95, 97, 98*n,* 102, 103, 106, 107, 109*n,* 111, 116*n,* 117, 119, 128*n,* 131, 138*n,* 147*n,* 148, 151, 154, 161, 175*n,* 177, 179*n,* 189, 190*n,* 191, 192, 194, 199, 208, 211, 217, 219, 220, 222, 224, 227, 231*n,* 238, 250, 254, 261, 262, 268*n,* 278, 290, 298, 307, 317*n,* 345*n,* 357*n,* 381, 406, 413, 431, 432, 434, 435, 436; *4.* 16, 21, 35, 51, 64, 65, 72, 78, 79, 82, 89, 94, 98, 105, 107, 113, 138, 163, 185, 191, 206, 244, 282, 317, 326, 342, 359, 361, 362; *5.* 33, 55, 74, 91, 111, 116, 126, 139, 152, 155, 175, 183, 211, 257, 258, 276, 309, 310, 311, 313. Letters to, *3.* 183-84, 206-7, 220-21, 270, 356, 359, 365, 366-67; *5.* 17, 51, 116-17, 128-29, 200, 239, 307-8

Stafford, George Lamb (Harry's brother), *3.* 178, 238, 261, 323; *4.* 80, 361; *5.* 55, 309

Stafford, George Wescott (Harry's son), *5.* 27, 30, 32

Stafford, Harry *1.* 5; *3.* 2-9, 37, 41, 68, 70, 77, 79, 80, 91*n,* 100, 102, 103*n,* 106, 108*n,* 111, 114, 131, 136, 139, 147, 148, 151, 160, 176, 178, 179, 184, 192, 207, 208, 211, 221, 222, 227, 250, 251, 253, 256, 261, 262, 272, 278, 299, 307, 324, 329*n,* 356, 359, 365, 367, 405, 406, 413, 431, 432, 435, 436, 437, 438, 442, 443, 444, 445, 446, 450; *4.* 17*n,* 30, 51, 65, 78, 80, 82, 85, 90, 93, 113, 138, 139, 156, 163, 167, 201, 206, 209, 212, 229, 282, 317, 326, 337, 361, 366, 382, 425, 426; *5.* 6, 7, 17, 27, 30, 31, 32, 50, 51, 53, 55, 66, 70, 111, 126, 129, 139, 141*n,* 152, 155, 160, 175, 183, 200, 207-8, 239, 256, 266, 269, 307, 308, 309, 311, 315*n,* 317; *6.* 17*n.* Letters to, *3.* 86-87, 93-95, 126-27, 133-34, 154, 155-56, 176, 177, 191-92, 194, 198, 203-4, 207-8, 211, 212, 214-16, 223-

24, 233-34, 235-36, 237-38, 240-41, 242-43, 264, 265-66, 322-23, 354-55, 357, 361, 363-64, 371, 381-82, 392; *4.* 88-89, 111, 236, 283; *5.* 51, 211

Stafford, Jacob Horner, *3.* 204, 223; *6.* 17

Stafford, John, *3.* 361

Stafford, Mrs. Lizzie Hider (Wesley's wife), *3.* 194, 210, 262

Stafford, Montgomery (George's brother), *3.* 147, 160, 206, 278; *4.* 80, 326; *6.* 17

Stafford, Montgomery (George's son), *3.* 178, 189, 194, 208, 238, 240, 250, 251, 261, 272, 346; *5.* 307, 308, 310. Letter to, *5.* 308-10

Stafford, Richard C., *3.* 363*n*

Stafford, Ruth (later Mrs. Goldy), *3.* 98*n,* 131, 178, 194, 208, 234, 238, 261, 278, 290, 307, 324, 346, 361, 381, 404*n,* 405, 406, 437; *4.* 30, 361; *5.* 309, 315. Letters to, *3.* 160, 217, 222-23, 225, 250-51, 256-57, 293

Stafford, Mrs. Susan, *3.* 2, 3, 8, 37, 41, 77, 91, 93, 95, 98, 102*n,* 106, 111, 118, 130-31, 135, 136, 139, 140, 154, 160, 161, 177, 189, 191, 192, 193, 194, 199, 203, 211, 215, 217, 219, 220, 222, 224, 234, 238, 240, 250, 261, 262, 272, 290, 294*n,* 298, 303, 323, 329, 339, 340, 361, 371, 382, 405, 406, 409, 414, 431, 432, 434, 435, 436, 438, 441, 443, 445; *4.* 30, 44, 79, 127, 156, 163, 189, 229, 238, 283, 433, 435, 440; *5.* 7, 309, 338, 340. Letters to, *3.* 145, 208, 210-11, 213, 220, 277-79, 306-7, 323-24, 337, 345-46, 380-81, 413; *4.* 16-17, 19-21, 34-35, 51, 64-65, 72, 78, 82, 85, 90, 92-94, 97, 98, 105-6, 108-9, 113, 123, 138, 145-46, 166-67, 185, 190, 191, 199, 201-2, 205-6, 208-9, 282, 317-18, 326, 360-61, 366; *5.* 17, 33, 51, 54, 116-17, 126, 128-29, 152, 200, 239, 307-8, 310-14, 316-17

Stafford, Van Doran, *3.* 178, 194, 206, 238, 240, 251, 261, 366, 447; *4.* 80, 185, 282, 326, 361; *5.* 126, 183, 307, 309, 310, 315. Letter to, *3.* 290

Stafford, Wesley, *3.* 194, 210, 262

Stagg, W. A., *3.* 441

Stanbery, Henry, *1.* 275, 289, 294, 296, 298, 304, 308, 312, 324, 329*n;* *5.* 288-89, 290, 291. Letter to, *1.* 289-91

Stanford, Sir Charles Villiers. Letter to, *5.* 318

Stanley, Arthur, *3.* 233

Stanley, Sir Henry Morton, *5.* 118, 121; *6.* 53

Stanley, M. E., *5.* 86*n*

Stanley, Samuel G., *4.* 429; *5.* 332, 345; *6.* 69. Letter to, *6.* 58

Stansberry, Mrs. Jane, *2.* 371

Stansberry, William, *2.* 363, 364, 371, 372. Letter to, *2.* 298-99

Stanton, Mr., *2.* 146, 149, 157

Stanton, Edwin McMasters, *1.* 78, 113, 220,

245*n*, 262

Stanton, Mrs. Elizabeth, 6. 74

Starr, Louis M., *1*. 190*n*

Starr & Co., H., *3*. 33

Starr's Foundry, *2*. 203

Statesman, The, 1. 9

Stead, Edwin R., *5*. 47, 48*n*, 107, 125

Stead, William T., *4*. 1-2; *5*. 20, 28-29, 32, 223, 333, 338, 340; *6*. 41*n*. Letters to, *4*. 116-17; *5*. 146

Stedman, Arthur, *5*. 151, 159, 182*n*, 347

Stedman, Edmund Clarence, *1*. 167-68, 184*n*, 339; *2*. 372; *3*. 38, 45, 108*n*, 179, 193, 198, 209, 214*n*, 251, 282, 316*n*, 410, 431; *4*. 15*n*, 18, 32, 82*n*, 83, 118*n*, 124, 126, 164, 171*n*, 172*n*, 173*n*, 196, 197, 210, 228, 301, 313, 314, 316, 318, 320, 321, 324, 325, 326, 331, 333, 340, 341, 378, 404, 407, 435, 437; *5*. 36, 151*n*, 159, 178, 182*n*, 334; *6*. 13, 31. Letters to, *2*. 334; *4*. 315; *5*. 49, 303; *6*. 13

Steiger, E., *3*. 444

Steinninger, G. E., *5*. 337

Stennett, W. H., *3*. 431

Stepnyak (or Stepniak), Sergei Mikhailovich, *4*. 340

Sterling, Louisa, *5*. 335

Stern, Louis E., *4*. viii

Sterrit, Charles, *4*. 385

Stevens, David, *2*. 52, 57, 58

Stevens, Gen. Isaac 1., *1*. 87*n*

Stevens, Oliver, *3*. 267*n*, 279, 283, 348*n* 4. 235*n*

Stevens, Thaddeus, *1*. 275

Stevenson, Hannah E., *1*. 153*n*, 164, 175, 188*n*, 374. Letter to, *1*. 160-61

Stevenson, Robert Louis, *2*. 139*n*; *3*. 406*n*; *4*. 30*n*

Stewart, B. P., *3*. 453

Stewart, Edward C. ("Ned"), *2*. 108, 373

Stewart, William, *1*. 376

Stillman, William J. Letter to, *3*. 63

Stilwell, James, *1*. 154, 169-70, 176, 177, 181, 184, 368, 375

Stilwell, John, *1*. 367, 374

Stilwell, Julia Elizabeth, *1*. 374. Letter to, *1*. 169-70

Stilwell, Margaret, *1*. 374, 377

Stitt, Frank N., *1*. 284, 311*n*; *5*. 289

Stoddard, Charles Warren, *1*. 339*n*, 377; *2*. 367, 368; *3*. 435, 445. Letters to, *2*. 81-82, 97-98

Stoddard, Richard Henry, *1*. 339; *3*. 282, 292*n*, 314, 327

Stoddart, James, *5*. 347

Stoddart, Joseph M., *3*. 447; *4*. 1; *5*. 112*n*, 120, 127, 134, 140, 147, 151, 156, 158, 162, 171, 183*n*, 212, 214, 215, 261, 331, 332, 334, 337, 339, 340, 343. Letters to, *3*. 263, 329-30; *5*. 41, 120, 128, 147-48, 161, 211, 213

Stodtman, Dr. Adolf, *3*. 351

Stoker, Abraham ("Bram"), *2*. 369; *3*. 27, 440; *4*. 41, 348*n*, 384*n*; *6*. 69. Letter to, *3*. 28

Stokes, Frederick A., *4*. 425, 430

Stone, Horatio, *1*. 70, 82

Stone, Mrs. Pearl, *6*. 65

Stories from Homer, 3. 118

Storms, George I., *1*. 364, 371; *5*. 215*n*

Storms, Herman, *1*. 368, 376

Storms, Walt Whitman, *2*. 363, 364, 371, 372; *3*. 431, 442; *5*. 215*n*

Story, W. W., *3*. 105*n*

Stott, Jno. S., *3*. 445

Stowe, Mrs. C. F., *4*. 433

Stowe, Harriet Beecher, *1*. 43*n*, 52; *2*. 86

Strachey, St. Loe, *3*. 442

Strahan, Messrs., *3*. 64

Strand, 5. 160

Strauss, Ida, *5*. 345

Street, John Phillips, *5*. 343. Letter to, *5*. 226

Strickland, Jr., E. F., *3*. 440

String, Emma M., *3*. 446

Stuart, Carlos D., *5*. 282. Letter to, *1*. 38

Stuart, Queen Mary, *4*. 396

Stuart, Gen. J. E. B., *1*. 150

Stuart, Richard A., *3*. 453

Studies in Bibliography, 1. viii

Studies of the Greek Poets, 3. 174; *5*. 300

Sturgis, Lt., *1*. 222

Sullivan, Louis, *3*. 150*n*; *4*. 430

Sullivan, Thomas, *1*. 98

"Summer Days in Canada," *3*. 181, 182; *5*. 308; *6*. 22

Summers, Gen. Edwin Vose, *1*. 59*n*

Summers, William, *4*. 215-16, 230

"Summer's Invocation, A" (later "Thou Orb Aloft Full-Dazzling"), *3*. 204*n*, 223*n*, 231*n*, 239*n*

Sumner, Charles, *1*. 61, 73-74, 83, 235*n*; *2*. 150*n*, 286, 289

Sunderland (England) *Times, 2.* 217

Surratt, Anna, *1*. 315

Surratt, John, H., *2*. 232*n*

Surratt, Isaac, *1*. 334

Surratt, John H., *1*. 315, 320, 334

Surridge, Edith, *5*. 343

Sutherland, Byron, *1*. 377; *2*. 366, 367, 368. Letters to, *1*. 266-67, 268-69; *2*. 44-45, 95, 238

Swalm, Dr. Samuel J., *1*. 211

Swanson, Mrs. Bernice, *5*. ix

Swertfager, Mrs. Walter, *5*. ix

Swinburne, Algernon, *1*. 298*n*, 332*n*, 346*n*; *2*. 16, 20, 22, 49, 130, 133*n*, 152, 158*n*, 161; *3*. 60, 258, 263*n*, 384*n*; *4*. 63*n*, 119*n*, 121, 137*n*; *6*. 43, 44

Swinton, John, *1*. 124*n*, 269*n*, 372, 376; *2*. 30, 48, 54, 313, 327, 366, 368, 371; *3*. 38, 66*n*,

109, 111, 342n, 348n, 441, 442, 448, 449, 451; 5. 52, 160, 303, 333, 334, 335, 347; 6. 8. Letters to, 1. 75-76, 252-53, 263; 2. 49-50, 138-39, 306, 324, 325; 3. 45-46, 49, 416; 5. 293; 6. 13

Swinton, William, 1. 76, 227n, 232, 269n, 300; 2. 103; 3. 38, 45, 46; 6. 13

Sydnor, William, 2. 45, 54

Symonds, John Adington, 2. 162, 369, 372; 3. 163n, 171, 173-74, 179, 362n, 405, 410, 434, 435, 437, 441, 442, 451; 4. 4, 30n, 32, 33, 35, 94, 119, 120, 121, 122, 125, 224, 239, 267, 271, 286, 287, 375, 384, 408, 436, 441; 5. vii, 19, 33n, 49, 63, 66, 68, 69, 71, 75, 77, 87, 127, 148, 149, 157, 181, 200n, 206, 220, 300, 305, 332, 335, 336, 344; 6. 41, 43n. Letters to, 2. 158-59; 4. 34; 5. 72-73, 182; 6. 25, 52-53

Taber (or Tabor), J.A., 1. 120, 133, 331

Talbot, Jesse, 2. 90; 5. 346

Tappan, Cora L. V.; 1. 43. Letter to, 2. 120-21

Tarr, Squire Frederick W., 5. 86

Tarr, Horace, 1. 99; 5. 338. Letter to, 5. 131

Tarrytown (N. Y.) Sunnyside Press, 3. 178

Tasistro, Louis Fitzgerald, 2. 172, 175, 178, 228, 229, 233, 236, 296, 311, 335, 338

Tatler, The, 1. 9

Taylor, Bayard, 1. 305, 377; 2. 121n, 132n, 321n; 3. 39n, 111, 283; 5. 244. Letter to, 1. 295

Taylor, Father Edward Thompson, 3. 369, 374; 4. 37

Taylor, Mrs. Fannie L., 3. 69n

Taylor, Hannah, 3. 374, 436, 446

Taylor, Hudson, 1. 314

Taylor, Jessie E., 4. 433

Taylor, Mrs. Mentia, 3. 57

Taylor, Robert H., 1. ix; 3. ix, 429; 4. viii

Taylor, W. Curtis, 3. 435

Taylor, William, 3. 133n, 445

Taylor, William H., 2. 54n, 363, 364, 371; 3. 432, 442; 5. 215, 232, 342

Taylor's Saloon, 1. 74

Teall, J. J. Harris, 3. 100. Letter to, 3. 101

Temple, Lady Mount, 4. 170

Templeton, Clement, 3. 100

Temps, Le, 4. 396

Teniers, David, 4. 157n

Tennant(?), J. H., 5. 338

Tennyson, Lord, 2. vi, 184n

Tennyson, Alfred Lord, 1. 5, 6; 2. 152, 155, 158, 161, 164, 270, 313, 321n, 344n, 362, 368, 371, 372; 3. 47n, 56, 132, 139, 140, 141, 144, 169n, 180, 188n, 239n, 384n, 391, 394, 401, 410, 430, 434, 443; 4. 58, 60, 70, 75n, 134, 141, 207, 312, 330, 362, 387, 389, 392, 430,

431; 5. 33n, 42, 127, 200n, 204, 205, 217, 219, 221, 223, 236, 237, 243, 276n, 294, 295, 301, 302, 305, 342; 6. 18, 35. Letters to, 2. 174-75, 184, 301, 335; 3. 133; 4. 63-64, 131; 5. 219. Letters from, 2. 125-26, 307-8, 339; 3. 134-35

Tennyson, Sir Charles, 2. vi, 184n

Tennyson, Hallam, 5. 276n, 347

Tennyson, Lionel, 3. 132, 133, 134, 179n

"Tennyson at 81," 4. 366

Teraud, T. A., 3. 390n

Terry, Ellen, 3. 383; 4. 41n, 431

Thackeray, William Makepiece, 2. 344n; 4. 223, 392

"Thanks in Old Age," 4. 135; 5. 118n

Tharpe, Josephine M., 4. 60n

Thayer, J. B., 2. 363

Thayer, Dr. Samuel W. Letter to, 2. 73-74

Thayer, W. W., 1. 339n, 365, 372

Thayer, William Roscoe, 3. 449, 453; 4. 15n. Letter to, 3. 408

Thayer & Eldridge, 1. 10, 11, 49, 51, 52-53, 54n, 190n, 364, 365, 371, 372; 2. 30n, 151n; 3. 92, 196-98, 226, 299. Letters to, 1. 54-55

Theatre, The, 3. 356n

Theobald, H. S. Letter to, 3. 63

"There Was a Child Went Forth," 1. 7-8; 4. 6

"These May Afternoons," 3. 154, 155

This World (Boston), 3. 294n

Thomas, Dr., 5. 103, 105, 117

Thomas, Dionysus, 1. 337, 350n; 6. 8. Letter to, 1. 344

Thomas, Gen. George Henry, 1. 262

Thomas, Mary Grace, 4. 39n, 429

Thomas, Serelda G., 5. 346

Thompson, Arthur, 4. 341; 5. 207

Thompson, Ben, 2. 53

Thompson, Bert A., 4. 227n

Thompson, Billy, 4. 27n, 89, 165, 166

Thompson, Ethel, 4. 341; 5. 207

Thompson, H. B. (?), 1. 331, 369, 377; 2. 367

Thompson, Honora E., 3. 433

Thompson, James W., 3. 159n, 433, 434, 444

Thompson, Percy W., 4. 430, 432

Thompson, Sam G., 5. 348

Thompson, Seymer, 3. 100

Thompson, William, 4. 29, 341; 5. 50, 207

Thoreau, Henry David, 1. 10, 42n; 2. 30n, 33; 3. 40n, 244n, 316

Thoreau, Sophia, 4. 257n

Thorek, Dr. Max, 1. ix; 2. vi; 3. ix, 429

Thornton, Sir Edward, 4. 49

Thornett, Alfred R., 2. 114

Thorsteinsson, Steingrimur, 3. 258, 310

"Thou Mother with Thy Equal Brood," see "As A Strong Bird on Pinions Free"

"Thou Orb Aloft Full-Dazzling," see "A Summer's Invocation"

"Thou Vast Rondure, Swimming in Space" (later part of "Passage to India"), 2. 75, 77

"Thou who hast slept all night upon the storm," *see* "To the Man-of-War-Bird"

"Thought on Shakspere, A," 4. 43, 45, 424

"Thoughts," 1. 47

Thrasher, Marion, 3. 453

Three Tales, see The Brazen Android and Other Tales

"Three Young Men's Deaths," 3. 141n, 158, 159; 5. 305; 6. 20

"Throstle," 4. 387, 389, 392

Ticknor, Benjamin H., 3. 228n, 253n, 255n, 279, 280, 437, 446, 447. Letters to, 3. 258, 280, 295

Ticknor & Fields, 1. 48n, 303n, 371

Tiffany, W. L., 3. 443

Tiffany's, 1. 74

Tilton, John W., 3. 311n. Letter to, 4. 264

Tilton, Josephine S., 3. 315

Tilton, Theodore, 2. 219

Time: A Monthly Magazine, 4. 137, 139

Tip (WW's dog), 3. 69, 96, 99, 115, 233

"'Tis But Ten Years Since," 2. 5, 266-67, 268, 277, 278, 280, 285; 5. 298

Titcomb, Timothy (Josiah Gilbert Holland), 1. 343

"To a Common Prostitute," 3. 270n, 273, 277, 279, 294n, 312n, 314; 5. 317

"To Get the Final Lilt of Song," 4. 145n, 160, 161, 164

"To Him That Was Crucified," 3. 334

"To the Man-of-War-Bird," 3. 23, 52, 56

"To the Pending Year," 4. 254n, 426

"To the Sun-Set Breeze," 4. 385n; 5. 41n, 113, 118, 120, 121, 122, 145n

"To the Year 1889," *see* "To the Pending Year"

"To Those Who've Failed," 4. 144n

Tobey, Edward S., 3. 296n, 348n

To-day, 3. 358-59n, 388, 393, 395, 396; 4. 189

"To-day and Thee," 4. 145n

Todhunter, Dr. John, 2. 153; 3. 60

Tolstoi; Count Leo, 4. 255, 261, 263; 5. 84

"Tomb-Blossoms, The," 1. 26n

Tombs, Andrew W. (?), 1. 29-30

Tooley, Sarah A. Letter to, 4. 108

Toronto *Globe*. Letter to, 3. 182; 6. 22

Tottie, Oscar, 3. 443. Letter to, 3. 129

Towers, John, 2. 53, 58

Towle, Mr., 1. 85

Towner, Charles, 2. 233, 243, 245, 260

Townley, E. L., 5. 343

Townsend, George A., 1. 329n; 3. 45; 5. 291

Townsend, Henry, 2. 276

Townsend, James, 5. 210

Townsend, Lillie, 2. 202, 210, 211, 363

Townsend, Patience, 3. 147n

Townsend, Priscilla, 2. 215; 3. 431, 432, 435; 5. 210

Townsend, Capt. Vandoren, 3. 147

Toynbee, Arnold, 3. 396n

Toynbee Hall, 3. 397, 401; 5. 320

Tracy, Gilbert A. Letter to, 1. 354

Transatlantic Magazine, 4. 385; 5. 22

Traubel, Agnes, 4. 202; 5. 121

Traubel, Anne Montgomerie, 5. 206n, 209, 210, 214, 225, 238, 240, 264

Traubel, Gertrude, 1. vii, x

Traubel, Horace 1. vii, x, 2, 3, 57n, 121n, 124n, 125n, 126n, 127n, 152n, 153n, 158n, 169n, 171n, 175n, 188n, 252n, 274n, 328n, 341n, 347n; 2. 1, 23n, 47n, 71n, 74n, 82n, 96n, 100n, 133n, 141n, 151n, 231n, 263n; 3. 274n, 298n, 331n, 349n; 4. 1, 2, 4, 18n, 136n, 142n, 158n, 160n, 168, 170, 171, 173n, 174, 178, 179, 180, 182, 186, 187, 191, 195, 196n, 200, 202, 203, 207, 212, 213, 214, 217, 218, 219, 221, 225, 228, 229, 231, 232, 242, 244, 245, 247, 256, 263, 266, 267, 270, 271, 274, 277, 284, 285, 289, 292, 293, 294n, 297, 298, 301, 302, 303, 304, 305, 307, 309, 312, 317, 320, 322, 325, 328, 329, 330, 333, 334, 336, 337, 339, 341, 346, 351, 352, 355, 356, 360, 363, 365, 367, 368, 370, 371, 372, 373, 374, 375, 377, 379, 380, 382, 384, 386, 387, 388, 390, 391, 395, 396, 401, 405, 406, 408; 5. 1, 19, 20, 22, 36, 37, 41, 43, 47, 48, 49, 51n, 58, 59, 60, 64, 65-66, 68, 69, 74, 77, 80, 81, 83, 89, 92, 93, 94, 97, 100, 101, 106, 108, 109, 110, 115, 116, 119, 120, 121, 122, 125, 129, 132, 134, 137, 140, 141n, 142, 144, 147-48, 150n, 151, 153, 154, 155, 157, 161, 164, 165, 171, 177, 179, 181, 184, 185n, 189, 190, 191, 193, 194, 200, 202n, 205, 207, 208, 209, 211, 213, 214, 215, 216, 217, 220, 222, 223-24, 225, 226, 227, 228, 229, 230, 231, 234, 235, 237, 238, 239, 240, 241, 243, 245n, 249, 250, 251, 252, 253, 254, 255, 256, 264, 265, 266, 267, 269, 272, 274, 335, 337, 342; 6. 55, 56, 58, 69. Letters to, 4. 343-44; 5. 103-5, 156, 162, 185, 209-10, 212

Traubel, Maurice, 4. 202, 352

Trautwine, Lucy L., 5. 340

Trelawney, Edward John, 3. 314n

Trent Collection (Duke University), 1. viii, 8

Tripp, Mrs. Maggy, 2. 215

Il Trovatore, 1. 185; 2. 169

Trowbridge, John T., 1. 184n, 294n, 329n, 374, 375, 376, 377, 378; 2. 126n, 144n, 214n, 364, 372; 3. 441, 442; 4. 50n, 69. Letters to, 1. 191, 195-96, 224, 254-55, 255-56; 2. 113-14

Trowbridge, Windsor Warren, 2. 114n

Trübner & Co., 3. 132, 134, 140, 141, 157n, 193n, 228n, 242, 253, 255, 319, 340, 357, 431,

433, 434, 436, 442; *4.* 235*n*; *6.* 10, 20, 25.
  Letters to, *2.* 263; *3.* 137-38, 247-48; *5.* 298
True, O. W., *4.* 436, 439
"True Conquerors," *4.* 144*n*
Trumbull, Jonathan, *5.* 64
Truth, 5. 179, 183, 332
Truth Seeker, The, 3. 314*n; 5.* 115, 151
Tucker, Benjamin R., *3.* 314*n,* 349, 447; *4.* 372
Tufts College, *2.* 5, 290, 305
Tuke, Henry S., *5.* 340. Letter to, *5.* 180-81
Tully, Vivas (?), *3.* 445
Turner, Joseph Mallord William, *3.* 63*n; 4.* 33*n*
Twain, Mark, *see* Samuel Clemens
"Twenty Years," *4.* 147, 148
"Twilight." *4.* 108, 425
"Twilight Song, A," *5.* 24*n,* 27, 28, 29, 32, 43,
  44; *6.* 50*n*
Two Rivulets, 2. 7, 330, 332, 334, 335, 337,
  338*n,* 343, 344, 345, 346; *3.* 21, 26, 27, 29, 31,
  32, 33, 34, 35, 37, 38, 39, 40, 41, 42, 43, 44,
  45, 47, 48, 49, 51, 52, 53, 55, 56, 57, 58-59,
  61, 62, 63, 64, 67, 68, 72, 73, 88, 92, 96, 99,
  101, 103, 116, 120, 128, 129, 130, 132, 133,
  137-38, 141, 142, 157, 159*n,* 174, 183*n,* 190,
  191, 192, 193, 195, 201, 206, 209, 211, 215,
  218, 252, 256, 282, 288, 307, 322; *4.* 25*n,* 53,
  54, 137, 152, 207; *5.* 251, 281*n,* 301, 303,
  306*n,* 307; *6.* 13, 14, 15, 16, 23, 24, 26, 27, 30
Tyndale, Hector, *1.* 42, 53*n,* 279; *3.* 25, 26
Tyndale, Sarah, *1.* 364, 371. Letter to, *1.* 42-44
Tyndall, John, *3.* 108
Tyrrell, Henry, *3.* 450. Letter to, *3.* 372
Tyrrell, R. Y., *2.* 134, 153

Ueber Wordsworth und Walt Whitman, 3. 349*n*
Uncle Tom's Cabin, 1. 52
"Unexpress'd, The," *5.* 41*n,* 120*n*
"Unfolded Out of the Folds," *3.* 270*n*
Unger, Mr., *4.* 120
Union Club (Philadelphia), *5.* 256*n*
Union Hotel (Georgetown), *2.* 115
Unitarian Society, *4.* 78
United States Christian Association, *1.* 111,
  125*n,* 127*n*
"United States to Old World Critics, The" *4.*
  145*n*
Unity, 4. 353; *5.* 51*n*
"Unknown Names," *see* "A Twilight Song"
"Unseen Buds," *5.* 201*n*
Upward, Allen, *6.* 69
Urie, Marie, *4.* 16
Urner, Benjamin, *1.* 45*n*
Urner, Mrs. Benjamin, *1.* 161
Usher, Judge John P., *3.* 163*n,* 173*n*
Usher, Jr., John P. Letter to, *3.* 173
Usher, Linton, *3.* 173

*V*ale, Thomas E., *5.* 338
Van Anden, Isaac, *1.* 27, 87
Vandermark, William E., *1.* 366, 367, 373, 374,
  375
Van Duren, Gertrude, *4.* 429
Van Laun, Henri, *3.* 320*n*
Van Nostrand, Ansel, *1.* 9, 151, 233; *2.* 80*n; 5.*
  273
Van Nostrand, Fanny, *1.* 131, 135, 138, 151,
  374; *2.* 41, 80*n,* 204, 372
Van Nostrand, Mary Whitman, *1.* 9, 29, 33,
  36, 79, 117, 131, 135, 138, 140, 151, 188*n,*
  204, 229, 233, 325, 364; *3.* 24, 166, 180*n,* 431,
  432, 433, 434, 435, 436, 438, 439, 443, 450; *4.*
  179, 282, 425, 426, 427; *5.* vii, 124, 127, 142,
  152, 160, 226, 259-60, 273, 275, 332. Letter to,
  5. 122-23
Van Rensellaer, A., *1.* 376
Van Tassel, Alice Hicks, *4.* 438
Van Wyck, Samuel. Letter to, *3.* 157
Vassar College, *3.* 153
Vaughan, Fred, *1.* 182*n,* 364, 365, 371, 372; *2.*
  371
Vedder, Elihu, *3.* 446
Velasquez, Diego Rodrigues, *4.* 393
Velsor, Joseph A., *1.* 280; *2.* 27*n*
Velsor, William H., *2.* 27
Verdi, Giuseppe, *1.* 185; *2.* 169
Vergil, *1.* 82
Vick, James, *3.* 432
Victor Emmanuel II, *2.* 112, 113
Victoria, Queen, *4.* 341; *5.* 46, 53
Vielé-Griffin, Francis, *4.* 248*n,* 426, 432
"Vigil Strange I Kept on the Fields One
  Night," *3.* 272*n*
Viking Age, The, 4. 390
Vincent, Minnie, *2.* 371
Vines, Sidney H., *3.* 103
"Virginia–The West," *2.* 157*n*
Vliet, Amos H., *1.* 64, 366
"Voice from Death, A," *4.* 345*n,* 346, 347, 348
"Voices of the Rain, The," *3.* 391-92, 396,
  409*n*
de Volney, Constantin François Chasseboeuf,
  Comte, *5.* 57
Volney's Ruins, 5. 57
Voltaire, *4.* 391
Voorhees, Mrs. *3.* 118
Voorhees, Judah B., *4.* 432

*W*ade, Benjamin Franklin, *2.* 26
Wager-Fisher, Mary E., *3.* 235*n,* 434; *5.* 334
Wagner, Richard, *2.* 5; *3.* 290*n,* 339*n; 4.* 329
Wainer, J. E., *3.* 263*n*
Wainwright, Mary, *3.* 363
Wakefield, Mrs. Eva Ingersoll, *5.* ix

Waldo, R. W., 2. 370

Waldron, Randall, 6. 74

Walker, Mrs. Elaine W., 3. vii

"Wallabout Martyrs, The" 4. 145n

Wallace, J. W., 1. vii; 4. 3, 346, 430, 432, 437,
439, 441; 5. 1, 2, 3-4, 7, 70, 80n, 81, 83, 85,
88, 95, 104, 110, 118, 122, 124, 134, 146, 155,
157, 160, 163, 165, 166, 167, 168, 170, 171,
174, 178, 180, 181, 182, 183, 184, 189, 191,
192n, 194, 195, 196, 206n, 208, 211, 213, 216,
218, 219, 220, 223, 224, 229, 231, 232, 234,
235, 236, 237, 238, 240, 241, 243, 244, 245,
246, 248, 250, 251, 252, 253, 254, 255, 256,
257, 258, 259, 260, 261, 262, 263, 265, 267,
268, 269, 271, 272, 334-48; 6. 58. Letters to,
4. 96, 345; 5. 62-63, 71, 76, 79, 82, 83, 90-91,
97, 135-36, 164, 169, 175-76, 180, 188, 198-99,
203, 205, 215, 221, 222, 227, 228, 233, 241-42,
245, 247, 251-52, 266; 6. 57

Wallace, Marie, 5. 349

Wallace, Will W., 1. 101n, 366, 373; 2. 361,
366

Wallack's Theatre, 2. 107-8

Wallis, George, 3. 51

Walsh, Dr., 4. 245, 246, 247, 248, 253, 260,
264, 266, 267

Walsh, Harry C., 5. 335

Walsh, Moses A., 4. 428

Walsh, William S., 3. 437; 4. 91n, 100, 245n,
330, 424, 425, 426, 429, 437

Walt Whitman (Bucke's biography), 3. 174,
209, 221n, 258, 266-67, 268-69, 291, 292, 294,
301, 310, 317, 325, 328, 329, 330n, 332, 337,
338-39, 340, 341, 342, 343, 344, 347n, 349,
351, 352, 355n, 357, 375; 4. 32n, 65n, 159,
215, 216-17, 312, 332, 352n, 362, 388; 5. 89n,
98, 100, 112, 140, 226, 243; 6. 29, 48n

"Walt Whitman and Ingersoll," 5. 106

"Walt Whitman and the Poetry of the
Future," 3. 253n

"Walt Whitman at Camden," 4. 52n

"Walt Whitman at Date," 5. 69, 77, 81, 83; 6.
56

"Walt Whitman Calendar," 4. 196-97

Walt Whitman Debating Club, 3. 21n

"Walt Whitman in Camden," 3. 387n, 388

"Walt Whitman in Europe," 5. 295n

"Walt Whitman in Russia," 3. 342

"Walt Whitman Last Night," 3. 176n

"Walt Whitman: Poet and Philospher and
Man," 5. 147, 154, 156n

"Walt Whitman Safe Home," 3. 188n

Walt Whitman Society, 4. 108, 113, 122, 136

"Walt Whitman, the Poet of Humanity," 4.
33-34, 35, 36, 39, 40, 41, 42, 43-44, 52, 53, 68,
69, 77, 81, 94, 99, 139n, 140, 141, 144, 146,
149, 150, 152, 153n, 159, 162, 167, 208, 270,

273n, 279n, 321n, 350n, 355, 359, 395; 5. 23n,
69n

"Walt Whitman: the Poet of Joy," 3. 21n

"Walt Whitman's Actual American Position,"
3. 20n, 22

"Walt Whitman's Art," 5. 74n

"Walt Whitman's Birthday," 5. 51n

"Walt Whitman's Dutch Traits," 5. 77, 78, 79-
80, 84, 97n, 140, 147n, 153, 154, 155, 159,
160, 162, 163, 164, 167, 171, 213

"Walt Whitman's Last," 5. 210n, 212, 213; 6.
57-58

"Walt Whitman's Last 'Public,' " 5. 40n

"Walt Whitman's Life," 5. 28n

"Walt Whitman's Quaker Traits," 5. 58, 59,
64, 78, 147

"Walt Whitman's Thanksgiving," 5. 118, 119

"Walt Whitman's Tuesday Night," 5. 40n

"Walt Whitman's View of Shakspere," 5. 64

Walters, Frank W., 6. 20

Walton, Mrs., 1. 43-44

Walton, Wilhelmina, 1. 372

"Wandering at Noon," *see* "Singing Thrust,
The"

War Memoranda 2. 5, 337

"Warble for Lilac-Time," 2. 93, 94, 204n, 220n;
6. 7

Ward, Mr., 5. 52

Ward, Artemus, 1. 191n, 346n; 2. 176n

Ward, Genevieve, *see* Genevra Guerrabella

Ward, Mrs. Humphrey, 4. 355

Ward, John Quincy Adams, 3. 38, 45, 441; 6.
13. Letters to, 3. 39; 5. 303; 6. 14

Ward, Samuel. Letter to, 2. 173

Ward & Downey, 5. 269

Ware, R. M., 3. 437

Warner, Dr. E., 2. 367

Warren, John Byrne Leicester, 3. 34, 44, 51; 5.
305

Warren, Robert Penn, 1. 274n

Washburne, Elihu Benjamin, 2. 81

Washington *Daily Morning Chronicle*, 2. 23n,
31n, 34n, 47n, 51n, 53n, 64n, 72n, 80n, 83n,
84n, 105n, 125n, 132n, 148n, 155n, 164n, 174n,
180, 191n, 238n, 260n, 261n

Washington *Daily Patriot*, 2. 180

Washington *Express*, 2. 38

Washington, George, 3. 115n; 4. 327n

"Washington in the Hot Season," 1. 136, 138

Washington *National Intelligencer*, 1. 300n, 337n

Washington *National Republican*, 1. 77n, 120n,
132n, 300n, 324n; 2. 14n

Washington *Post*, 3. 181n, 435

Washington *Star*, 1. 311; 2. 20, 29, 46, 50, 50n,
56, 58, 77n, 79n, 180n, 222, 223n, 229, 329,
342n; 3. 25, 88n, 90n, 170n, 265, 280n; 4. 114,
425

Washington *Sunday Herald, 2.* 189*n*, 237*n*; *3.* 184*n*

Washington *Sunday Morning Chronicle, 3.* 150*n*; *5.* 290

"Washington's Monument, February, 1885," *3.* 387*n*, 409*n*

Wassall, J. W., *4.* 358*n*

Waters, George W., *3.* 68, 80, 99. Letters to, *3.* 83-84, 115-16, 139

Watson, Mr., *4.* 410

Watson, R. Spence, *3.* 451. Letters to, *6.* 15, 16

Watson's Art Journal, 2. 33

Watt, Alvin R., *5.* ix

Watt, James, *5.* 345

Waugh, Albert, *6.* 59*n*

Weaver, George, *3.* 452

Webb, Alfred, *3.* 440

Webb, Ellen, *5.* 347

Webb, Frank, *5.* 347

Webb, James Watson, *1.* 301

Webb, Walter Whitman, *5.* 347

Weber, Mrs. William R., *4.* viii

Webling, Ethel, *5.* 345

Webling, Josephine, *5.* 346

Webster, Augusta, *3.* 100*n*

Webster, C. E., *4.* 315

Webster, E. D., *1.* 73

Wechter, Dixon, *2.* 306*n*

Wedmore, Frederick, *6.* 69

"Week at West Hills, A," *3.* 235; *5.* 314*n*

Weitzel, Conrad F., *3.* vii

Wells, S. R., *1.* 371

Wentworth, Horace, *1.* 49*n*, 377; *3.* 200

Wescott, Rev. J. B., *3.* 210*n*

Wesselhoeft, Dr., *4.* 114

West, Elizabeth D., *2.* 153, 330*n*

West Jersey & Seashore Railroad Co., *3.* 437

West Jersey Courier, 3. 234

West Jersey Press, 2. 345*n*; *3.* 20*n*, 21*n*, 22*n*, 29*n*, 30*n*, 87*n*, 115*n*, 116*n*

Westcott, Dr., *4.* 78*n*

Westermann, Bernard, *2.* 48; *3.* 432

Westgate, Lizzie, *3.* 445

Westlake, Mrs. Neda M., *1.* x

Westminster Hotel, *4.* 82, 83, 87. Letter to, *4.* 83

Westminster Review, The, 2. 127-28, 130, 131-32, 133-34, 153, 161

Westness, T. D., *6.* 20

Wharton, Dr., *4.* 242, 243

"What Best I See in Thee," *3.* 170*n*

"What Lurks Behind Shakspeare's Historical Plays?" *3.* 377, 378, 379

Wheeler, A. C., *3.* 434

Wheeler, Dora, *4.* 83*n*, 133

Wheeler, George, *1.* 169

Wheeler, John H., *1.* 169

"When I Heard at the Close of the Day," *2.* 82*n*

"When Lilacs Last in the Dooryard Bloom'd," *1.* 350; *2.* 16*n*; *3.* 272*n*, 319*n*; *4.* 5; *5.* 318; *6.* 40*n*

"When the Full-Grown Poet Came," *3.* 43*n*

"Whispers of Heavenly Death," *1.* 355*n*; *2.* 17, 21*n*, 24, 26, 44, 46, 47, 47*n*; *3.* 314*n*

Whitaker, A. H., *3.* 445

White, Dr. George A., *2.* 230, 250-51, 308, 370

White, Gleason, *4.* 437; *5.* 115, 337

White, Isabella A., *2.* 363, 371

White, Laura Lyon, *5.* 162*n*, 339

White, R. G., *4.* 25*n*

White, William, *5.* 172*n*

White, William Hale, *3.* 448. Letter to, *6.* 28

White, Stokes & Allen. Letter to, *6.* 40

Whitestone School, *6.* 3

Whiting, W. I., *4.* 32*n*, 428

Whitman, Andrew (son of Andrew Jackson Whitman), *2.* 42

Whitman, Andrew Jackson, *1.* 8, 10, 30, 32, 50*n*, 60, 64, 88-89, 95, 97, 103, 105, 130, 135, 137-38, 140, 143-44, 148, 151, 156, 158, 165, 166-67, 172, 174, 179, 183, 185, 186, 189, 190, 280*n*; *2.* 41*n*, 149*n*

Whitman, C. B., *3.* 443

Whitman, Edward, *1.* 8, 10, 30, 31, 32, 56, 64, 97, 105, 132, 144, 145, 217, 281, 305, 339; *2.* 3, 40, 48, 64, 68, 79, 86, 130*n*, 157, 167, 183, 186*n*, 194*n*, 203, 208, 241, 248, 254, 282, 311, 315; *3.* 33, 69, 99, 165, 180*n*, 215*n*, 222, 249; *4.* 73, 179, 201, 208, 282, 332, 427; *5.* 51, 67, 122, 124, 160, 163, 178, 239, 268, 317; *6.* 31. Letter to, *5.* 123

Whitman, George (son of Andrew Jackson Whitman), *1.* 156; *2.* 149

Whitman, Capt. George J., *1.* 76

Whitman, George Washington, *1.* 6, 9, 10, 14, 30, 32, 54, 58-60, 62, 63, 68, 71, 72, 76, 77, 78, 79, 80, 85, 87-88, 95, 97, 98, 100, 102, 104, 105, 107, 109, 111, 116, 118, 130, 135, 136, 137, 138, 140, 145, 146, 151, 156, 165, 167, 172-73, 179-80, 186, 190, 192, 193, 194, 195, 198, 200, 203, 204, 206, 207, 209, 210, 211-12, 215-16, 217, 218, 219, 221, 222, 223, 224, 225, 226, 227, 229, 231, 232, 233, 234, 235, 237, 239, 240, 243, 244, 247, 249, 250, 252-53, 255, 256-57, 258, 262, 268, 270, 273, 276, 277, 279, 285, 289, 292, 294, 296, 297, 300, 306, 308, 311, 312, 313, 314, 315, 317, 318, 320, 321, 327-28, 329, 339, 342, 356*n*, 365, 367, 368, 369, 372, 375, 376; *2.* 3, 6, 27, 30, 32, 35, 37, 38, 39, 41, 48, 64, 68, 71, 79, 85, 102, 116, 130*n*, 145, 147, 148, 149, 156, 157, 170, 178, 179, 182, 186, 187*n*, 192, 194, 195, 197, 201, 202, 203, 204, 206, 207, 208,

211, 213, 215, 219*n,* 222, 235, 237, 241, 242,
258, 262, 264, 267, 279, 282, 287, 311, 314,
315, 316, 325, 364, 369, 373; *3.* 2, 24, 45, 47,
51, 54, 69, 74*n,* 86, 87, 89, 91, 97, 99, 106*n,*
110*n,* 114-15, 117, 126, 127, 128, 135, 139,
142, 144, 147, 151, 160, 161, 165, 170, 180*n,*
187, 201, 204, 206*n,* 220, 222, 232, 233, 254,
303, 328, 348, 361*n,* 384*n,* 405*n,* 433, 434,
435; *4.* 47*n,* 50, 73, 167, 227, 235, 253, 261,
282, 348; *5.* 122, 123, 124, 125, 128, 134*n,*
157, 221, 226, 232*n,* 239, 260, 268, 274, 275,
276, 277, 285; *6.* 15*n,* 31*n.* Letters to, *1.* 56-
57, 189, 208-9; *2.* 187
Whitman, H. N., *3.* 438, 450
Whitman, Hannah Brush, *1.* 309
Whitman, James (son of Andrew Jackson
    Whitman), *1.* 207, 281; *2.* 149
Whitman, Jesse, *1.* 8, 10, 50*n,* 56, 64, 105, 132,
    144, 145, 164*n,* 189*n,* 338*n;* *2.* 3
Whitman, Jessie Louisa, *1.* 9, 110, 118, 132,
    138, 173, 183, 190, 192, 195, 207, 208, 213,
    216, 218, 219, 224, 229, 248, 252, 268, 269,
    281, 319, 320, 323; *2.* 64, 67, 68, 158, 203,
    279, 282, 315, 367; *3.* 24, 51, 54, 84, 85, 95,
    97, 98, 121, 123, 127, 135, 160, 161, 164, 166,
    170, 180*n,* 359*n,* 373*n;* *4.* 46, 47, 49, 51, 71,
    83, 199, 202*n,* 440; *5.* 87, 122, 123, 125, 126,
    127, 129, 131, 135, 144, 148, 152, 157, 160,
    175, 178, 185, 268, 273*n,* 274, 277; *6.* 58.
    Letters to, *3.* 69, 99-100, 359; *4.* 47, 48, 72-73;
    5. 124, 142, 143-44
Whitman, Lavinia F., *4.* 429; *5.* 334, 343, 346,
    347, 349
Whitman, Louisa Orr, *2.* 3, 6, 130*n,* 145, 146,
    147, 148, 149, 156, 178, 186, 187*n,* 192, 194,
    195, 197, 201, 202, 204, 205, 207, 208, 211,
    212*n,* 213, 215-16, 219*n,* 220, 222, 225*n,* 241,
    245, 262, 264, 282, 287, 296, 298, 311, 314,
    315, 325, 329, 344, 363, 369, 370; *3.* 2, 24, 47,
    51, 54, 65, 69, 84, 87, 88, 89, 90-91, 95, 97,
    98, 99, 104, 106*n,* 117, 123, 126, 127, 128,
    135, 139, 142, 144, 147, 148, 151, 156, 160,
    161, 170, 180*n,* 187, 192*n,* 201, 220, 222, 234,
    254, 303, 328, 364*n,* 368*n,* 405*n,* 432, 433,
    434, 435, 436, 437, 445; *4.* 46, 47, 50-51, 73,
    83, 167, 181, 202*n,* 227, 253, 266*n,* 282, 316,
    332, 345, 391, 427, 435; *5.* 87, 122, 134*n,* 157,
    160-61, 185, 193, 214*n,* 226, 232*n,* 239, 264,
    268, 273, 274, 277, 310, 314, 331; *6.* 15*n.*
    Letters to, *3.* 114-15, 120-21, 163-66, 232-33,
    238-39, 244, 249-50; *4.* 199-200, 235, 348, 355-
    56; *6.* 31
Whitman, Louisa Van Velsor, *1.* vii, 1, 5, 6, 7,
    8, 9, 13, 43, 50, 53, 56, 62, 64, 67, 68, 79, 130,
    146, 176, 179, 185, 208, 225, 226, 235, 239,
    240, 242, 244, 247, 250, 252, 256, 257, 258,
    267, 269, 274-75, 282, 283, 285, 286, 292, 301,

319, 326, 330, 335, 338, 341, 342, 345, 356*n,*
364, 365, 366, 367, 368, 369, 370, 371, 372,
373, 374, 376, 377, 378, 379; *2.* 6, 20, 29, 34*n,*
39*n,* 43, 45, 46, 48, 55, 58, 61, 64, 67, 68, 72*n,*
79*n,* 83, 84, 85, 86, 88, 98*n,* 99, 101, 102, 103,
106, 113, 114, 116, 122, 123, 126, 127, 129-30,
131, 157, 158, 165, 167, 169, 170, 171, 172,
173, 175, 176, 177, 178, 179, 180, 181, 182,
196*n,* 202, 216, 223, 225, 228, 230, 233, 234,
235, 239, 240, 242, 246, 285, 299, 301, 360,
361, 362, 363, 365, 366, 367, 368, 369, 370; *3.*
33, 56, 62*n,* 145, 235, 366; *4.* 3, 35*n,* 90, 188,
195, 391, 398; *5.* 7, 199*n,* 203, 210, 213, 233*n,*
240, 248, 265, 288, 290; *6.* 4, 48*n,* 66. Letters
to, 1. 58-60, 71-72, 77-78, 85-90, 95-98, 99-
101, 102-6, 107-18, 130-32, 135-38, 139-41,
143-45, 146-49, 150-52, 156-58, 165-69, 172-74,
189-90, 192-95, 197-98, 200-1, 202-8, 209-13,
215-24, 227-34, 251-52, 260-63, 272-74, 276,
277-81, 288-89, 292-95, 296-98, 298-301, 302-4,
305-10, 310-14, 314-15, 316-18, 319-21, 322-23,
324-26; *2.* 14-15, 27-28, 30-32, 34-40, 41-43,
70-71, 78-79, 144-45, 146-50, 156-57, 183-84,
186-88, 191-95, 196-200, 200-2, 203-12, 213,
214-16, 217, 218-21; *5.* 283-85
Whitman, Mannahatta, *1.* 9, 56, 60, 62, 71, 87,
    89, 97, 103, 108, 118, 132, 137, 138, 141, 145,
    149, 157, 168, 173, 183, 190, 193, 195, 200,
    207, 208, 213, 216, 252, 281, 302, 312, 323,
    325; *2.* 64, 67, 68, 149*n,* 158, 198*n,* 205, 220,
    279, 282, 315, 363, 367, 370; *3.* 24, 51, 54, 84,
    85, 95, 97, 98, 121, 126, 127, 135, 160, 161,
    164, 166, 170, 180*n,* 359*n,* 373*n,* 431, 434; *4.*
    46, 47, 48-49, 51. Letters to, *2.* 202-3; *3.* 69,
    99-100, 122-23, 359
Whitman, Martha, *1.* 9, 54, 56, 59, 60, 71, 77,
    86, 87, 89, 90, 96, 101, 104, 105, 106, 108,
    109, 110, 111, 116, 117, 118, 132, 136, 138,
    141, 144, 145, 148, 149, 151, 156, 166, 173,
    174, 179, 183, 190, 192, 194, 195, 198, 201,
    203, 204, 206, 210, 211, 213, 216, 218, 219,
    220, 221, 224, 226, 228, 229, 230, 232, 233,
    239, 251, 257, 272, 273, 274, 275, 280, 289,
    292, 294, 306, 308, 310, 312, 313, 314, 315,
    318, 321, 327, 340, 342, 356*n,* 366; *2.* 3, 6, 38,
    39, 64, 67-68, 71, 80*n,* 86, 103, 123, 130*n,* 145,
    157, 158, 182, 187, 192, 194, 196, 197, 198,
    199, 200, 201, 202, 203, 211, 234, 240, 272,
    362, 363; *6.* 66, 68. Letters to, *1.* 62-64
Whitman, Nancy, *1.* 8, 50*n,* 89, 130*n,* 144*n,*
    156, 165, 189*n,* 190, 207, 227, 252, 304; *2.*
    42*n,* 149*n;* *3.* 432, 444
Whitman, Sarah Helen, *2.* 64, 66
Whitman, Thomas Jefferson, *1.* 8, 9, 10, 12,
    56, 58, 59, 60, 62, 63, 64, 71, 72, 77, 78, 85,
    86, 87, 89, 95, 96, 97, 99, 100, 101, 103, 105,
    106, 109, 110, 111, 116, 117, 118, 130, 131,

136, 137, 138, 139, 141, 143, 144, 145, 151,
156, 158, 165, 167-68, 169, 172, 173, 174, 183,
189, 190, 192, 194, 195, 198, 200, 202, 203,
204, 206, 207, 208, 209, 210, 211, 213, 216,
218, 219, 220, 221, 224, 227, 228, 229, 230,
232, 233, 234, 237, 249, 250, 251, 257, 262,
272, 273, 278, 279, 280, 285, 289, 292, 294,
296, 297, 300, 302, 303, 306, 308, 310, 312,
313, 314, 315, 317, 318, 321, 324, 325, 326,
328, 330, 342, 356*n*, 365, 366, 367, 369, 370,
371, 372, 373, 374, 375, 377, 378; *2.* 3, 6, 14,
27*n*, 30, 37, 71, 79*n*, 130*n*, 149*n*, 150, 182,
187, 192, 196, 197, 198, 199, 200, 202, 203,
207, 208, 209, 211, 213, 219-20, 241, 242, 254,
279, 282, 306, 315, 360, 363, 365, 366, 367,
369, 370, 372; *3.* 25, 50*n*, 54, 69, 123, 127,
160*n*, 164, 166, 264*n*, 311*n*, 323, 359*n*, 373*n*,
431, 432, 434, 435, 439, 442, 443, 448, 451,
452, 453; *4.* 199, 293, 426, 429, 431, 433; *5.*
122, 123, 124, 125, 126, 127, 130, 131, 132,
133, 134, 136, 178, 338; *6.* 21*n*, 58, 66. Letters
to, *1.* 50-51, 52-54, 67-68, 73-75, 76-77, 79-80,
225-26, 249-51, 274-76, 326-27; *2.* 67-69, 157-
58, 196; *3.* 185-86; *4.* 46-51, 71, 83. Letters
from, *1.* 27-36

Whitman, Walter (father), *1.* 7, 27, 36, 147,
179; *2.* 170; *3.* 3, 91, 157, 235; *4.* 5, 90, 195;
5. 57, 69, 203, 240, 265, 272

Whitman, Walter B., *4.* 439

Whitman, Walter Orr (son of George), *2.*
344; *3.* 24, 26, 32, 45, 51, 54, 56, 91*n*, 160; *4.*
35*n*, 391; *6.* 15*n*

Whitney & Adams, *3.* 430

Whittaker, Clarence, *3.* 433

Whittaker, Daniel. Letter to, *3.* 37

Whittier, John Greenleaf, *1.* 26*n*; *2.* 171*n*; *3.*
167*n*, 214*n*, 317, 405*n*; *4.* 136, 141, 142, 164,
248, 270, 329, 381, 382, 407, 426, 431; *5.* 206;
6. 46

Wickware, Dr. D. M., *3.* vii-viii, 191*n*

Wide Awake Pleasure Book, 3. 235*n*

Wiggins, John W., *4.* 432

Wigglesworth, Anne, *1.* 160, 161, 175

Wigglesworth, Jane, *1.* 160, 161, 175

Wigglesworth, Mary, *1.* 160, 161, 175

Wilcox & Gibbs, *2.* 123

Wild, Fred, *5.* 135, 157, 250, 256, 263, 348

"Wild Frank's Return," *1.* 26*n*

Wilde, Oscar, *2.* 138*n*; *3.* 263, 264, 266, 283*n*,
447. Letter to, *3.* 263

Wiley & Sons, *3.* 138

Wilkie, James, *4.* 425, 429

Wilkins, Edward, *4.* 227, 231, 232, 233, 238,
240, 241, 243, 244, 245, 247, 253, 254, 259,
263, 264, 265, 267, 269, 270, 271, 274, 278,
279, 282, 283, 284, 307, 309, 312, 313, 316,
320, 324, 325, 328, 329, 333, 334, 336, 339,

340, 342, 345, 346, 349, 354, 355, 361, 363,
364*n*, 365, 366, 369, 372, 373, 376, 383, 384,
385, 386, 389, 390, 391, 392, 393, 402, 427,
441; *5.* 24, 31, 137, 279*n*, 345. Letters to, *4.*
409-10; *5.* 30-31, 43, 48, 61-62, 137, 248-49

Wilkinson, Anna M., *3.* 450

Willard, Miss, *3.* 321*n*

Willard's Hotel, *1.* 216, 228; *2.* 109

Williams, Mr., *3.* 200; *4.* 244

Williams, F. Churchill, *3.* 365

Williams, Francis (Frank) H., *3.* 360*n*, 361,
365; *4.* 151*n*, 437; *5.* 42*n*, 94, 259

Williams, George Henry, *2.* 146, 148, 150, 158,
232*n*, 370, 371

Williams, Mary B. N., *3.* 451; *4.* 433

Williams, Talcott, *3.* 297, 375; *4.* 1, 24, 27, 81,
428, 429; *5.* 121, 127, 129*n*, 130, 133, 243-44,
332, 337, 338, 341, 344, 349. Letters to, *3.*
378-80, 383; *4.* 27-28, 32, 66, 96-97, 115, 135,
155; *5.* 133, 316; *6.* 43, 54

Williams, Mrs. Talcott, *4.* 32, 81, 153, 431; *5.*
337, 349

Williams, Thomas, *5.* 79-80

Williams, Will, *2.* 372

Williams & Co., A., *3.* 446. Letters to, *3.* 103-
4, 192

Williamson, Mr., *2.* 366

Williamson, George M., *4.* 424, 429, 430, 432,
436. Letter to, *4.* 123-24

Willson, John G., *3.* 447

Wilmans, Helen, *3.* 447

Wilson, Dr. A. D., *2.* 68

Wilson, Benton H., *1.* 12, 176, 369, 370, 377,
378; *2.* 360, 361, 365, 366, 367, 372. Letters
to, *1.* 323-24; *2.* 95-96

Wilson, Bluford, *2.* 308, 313

Wilson, Francis, *5.* 151*n*, 339

Wilson, Frederick W., *3.* 450; *4.* 33*n*, 66*n*, 72,
81*n*, 139*n*, 141, 150*n*, 159, 160, 167, 270, 272,
295*n*, 359*n*; *5.* 23*n*, 69*n*; *6.* 37

Wilson, H. B., *3.* 444

Wilson, Henry, *1.* 377; *2.* 360, 365

Wilson, Gen. James Grant, *3.* 406; *4.* 430.
Letters to, *3.* 154; *4.* 56; *5.* 335

Wilson, John L., *3.* 144*n*, 177*n*

Wilson, Peter W.(?), *1.* 28, 35

Wilson, Thomas A., *2.* 308*n*, 371

Wilson, Walt Whitman, *2.* 95*n*

Wilson & McCormack, *3.* 323*n*, 329, 344, 438

Winant, Stephen, *2.* 368

Wineburgh, Lazarus, *1.* 51*n*; *3.* 271

Wingate, Charles F., *1.* 378; *4.* 429; *5.* 334

Winter, William, *1.* 84*n*, 124*n*, 328*n*, 339; *3.*
282, 314

"Winter-Sunshine. A Trip from Camden to
the Coast," *3.* 146, 161

Winterstein, Manville, *1.* 177; *2.* 364, 372

Wise, Alfred, *2.* 366

Witcraft, John R., *4.* 432

"With Husky—Haughty Lips, O Sea," *3.* 355, 357, 360, 364

Wixon, Miss, *5.* 113

"Woman Waits for Me, A," *3.* 270*n*, 271*n*, 273, 277, 279, 312*n*, 314

"Woman's Estimate of Walt Whitman, A," *4.* 92*n*

Woman's Journal, The, 3. 283*n*

Wood (soldier), *5.* 286, 290

Wood, Charles, *3.* 433

Wood, Edward T., *5.* 347

Wood, George, *1.* 372. Letters to, *1.* 71, 304

Wood, J. B., *4.* 407, 441

Wood, W. R., *3.* 433

Wood, Wallace, *5.* 339, 340. Letter to, *5.* 172

Woodbury, Augustus, *1.* 308*n*

Woodbury, Charles J., *1.* 377; *5.* 70, 72, 222, 343

Woodbury, John P., *3.* 201*n*

Woodbury (N.J.) *Constitution, 3.* 94

Woodhall, Judge, *5.* 311

Woodruff, Edwin H., *3.* 447. Letter to, *4.* 59

Woods, Fred, *5.* 113, 138, 150, 168, 176

Woodstown (N.J.) *Constitution, 3.* 133*n*

Woodstown (N.J.) *Register, 3.* 181*n*, 281*n*, 435

Woodworth, Thomas M., *1.* 12; *2.* 368

Wooldridge, Andrew J., *2.* 105

Word, The, 3. 312*n*, 314*n*

"Word about Tennyson, A," *4.* 60, 63*n*; *6.* 35

"Word for Dead Soldiers, A," *2.* 264*n*

Wordsworth, William, *3.* 171*n*, 349*n*; *4.* 325*n*, 330

Wormwood, R. F. Letter to, *4.* 400

Worster, Rodney R., *1.* 375

Worthen, William E., *1.* 226, 228, 302*n*, 368, 369, 375; *5.* 131*n*

Worthington (Minn.) *Advance, 3.* 437

Worthington, Richard, *3.* 196-98, 199, 226, 320*n*, 409*n*, 433, 435, 444, 448; *4.* 160. Letter to, *3.* 186

Wraymond (or Raymond), Lewis, *2.* 51. Letter to, *2.* 53-54

Wren, Jennie, *5.* 340

Wright, Dana F., *1.* 247*n*, 376. Letter to, *5.* 285

Wright, Mrs. H. J., *1.* 332

Wright, Col. John Gibson, *1.* 240*n*, 262; *4.* 235; *5.* 285

Wright, Max A., *5.* 348

Wright, Samuel B., *3.* 452

Wroth, Alice, *3.* 233

Wroth, Mrs. Caroline, *3.* 233, 234

Wroth, Carric E., *5.* 333

Wroth, James Henry ("Harry"), *3.* 438; *4.* 113

Wroth, James Stewart, *3.* viii; *4.* viii, 441. Letter to, *4.* 113

Wroth, John W., *4.* 113, 425, 430, 440; *5.* 338

Wyckoff, Nicholas, *1.* 98, 99; *5.* 284*n*. Letter to, *1.* 101-2

Wyld, Mr., *3.* 346

Wyman, Bayard, *5.* 349

Wyse, Charles Bonaparte, *3.* 171*n*

Yard, Major Thomas W., *1.* 86

Yates, Edmund, *2.* 30*n*. Letter to, *2.* 218

Yeats, John Butler, *2.* 153

Yeats, William Butler, *2.* 153*n*; *4.* 303*n*

Yesterdays with Authors, 4. 388, 390, 396

"Yonnondio," *4.* 131

Young, James B., *2.* 132, 368

Young, John Russell, *3.* 448; *5.* 257, 260, 261-62, 345, 346. Letters to, *5.* 256, 262

Young & Co., J. P., *2.* 371

Youth's Companion, The, 5. 153, 154, 339. Letter to, *5.* 153

Zagranichnyi Viestnik, *3.* 343*n*

Zahle, Nathalie, *2.* 282*n*

Ziegler & Swearingen, *3.* 88*n*

Zimmerman, D. M., *3.* 431, 436, 441. Letter to, *3.* 207